WHAT INFANTS KNOW

WHAT INFANTS KNOW

The New Cognitive Science of Early Development

Jacques Mehler and Emmanuel Dupoux

Translated by Patsy Southgate

BLACKWELL
Cambridge MA & Oxford UK

Copyright © Editions Odile Jacob, 1990
English translation © Basil Blackwell, 1994

The rights of Jacques Mehler and Emmanuel Dupoux to be identified as authors of this work has been asserted in accordance with the Copyright, Designs and Patents Act 1988.

First published 1994

Blackwell Publishers
238 Main Street
Cambridge, Massachusetts 02142
USA

108 Cowley Road
Oxford OX4 1JF
UK

Library of Congress Cataloging-in Publication Data

Mehler, Jacques.
     [Naître humain. English]
     What infants know : the new cognitive science of early development
  / Jacques Mehler and Emmanuel Dupoux ; translated by Patsy
  Southgate.
     Includes bibliographical references and index.
     ISBN 1-55786-369-5 (hb) ISBN 1-55786-370-9 (pb)
     1. Infants (Newborn)—Psychology. 2. Genetic psychology.
  3. Cognition in children. I. Dupoux, Emmanuel. II. Title.
  BF719.M4413   1993
  155.42'23—dc20   93-10147
                                                    CIP

British Library Cataloguing in Publication Data

A CIP catalogue record for this book is available from the British Library.

Typeset in 10.5 on 13 pt Plantin by Lorrie LeJeune and David Niergarth
Printed in the USA
This book is printed on acid-free paper

Contents

Preface

Unlike all 1965 model Volkwagon Beetles, and most lower species of animals, humans do not look alike nor do they behave as if they were all copies from a single model. True, animals who belong to one species behave alike. Cows, to the best of our knowledge, sleep and eat grass, flies try to get out of the room by flying into windows, and parakeets screech and flap. In contrast, humans differ enormously in the behaviors they display. We all have unique histories, and will react to a situation in our own specific fashions. John is an athlete while Peter sits and broods. Mary is a lawyer with great verbal ability while Hillary stays at home and paints. Who could argue that Gandhi and Jack the Ripper had much in common? Who would think of replacing an orchestra conductor with a professional wrestler, or for that matter, a politician with an actor? Humans differ not only in their behavioral repertoires but in their personalities, aptitudes, and outlooks.

Humans believe that every member of the species has a unique essence which is not replicated exactly alike in anybody else. At the same time, we recognize that though any two humans do not look completely alike, they resemble each other a great deal. Whether our eyes are slanted or not, our skin pale or dark, our bodies hirsute or smooth, what unites us far outweighs what separates us. We all have a mouth, two eyes, a nose, a chin, two legs to walk on, two arms, two hands, and ten fingers, giving us a typically human appearance distinct from the physiognomy of a horse, for example. And while we feel pity or even disgust for the deformed person glimpsed on the street or for the elephant man in the movies, we do not judge either one to be any the less human. A wax model at Madame Tussaud's wax museum might excite our amazement or admiration, but we would never think of speaking to it. The resemblances that unite us are therefore not only physical. To recognize a person as a fellow human is also, and perhaps especially, to endow him or her with certain psychological characteristics which, like the key elements of our physiology, are common to all members of the species and make up our *human nature*.

For a long time, philosophy and the humanities had accustomed us to thinking that while our bodies are genetically determined, our minds can never be limited by a predetermined "nature." That would be like binding us to a "destiny" that would exclude all freedom of choice. The notion of a genetic heritage has indeed been accepted, but only in the biological and physical realms. The mind has remained exempt. Man and woman, since they are, above all, thinking beings, could not have a preprogrammed "nature." Virtually anything must be possible for them, and confronting the self, limited only by what it learns and its personal history, there can only be "others." Here modern relativism, the cult of differences, finds its justification.

There is no lack of arguments that exalt the infinite diversity of human beings. Since no two individuals are ever identical, how could one possibly come up with a model of *the* human nature? This is true enough, but scientific knowledge, in order to advance, must look beyond certain obvious facts and operate by simplification and generalization.

Cognitive science, at least as we see it, proposes specifically to determine, by precise empirical studies, the psychological properties which are common to human beings, regardless of cultural or individual differences. It will describe the functioning of memory, language, attention, and interaction with or perception of others, and it will also determine which nervous structures regulate them. The study of behavior requires, therefore, the collaboration, indeed the integration of many disciplines, from linguistics to neurobiology and computer science.

This investigation, begun almost thirty years ago, has already yielded promising results. New findings enable us to answer questions some of the greatest thinkers have asked about human nature. What is the nature of our mental life? What are the links between language and thought, thought and matter? Does intelligence depend on a unique mental capacity or on a body of specialized aptitudes? Is Peter's intelligence comparable to Mary's, or is each human being unique? Is our mental life merely the reflection of our culture and our personal history, or is it determined by our genes? Is our ability to adapt to new situations limitless? To what extent can we be influenced and manipulated from the outside? Is the newborn's mind a blank slate? Does it fill like a water pitcher with the knowledge of its elders? What are the links between the mental life of the adult and that of the child, the mentally ill person, the animal?

These questions are far from original. But now we seem to have perfected new methods and models that allow us to approach them through experimental techniques with rigor and precision. A new age is dawning that tolls the death of general arguments and a priori opinions, and opens the way to an empirical investigation of the workings of the human psyche. Thus, by examining the experimental data obtained from the adult, the newborn, and the animal, we will be able to see that while human cognitive capacities are clearly very versatile, they are also very specific. Like other animals, humans are able to adapt in astonishing ways to new situations and new needs, but only in certain areas and within certain limits. While they can endlessly acquire new knowledge, it is only within a restricted framework. So their cognitive skills are not limitless. While these skills can evolve, they can do so only within the confines of a relatively narrow genetic envelope, which imparts to members of the species a fixed core of aptitudes that everyone possesses in common. It is precisely this core that we propose to explore here in order to restore the concept of a universal *human nature*, refined and renewed, to the place it deserves to occupy in the body of the human sciences.

1

Explaining Our Behavior

We are never indifferent to explanations of our behavior. We all possess the remarkable ability to examine, through introspection, the contents of our minds and to produce a multitude of interpretations – emotional or rational, convincing or dubious, but always varied – which purport to account for our actions and conduct in terms of our plans, desires, and beliefs. And we all exercise this ability with regard to others. Yet only the behavior of those around us and the stimuli they receive from the environment can actually be observed and evaluated. It is, therefore, possible to explain the behavior of living beings in two distinct ways: we can invoke subjective mental states, but we can also cite external circumstances and describe the interplay of stimulus and response.

These possibilities correspond to the approaches that have most deeply influenced the study of the psychological mechanism: *commonsense psychology*, in its academic form, and *behaviorism*.

The Psychology of Everyman and Everywoman

Commonsense psychology relies on the unconditional use of terms like "will," "consciousness," or "desire" that form the basis of a theory of human mental processes. However naive it may be, this "everyday" psychology possesses quasi-miraculous powers of prediction. For example, during a demonstration, you notice Mr. Smith marching, shouting, and waving a banner, demanding a salary increase for government employees. You know that in a month a local election will feature politician X, favorable to a salary increase, running against Y, who supports a policy of austerity. Even if you don't know Mr. Smith, you can predict with near certainty that he will vote for X. You have no idea when or where Mr. Smith will go to vote. You don't have the foggiest notion of the millions of atomic collisions, chemical reactions, physiological, hormonal, and neurological changes separating the present from the moment when Mr. Smith will cast his ballot. Yet you are sure he will choose X and not Y. The most highly developed of our physical theories cannot hold a candle to commonsense psychology when it comes to predicting the behavior of evolved organisms.

To understand and predict the behavior of others, it therefore seems natural to us to invoke subjective mental states or conditions similar to our own. Otherwise, we would simply not be able to live in society. It would be impossible for us to anticipate the consequences of our actions, to predict those of others, and to make the necessary adjustments. However, despite its undeniable usefulness, commonsense psychology is not infallible. Our intuitions can be in error. We see this clearly when we start trying to figure out the behavior of our children. To try to evaluate a problem in school, for example, we will get a vastly different explanation according to whether we consult a teacher, the school psychologist, a pediatrician, a neurologist, or our local hairstylist. Everyone has his or her piece to say. But a simple opinion is not always enough, as the following story will demonstrate.

Peter is a six-year-old boy, lively and bright. Curious by nature, he always seemed eager to learn, so his parents enrolled him in the local elementary school, which had an excellent reputation. After a week in class, his behavior changed. For no apparent reason, he started to cry several times a day. He became increasingly irritable, to the point of refusing to go to school entirely. His parents were worried, but saw in their child's reaction nothing but a passing rebelliousness since his older siblings had also put up a fuss about going to school. They therefore tried reasoning with the boy, but in vain; he continued to protest, and even started wetting his bed again.

One day Albert, a neuropsychologist who lived in their building, suggested that Peter's problem may have been caused by the presence of "atypical, ectopic or heterotopic" cells in one of the convolutions of the left hemisphere of his brain. They were shocked. It was indeed possible that some brain damage had produced the behavioral problems. But the correlation between Peter's behavior and his aversion to school led one to believe that his difficulties were related more to adjustment than to neurology.

Peter's parents' hypothesis was easy to verify: all they had to do was keep him out of school for a while. Sure enough, when they did this he improved immediately, and a little investigation turned up the fact that he couldn't stand his teacher.

In his new school, he met Paul, another adorable six-year-old boy with curly blond hair and blue eyes, who was a little shy. Although susceptible to passing migraines and allergies, he was very lively and loved to learn. Ambidextrous, he had played the piano since the age of four and could sight-read sheet music. He had a great deal of trouble learning to read, however, and, to a lesser degree, in learning to write. When Albert, our neuropsychologist, met Paul's parents by chance during dinner at a mutual friend's house, he once again suggested that their child's reading problems might stem from an anarchic proliferation of "atypical, ectopic or heterotopic" cells in one of the convolutions in the left hemisphere of his brain. In fact, a recent study had established that this type of abnormality is found in the left hemisphere of blond, allergic, ambidextrous, highly gifted, dyslexic children.[1] Paul's parents also were very shocked by these suggestions, for, as in Peter's case, Paul's problems had only emerged when he started school. He hated his classes, especially reading, and he, too, began wetting his bed again after a few weeks. These surely were symptoms of an aversion to school. Wouldn't simply changing schools effect a cure? In the end, they had to yield to Albert's arguments, however. Upon formal examination, it was discovered that Paul indeed suffered from a more serious condition, and changing schools was of no avail. As we know today, certain cases of dyslexia are caused by the pathological development of certain regions of the cerebral cortex during pregnancy.

Peter's story shows that our intuitions about behavior, though based on rough correlations, have a power of prediction that makes it worthwhile to take them seriously. As such, they are indispensable to our relationships with others. But, as Paul's case clearly illustrates, this approach has its limits. Intuitions may have only a superficial value. The profound sources of behavior are often less transparent than they seem. And scientists well know that the validity of a hypothesis only becomes clear once we understand the phenomenon it seeks to explain. We must keep our minds open to all sorts of hypotheses, or risk jumping to the wrong conclusions.

We are, therefore, justified in asking ourselves if the implicit understanding we have of the way the mind works, the commonsense psychology we currently use to predict the behavior of others, can yield a rigorous model of scientific explanation, if it can legitimately serve as the foundation of a scientific theory.

The Homunculus that Controls Us

We all think that our behavior can, more or less, be explained by the interaction of two component parts. On one level, a central intelligence, unique and indissociable, monitors and plans what we do at every moment; on another, a mindless mechanical system undertakes the execution of what has been decided.

This "dualist" concept, which underlies our commonsense psychology, can be illustrated by a metaphor. Let us imagine that there is an intelligent little person in our brain, a *homunculus* who can see through our eyes, hear through our ears, and control our organism with the aid of gears, levers, pedals, and buttons, as if our body were a robot. It is this homunculus that takes us for a walk, decides to direct our attention, for example, to a couple on our right or to an advertisement on the back of a bus. It also prompts us to sniff the perfume of a passing woman, or a man's cologne. This general intelligence regulates our most basic functions as well as our mathematical reasoning or our learning of Latin declensions.

Let us assume, then, that our homunculus is responsible for what we think and do. But who is in charge of it? Another homunculus, contained within the first? Then who controls this second one? A third, contained within the second? Where does this endless series of homunculi end? This metaphor embodies, as we can see, the major drawback of assuming what it intends to explain: the existence of a central "intelligence" that controls the organism. It begs the question, reflecting our profound ignorance of the real causes of "intelligent" behavior.

But, while it fails to explain adequately our mental processes, does it at least give us a good description of them? If we accept the image of the homunculus, our mental life seems unified to us. We have the impression of being able to direct our awareness toward different mental phenomena, a little like illuminating different parts of a dark room with a flashlight. We think we are able to control our reasoning, our perceptions, our imagination. But in fact, this impression is misleading. The metaphor of the homunculus cannot account for even our most basic acts, as a consideration of our oversights and mental slips will demonstrate.

We all occasionally find ourselves confronted by an unexpected problem when we're in a rush and lack the information necessary to deal with it effectively. In such cases, our homunculus certainly has the right to make a mistake: no one can be expected to do the impossible. But most of the time, we have enough information to cope with situations that arise, and yet we make mistakes anyhow. Who among us has

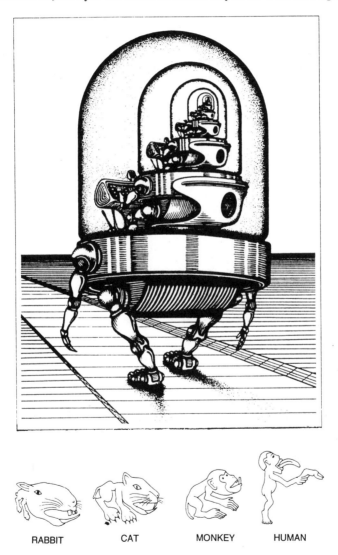

RABBIT   CAT   MONKEY   HUMAN

Figure 1.1   The homunculus and regression to infinity, according to Roger Shepard (above). Cortical representation of the bodies of four animals (below).

not unthinkingly done something really bizarre? Who has never sat down on a chair that wasn't there, or tried to unlock someone else's car, cursing at the key? Who has never forgotten an important date or birthday? What good then, is an absent-minded or blundering homunculus?

These errors are too stupid to be attributable to the homunculus, we say. Intelligent as it is, it could not be responsible for them. And yet they are too abstract, too systematic, to simply be mechanical failures of its vehicle, the automaton that executes its orders. Actually, it seems as if these errors follow certain laws. In the case of errors in "programming," as when we pour orange juice into our coffee cup, the goal "achieved" often bears a certain resemblance to the one that had been "envisioned." In the case of slips of the tongue, it is always linguistic units of the same kind that are affected: basic speech sounds or "phonemes" are inverted, as in "Larwin and Damarck," or even syllables and entire words, while the linguistic structure of the word or phrase is preserved. How is this possible? If the robot attending the homunculus is responsible for the slip, isn't it doing more than just following orders? Could it have a knowledge of language?

Certain mistakes are due to errors in "piloting," when one sequence of routine actions takes over for another, less habitual one. For example, you are absent-mindedly getting undressed to change for dinner, and you suddenly find yourself in bed with your pajamas on. Once in motion, the sequence of acts that go into getting undressed carried through to its usual conclusion, despite your firm intention to put on a dinner dress or jacket and go out. Musicians are only too familiar with the error of starting to play one piece and segueing into another, more familiar piece that resembles it. Once an action is launched, it is very hard to intercept it. Decisions have a certain inflexibility. Comic moments of no great importance can ensue, but so can tragedies.

1977, Tenerife, the Canary Islands. A Boeing 747 preparing for takeoff crashes into another plane taxiing down the same runway: 583 dead. The 747 attempting takeoff had not received authorization from the control tower, and the other plane should not have been on that runway. In both cases, the pilots had continued on course even though the control tower had clearly warned them that there was a problem.[2] Each pilot could see the other plane and would have had time to avert the collision.

Other fatal accidents can be traced to too-entrenched routines. For example, a few years ago, a flight from the United States crashed on a runway that was under reconstruction at the Mexico City airport. The pilot had been directed by the control tower to another runway, parallel to the first. At the last minute, however, he altered his course and tried to land on the first one, smashing into a group of trucks. The pilot was experienced, but for years he had always landed on the runway that, this time, was undergoing repairs.

Similarly, the tragic end of the Light Brigade was caused by a slip of the tongue on the part of Lord Cardigan. Instead of calling for a retreat, he gave the order to charge. His overtrained cavalry advanced as one man to their certain death, and nothing, not even Lord Cardigan's counterorders, could stop them.[3]

Is our homunculus responsible for these absent-minded mistakes? The fact that they happen against our will rules out this possibility. Are they the robot's fault, then? But how could a mindless automaton make such crucial, complex decisions? The naive image of an intelligent homunculus controlling a mindless robot thus cannot account for our unthinking blunders.

Shouldn't we then postulate a slightly more intelligent robot and slightly less brilliant homunculus? Must not we assume that some of the most sophisticated human aptitudes, like language and the ability to anticipate and adapt to new situations, are outside the control of the central intelligence and are partly "automatic"? The homunculus would, in this scenario, be content to supervise major mental operations like reasoning, judgment, or memory, while the robot would have rather more sophisticated chores than in our first hypothesis. But then how do we explain memory lapses?

We all live under the illusion that we can decide to remember something. And yet, our past eludes us as often as our present. Memory lapses have different forms and varying degrees of intensity. Between clear and detailed recollection and the "total blackout," our memory often yields fragmentary data. For example, sometimes we cannot remember the name of someone we know. In certain cases, we remember the meaning of a word, and can even supply various details about it, but the word itself escapes us. We can also block out ideas or intentions: we find ourselves in the kitchen with a screwdriver mysteriously in our hand, and only later do we remember that we were supposed to fix the toaster. It also happens that vital information eludes us when we need it most, as when we forget a very important appointment or leave our keys in our car. Complete memory lapses can also occur: a driver can suddenly "wake up" at the wheel of his or her car with no memory of what has happened for a period of time.

Our memory is therefore imperfect and, even when it works well, only approximate. Can you, for example, really remember your breakfast four days ago? You know that you had it, and even, probably, what you ate and drank. But you have forgotten the details of the arrangement of the cups, the color of the sky, what you said, heard, saw. All you remember is a "generic" breakfast, with average details: coffee with two lumps of sugar, a bran muffin, the news on the radio. The exceptional family dinner you attended three months ago, however, is much more clearly etched on your mind. So, our memory stores the stereotypical aspects of daily events and memorizes in detail only those which depart perceptibly from the norm.

That our memory is only approximate is of no importance in everyday life. But certain lapses can have fatal consequences: for example, when it comes to judging the guilt or innocence of an accused criminal. Certain trials during which an accused was convicted of murder only on the basis of a visual identification show this clearly.[4] In one case, two witnesses had seen the murderer for more than twenty minutes. In another, more than fifteen witnesses, of which eight were policemen, officially identified the suspect. "His features are etched in my mind," one of them even testified. But the accused were, in fact, innocent.

Each time, some of the witnesses had had occasion to see a photograph of the accused before the lineup. Thus, at the time of the lineup, his face was more familiar to them than those of the other suspects, leading them to make a positive identification of an innocent person. Our memories are thus more often influenced by the familiarity of a face than by the circumstances under which we saw it.

Similarly, the way we are asked a question about an event can influence our answer and even our memory of the event. After seeing a film about an automobile accident, students were asked what the speed of the vehicles was at the "time of the contact/bump/impact/collision." According to the word used, estimates varied between 30 and 45 mph.[5] When questioned, the subjects of the experiment denied having been influenced by the way the question was phrased.

Sometimes, we can even distort basic perceptual judgments. A simple visual test consists of asking whether two lines are of identical length. Actually, only one person is the subject of the experiment. The others are accomplices charged with making persuasive statements to the effect that the lines are of equal length when, quite obviously, one is longer than the other. Experimental subjects, going against their own perceptions, are won over by the general opinion. Questioned after the experiment, they blame their own vision, but deny having been influenced in any way by group pressure.[6] As we can see, the criteria actually used in making a judgment are not necessarily conscious.

Despite ourselves, discrepancies occur between what we want to do and what we actually accomplish. Everything seems to indicate that our memory is an autonomous system which we consult to recover precious facts, a system which sometimes gets its wires crossed. Its weaknesses would have no importance if we could be sure of the reliability of a particular memory, but unfortunately that is not the case. We have no direct information available to us about the limitations of our minds, and most of these oversimplifications, distortions, and omissions occur without our knowledge.

Our homunculus, then, instead of being the master of our psyche, is more like its unwitting plaything. What is supposed to be the source of our judgments is often ignorant of their provenance. We might think that the problem arises from the fact that it is incapable of studying itself. But neither is it capable of studying its presumed colleagues, in the heads of other humans.

Indeed, not only are we poor judges of our own behavior, but we also have a simplified notion of the mental processes of others and fail to take into account the particular limitations of our own minds. We place an exaggerated importance on certain aspects of behavior and minimize others. Errors in evaluating the behavior of others can result. The jurors at a trial, for example, are extremely susceptible to eyewitness accounts, even when the witnesses suffer from poor vision. They seem to place more importance on the self-assurance and personality of the witness than on his or her objective competence.[7]

The metaphor of the homunculus has no basis in reality, then. Indeed, how can we explain the fact that it doesn't always know why it formulates certain judgments? It should, at least, know what guides its choices, yet it only seems capable of rationalizing after the fact. Perhaps, then, it is not a homunculus that governs. . . .

Entire areas of our mental life elude us but these unconscious processes can be extremely useful upon occasion. Who has not suddenly found the solution to a problem upon waking after a good night's sleep? Many mathematicians even claim to have made their most important discoveries under such totally fortuitous circumstances.[8] From there, it is just a step to say that true intelligence does not reside in a process we can consciously control, but rather in a set of "passive" processes that unfold behind the scenes. Alongside our recently posited homunculus, then, in our deepest recesses, an "intelligent" little demon directs our gestures, memory, and attention from the shadows.

Observe figure 1.2 carefully. You recognize the face: two photographs of Margaret Thatcher, shown upside down. In one photo, the mouth and eyes have been inverted. Your intelligence, your homunculus, can readily accept the idea that one of the two faces is abnormal, but it is incapable of anticipating the sensation you feel when you look at these faces right side up.

Figure 1.2   Contrast between perception and comprehension: we must turn the page upside down to realize how monstrous one of these faces is (Thompson, 1980).

Freud has been most persuasive in convincing us of the essential role played by the hidden side of our psyche. "Certain apparently unintentional acts prove, when we submit them to psychoanalytical examination, to be fully motivated and determined by causes that elude our consciousness," he wrote.[9] According to him, involuntary actions demonstrate the existence of an unconscious that acts on our desires and influences our motivations.

Actually, this theory also posits a homunculus, but in this case, one that operates in darkness. And the problems found in our original metaphor arise once again: Who controls this "demon"? How does it manage to be intelligent? This concept is defective not because it postulates mental processes that elude our consciousness, but because it presupposes mental entities but does not say how they function effectively without the intervention of an increasingly mysterious intelligence.

Thus, as the stories of Peter and Paul show, our intuitions about our own behavior and the behavior of others are by no means reliable. And even when they actually allow us to predict certain behaviors, as in most ordinary situations, they are circular, like the metaphor of the homunculus. It therefore seems extremely risky to try to formulate a scientific psychology based only on our intuitions. And yet, the idea that the human mind is simple and transparent and that conscious introspection, with sufficient effort, can yield access to all psychological phenomena, has had considerable influence, and still does today. Certain psychologists have even undertaken the task of unveiling the nature of thought through the use of *introspection*.

Can We Know Ourselves?

In order to study the workings of simple mental tasks, introspectionist psychologists such as those of the Würzburg school developed a method that, at first glance, seems fairly straightforward.[10] It involved having each subject observe his or her own thoughts and give an oral account of the psychological phenomena observed during the performance of a certain task. The rapidity of mental operations is such that it was necessary to proceed in a stepwise fashion. For example, for the association of one word with another, the observation was divided into four stages: a preparatory stage, a word presentation stage, a searching stage, and finally a stage for the appearance of the response word. One observer was to concentrate on the first stage, another on the second, and so forth, until the total number of stages involved was covered. It was hoped that this method would lead to a more complete description of mental events.

Despite these precautions, the results were rather disappointing. While certain interesting phenomena were uncovered, no important information could be obtained regarding the psychological mechanisms involved. The introspectionists proved above all that the exclusive utilization of data from introspection is not sufficient for the study of psychological mechanisms. Thus, when a word was presented, the associated word appeared immediately, without the observer being able to tell how this response had been possible. Often, in fact, our consciousness has access only to a result, while the complex process that makes it possible happens "in the dark," in a very rapid, automatic fashion. It only takes a few tenths of a second to recognize a familiar face, to picture a map of the United States, or to remember one's telephone number. What then can be said about more complex acts like understanding a sentence, solving a problem, or making an impromptu speech? Is it actually even possible to observe in oneself the multitude of unconscious and automatic processes that mutually activate one another, simultaneously exchanging and processing masses of data? The essentials of our mental life take place without our knowledge and remain impenetrable to our introspection.

Nevertheless, the idea that mental processes are transparent has resurfaced recently, especially in the field of artificial intelligence. For example, Nobel-prize winner H. A. Simon, one of the founders of artificial intelligence, wrote:

> Human subjects are not schizophrenic creatures who produce a stream of words parallel but irrelevant to the cognitive task they are performing. On the contrary, their thinking aloud protocols and retrospective reports can reveal in remarkable detail what information they are attending to while performing their tasks, and by revealing this information, can provide and orderly picture of the exact way in which the tasks are being performed: the strategies employed, the inferences drawn from the information, the accessing of memory by recognition.[11]

The appearance of computers in the 1960s prompted a vague technological optimism.[12] Persuaded that mental phenomena were simple and accessible, researchers in artificial intelligence turned to interviews with mathematicians and chess players. They hoped, through conscious examination, to extract the knowledge, strategies, and heuristics used by these experts and to incorporate them into computer programs.[13] Certain researchers even predicted that it would soon be possible to build machines that would act like thinking beings. They would be able to see, talk, and think. It would just be a question of computational power.

Today we have infinitely more powerful computers than we had in the early stages of data processing, and yet these predictions are still unfulfilled: many elementary problems relative to vision cannot yet be resolved by simulation. We can speculate that this failure is not simply due to the fact that our machines are not yet powerful enough. Intelligence is not one single and transparent aptitude. Cognition involves, on the contrary, a great number of specialized and automatic systems that process data concurrently and that remain impenetrable to conscious examination.

Before simulating them, we must study and understand what these systems accomplish and how they function. It is therefore very problematic to claim that we can straightforwardly use commonsense psychology to construct a scientific psychological theory. This is precisely the objection that behaviorists have raised to psychology as a whole. For them, invoking grand abstract systems that assume what they profess to explain is futile. A scientific psychological theory should strive to explain "intelligent" behavior not by calling upon some vague notion of intelligence, nor by resorting to commonsense psychology, but by basing itself solely on solid experimental techniques.

The Human Mechanism

How can we reduce the idea of intelligence to a series of elementary mechanisms which, by their joint action and organization, can produce complex behaviors, just as inert molecules give birth to living matter? How can we reduce complex objects of psychological study to simple data that will lend themselves to rigorous observation? These are the questions that psychologists have always asked. The behaviorists proposed a radical solution: permitting nothing but behavior as an object of study, in the hope that broad concepts such as intelligence would vanish of their own accord. Actually, they said, animals develop complex behaviors that it seems possible to explain without invoking the idea of intelligence. One might counter that the behavior of a person has nothing in common with that of a dog, a rat, or, more notably, a sea slug. And yet, the obvious differences between species do not necessarily mean that theoretical descriptions obtained from animals are devoid of all pertinence to the description of certain human mental processes.[14]

From Toad to Human

From ignorant machines . . .   Take the toad: its behavior is rather limited, but highly "rational." All tastes being equal in nature, it leans toward the consumption of earthworms, centipedes, and other small invertebrates. It can spend hours lying in wait for its prey. When a tasty morsel appears in its visual field, it turns toward it, approaches, immobilizes itself, and snaps it up with its tongue. Naturally, it avoids approaching animals it deems inedible or that might pose a threat.

If we wished to use the vocabulary of commonsense psychology, we would say that the toad is hungry, that it knows a certain number of things about earthworms and potential predators, and that it has a goal: gobbling up its prey. As a result, it adopts an approach strategy and a plan of attack adapted to its goal. But do these intuitive concepts really help us to explain the toad's behavior? Do they permit us to predict the animal's behavior outside its normal habitat? Neuroethological studies have shown they do nothing of the sort.[15]

Let's put our toad in a Plexiglas aquarium, and offer it a live earthworm outside the glass. It turns toward the prey, approaches, tries to snap it up . . . but bangs into the aquarium wall. It is indifferent to this failure: we can offer it the earthworm ten, twenty, a hundred times from outside the wall, and it will lunge at it with the same greed, as if for the first time. We can replace the earthworm with any elongated object in a horizontal position, a pencil, for example. The toad responds to these schematic, inedible stimuli exactly as if they were earthworms. Its behavior is thus not only stupid, but also very specific. An object with a *vertical* elongated shape, an "anti-earthworm," even if it is edible, does not elicit the slightest reaction on its part and, if several potential prey move into its visual field simultaneously, its behavior is inhibited and it does not move.

How to explain these phenomena? This behavior is so rigid and so dependent on exterior stimuli that it brings an automaton to mind. Furthermore, if a toad is raised in isolation, its reactions are exactly the same as those of a "wild" toad. The rigidity of its behavior, and its lack of adaptability, lead us to think that it is determined by genetic heritage rather than by experience.

To describe behavior of this type, ethologists speak of *innate releasing mechanisms* which produce a rigid sequence of actions in response to a very specific stimulus. The toad has a repertoire of four actions: orientation (o), approach (a), fixation (f), and capture (c). Each is released by the presence of a configuration in its visual field. Every stimulus with an elongated shape moving in relation to the background in a direction parallel to its main axis is treated as a potential prey. If it appears at the periphery of the visual field, the orientation behavior is released so as to place it at the center of the visual field. If it happens to be at a distance, the approach response is released. If it is close by, the fixation behavior has the effect of placing the prey in the visual field of both eyes. When it is both close and centered in the binocular visual field, the capture behavior is produced.

These four releasing mechanisms are independent of each other. Under natural conditions, the toad's behavior essentially follows the sequence (o, a, f, c). But if the distance between the prey and the toad is short, the sequence becomes (o, f, c). If the prey appears directly in front of the toad, capture can follow immediately. Conversely, if the prey flees, we can observe various sequences unfolding in which orientation and approach alternate until the conditions for capture are achieved. If we keep the prey at a fixed distance from the animal, it will go around in circles. Once a behavior is released, it continues to completion, even if we withdraw the releasing stimulus. If, for example, we cause the prey to disappear right after the period of fixation, the toad strikes precisely the spot where it has been, then swallows and "licks its chops" as if nothing were amiss.

These stereotyped behaviors are based, in fact, on very specific neuronal mechanisms. Thus we have neurons that respond selectively to certain prey. These "earthworm detectors," for example, integrate data coming from the retina and are sensitive only to certain spatiotemporal properties of the stimuli. This neuronal wiring is connected to the toad's motor system. A fairly complex behavior is in fact released and controlled by a simple and rigid group of mechanisms.

This same type of mechanism explains much more complex behavior, like the mating display of certain fish, nest-building, or the construction of a spider web. To take another example, the Australian wasp builds a funnel to protect its nest from parasites. This operation involves several stages. The end of each stage triggers the next one, so that the various behaviors are linked in a fixed order. As in the toad's case, the behavior is the fruit of a "program," or a rigid, hierarchical chain of actions.

It is thus useless to attribute a psychology to the toad, the spider, or the wasp, or to speak of desires, intentions, goals, or indeed of anything that makes up the substance of our mental life. We are dealing here with rigid, specialized mechanisms within which intentions, strategies, and capabilities are directly "wired." The knowledge results from the way the visual and motor systems are organized, the intentions boil down to the existence of releasing mechanisms, and the strategies are nothing but the temporal chain of these mechanisms. A television set is built to transmit images, the toad to hunt earthworms. Who would attribute a psychology to their television set?

. . . to Pavlov's dogs   In the past, various philosophers, including the British empiricists, have maintained that rigid reflexes such as innate releasing mechanisms do not sufficiently account for the richness and adaptability of the behavior of higher organisms. In their view, the more evolved the creature, the greater its ability to learn from experience. Thus, complex behaviors might be forged from rudimentary behaviors by the expedient of what they called "association." An organism could thus enlarge its repertoire of behaviors by associating a new response with a stimulus.

The great Russian psychologist Pavlov noticed that a piece of meat released certain behaviors in a hungry dog, among them salivation. The piece of meat acted like the earthworm for the toad. It automatically caused an *unconditioned reflex*, salivation. If we simultaneously and repeatedly introduce another stimulus, the sound of a bell in Pavlov's experiments, the animal's responses are modified: the bell to which the dog at first was indifferent now triggers salivation by itself.[16] A *conditioned reflex* appears which, unlike the unconditioned reflex, is reversible. If we keep ringing the bell in the dog's presence, without following it up with meat, the association established by the conditioning grows progressively weaker and finally disappears.

Pavlov thought that this mechanism was one of the fundamental elements of the learning experience. Indeed, conditioning would explain why the behavior of an organism depended on its history and the characteristics of the environment in which it was placed. But Pavlovian conditioning is totally unintelligent and blind. It simply augments the frequency of a response by associating one stimulus with a new one. Once stabilized, a conditioned reflex can serve as a basis for another type of conditioning. This is what is called *secondary conditioning*. For example, if we associate the sound of the bell that accompanies the meat with a light that goes on, the latter alone will suffice to induce salivation.

Despite the initial attractiveness of this account, he concluded that this process was far too limited a device to constitute a universal learning mechanism. It is actually fairly difficult, by this method, to elicit even slightly complex behaviors. Similarly, voluntary behaviors hardly ever have their roots in this type of conditioning. So it's hard to see how they could serve as a basis for intelligent behavior. This is why scientists began to seek a different method.

. . . by way of trained pigeons   By what mechanism can animals acquire complex behaviors? This is the question asked by the celebrated psychologist B. F. Skinner.[17] Drawing inspiration from the methods used by animal trainers from time immemorial, he forged the concept of *operant conditioning*. Its extremely simple and powerful principles explain the appeal this concept held for generations of researchers and the influence it still exerts today. It rests on the cardinal idea of *reinforcement*.

Take a pigeon and place it in a Skinner box – a cage equipped with a button the bird can press with its beak. For a period of time a signal light goes on and off in the cage. At the end of this period, a hatch opens, giving access to food, but only if the pigeon has pressed the button with its beak while the light was on. If it has failed to do this, the hatch does not open, and the bird must tighten its belt. After a certain number of tries, we observe that the pigeon has a tendency to peck at

Figure 1.3   A pigeon during an experiment in a Skinner box (Skinner, 1972).

the button more frequently when the light is on, and less while it is off. This behavior is extremely well adapted to the situation, for it allows the bird to eat more with less expenditure of energy.

We are not dealing here with Pavlovian conditioning, since there is no unconditioned stimulus onto which a conditioned stimulus can graft itself. Couldn't we then say that the pigeon has "understood" the relationship between the button, the signal light, and access to food, and that it "thinks" that pecking the button at the right moment will activate the subsequent opening of the hatch? In fact, it is useless to credit it with such a rich inner life. During the learning phase, the pigeon pecks around just about everywhere in its cage: sometimes it presses the button when the light is off, sometimes when it is on. Some of these actions are followed by food, others not. Since food is agreeable to the pigeon, the actions which procure it happen to get reinforced, while the others tend to fade away. Thus, at the end of a transitional period, only the association signal-light/peck-the-button remains.

We can complicate the situation at will, and confront the pigeon with two buttons, one red, the other green. To obtain food, it must peck the green one as soon as the light goes on and the red one as soon as it goes off. After a certain number of tries, more than in the preceding situation, it will succeed in selecting the sequence of actions that provide reinforcement. In this way we can teach pigeons extremely complex sequences of actions, which they execute with stunning speed.

This mechanism also allows the bird to adapt to new situations. For example, if we replace the red button with an orange button of a different shape, it gets used to this new configuration very quickly. It doesn't have to start over from scratch, but can use its experience to generalize its behavior to fit a related group of stimuli.

For all that, this type of behavior does not imply that the bird is intelligent or that it understands what is happening to it. The repeated presentation of the stimulus and the food simply selects the behaviors that produce reinforcement. Over the course of the learning period, moreover, sometimes the bird will make a superfluous gesture, give a little flap of its wing, or jump on one foot at the same time as it produces a correct response. In this case, it is the entirety of the behavior that is reinforced, so that in subsequent attempts, the pigeon will systematically repeat that same gesture, useless and sometimes even cumbersome, which is called *superstitious behavior*.[18] Then the whole routine is selected, whether it contributes to obtaining the reinforcement or not.

The Behaviorist Temptation

Complex behaviors in animals can be explained by the direct connection between stimulus and response. These connections can be innate (as with the toad) or established by operant conditioning (as with the pigeon), but in both cases we can dispense with the evocation of notions like desires, beliefs, goals, and, with greater reason, consciousness. Why can't we draw the same conclusions with regard to humans?

This idea is at the very root of a movement that claimed to formulate an "objective" psychology free of mental notions, which were thought to be circular and antiscientific. According to the champions of this *behaviorist* psychology, language, reasoning, perception, memory, in short, the totality of human behavior, can be explained by a "mental chemistry" in which only elementary stimulations and actions occur. Furthermore, the behaviorists thought that these stimulations could be reduced to measurable physical dimensions like intensity, wavelength, etc. They considered language, for example, to be a collection of stimulus-response connections acquired by operant conditioning. Words, for them, were responses associated with visual images or elementary sensations. Learning the word "red" would involve its association with the visual stimulation of the color red. The laws of association themselves would be very simple, general, and their use would require no intelligence at all. As in the case of Pavlov's dog, the fundamental principles of association would rest on the spatial or temporal contiguity of two events, their intensity or frequency of appearance. As in the pigeon's case, sentences would result from associative sequences, each word serving as a stimulus for the production of the following word.

In fact, for behaviorists, the very notion of the "idea" should be replaced by "observable" terms. This is why they postulated that thought could only be "subvocal language": the slightest idea that crossed our minds would in fact correlate to the infinitesimal movements of our articulatory muscles.

The idea of tackling the complex phenomena of the human mind with the aid of simple, uniform mechanisms was very seductive. Besides, it suggested a continuity between human beings and the rest of the animal kingdom. In spite of all this, however, the behaviorist movement ended in failure. Not only did the analogy between the sea slug and the human fail to explain such mental aptitudes as language and reasoning, but the explanation of behavior on the basis of stimulus-response relations failed even with animals. The explanation of simple behaviors cannot omit the animal's mental states which, although not directly observable, play a role of primary importance. This fact emerges clearly when we try to define precisely what a simple stimulus and a simple response are.

The Ambiguity of Stimulations   How to define a "stimulus"? The behaviorists thought it could be reduced to a physical measurement like body temperature, the wavelength of a luminous stimulus, etc. However, it was proved that such definitions were entirely too restrictive. We must take into account not only the isolated stimulus, but also the relationships between stimuli.

Let us consider the following imaginary experiment, inspired by actual experiments: placing a rat in a maze fitted with a panel painted two shades of gray. The rat must learn to turn left when the top of the panel is darker than the bottom, and right under the opposite circumstance. It was proved that once this behavior was learned, the rat generalizes it for many stimuli, one darker the other lighter, even when the colors were changed. The stimulus the rat reacts to is therefore defined by a relationship rather than by an absolute physical attribute.

Other experiments showed that certain animals are sensitive to rather general characteristics and that they are capable of reacting in terms of the overall shape (round, square, triangular) rather than the physical composition of a particular stimulus. Thus pigeons can learn to sort quite different stimuli into complex categories: for example, they can place pictures of oak, beech, and even pine trees in the same category, seen close up or from the air. During the Vietnam War, incidentally, the American army studied this faculty and trained pigeons to recognize men in the jungle. They were familiarized through the use of photographs. The astonishing thing is that they were able, somehow, to generalize from head shots or full-length portraits: once trained, they could pick out a man in any position, even ones they hadn't learned from photographs and even in the midst of dense vegetation. They were also taught to estimate the number of men and to radio this information by means of a little transmitter attached to their foot.

David Premack (1976) demonstrated that chimpanzees can learn to match abstract characteristics. To determine if they were able to recognize not only a category of objects, but also a quantity or a fraction, they were shown, for example, half an apple and a quarter of an apple. Premack then noticed that they could add these up. To make sure, he asked them, in effect, to chose another object that corresponded to the sum of the portions represented by the first two: they answered, in essence, that a half an apple plus a quarter of an apple equaled a bottle that was three-quarters full. Despite the disparity between these objects, they learned to perform this task with amazing ease. More amazing still, they were able to solve the problem even when the objects were all different: for example, they answered that a quarter of an apple plus a quarter of a bottle corresponded to a semicircle.

In humans, it is clear that perception is more than the reception of a physical energy. In fact, we've known for some time that visual stimuli can be ambiguous. For example, in figure 1.4 we can perceive either a young woman looking back over her shoulder or a three-quarter view of an old woman. But we can never see both images at the same time. Sev-

Figure 1.4 Boring's ambiguity: the reader can see an old woman looking down, or a young woman with her head turned away (Gregory, 1970).

eral different mental constructions can correspond to the same physical image. Visual perception therefore cannot be limited to stimulation by luminous energy: it also consists of a process of reconstructing and interpreting the image.

Our perceptual mechanism can even make us see objects that do not exist. Figure 1.5 is made up of four truncated octagons, but that is not what we perceive: we get a very distinct impression of a white rectangle standing out against the background. We see the shape of an object that is not there. It is as if our perceptual mechanism were attempting to depict the scene with a minimum of elements.

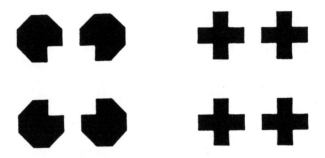

Figure 1.5   On the left, a cognitive shape. The reader sees a rectangle that stands out clearly on the page, when only a quarter of each black octagon has been removed. On the right, the rectangle does not appear because we do not see the crosses as truncated (Schiffmann, 1990).

These examples show that the relationship between the stimulus and its perception is not direct: our mind makes calculations and calls on abstract notions like those of object, form, and space. Perception is far from being a direct copy of reality. It is also a process of interpretation, of representation. It is therefore impossible to define a stimulus in purely physical terms without taking into account the mental constructs imposed by the organism.

The Intentionality of Responses   We run into problems the minute we try to define what a response is. For the behaviorists, a response should be quantifiable in terms of a muscular reaction or a set sequence of movements. Actually, in certain cases, that is what we observe – for example, when an animal, like our pigeon in its Skinner box, has no other option than to proceed by trial and error until it can execute the relatively arbitrary sequence the experimenter wants it to learn. However, most of the time, if we give an animal a chance to use its head in a more creative way, the response will be defined more by the goal sought than by, say, a determined muscular movement.

Take a dog and teach it to obtain food by opening a box with its right paw. Then, tie it up in such a way that this paw can no longer reach the box. Will it go on contracting the muscles of its right paw as if nothing were wrong? No, it will use its muzzle or another paw instead. It will respond with a motor sequence that is new and original, but adapted to the situation. It is the sought-after goal that counts.

This phenomenon is very common. For example, we can condition a rat to follow a precise path in a maze in order to obtain food. But if by making an opening in a wall we give it an opportunity to avoid an unnecessary detour, it will modify its usual behavior and take the shortcut.

Studies of primates have shown that their responses can be even more complex. For example, a chimpanzee accompanies its trainer into a field, where it sees her placing food in certain hiding places. Then it is set free. What does it do? It naturally seeks out the food wherever the trainer hid it. But it proceeds neither by hit or miss, nor by retracing the experimenter's steps. It follows a very precise path: the shortest distance between all the hiding places.[20] How then can we define a response without knowing the goal, the intentionality of the behavior studied?

These observations show not only that an animal acts in terms of a goal, but also that it possesses and uses an internal representation of its environment, a map of the maze in the rat's case, a map of the field in the chimpanzee's. This representation allows it to choose the response most suitable to the goal pursued. We cannot, then, say that an animal always acts in a mindless and mechanical way, or that it gropes for a reinforcement that will select, as if by magic, the behavior appropriate to the given situation. It clearly has a mental life of its own that casts doubt on behaviorist assumptions.

Mental Terms Are Necessary

The behaviorist school must be credited with demonstrating that the interpretation of behavior has a responsibility to be economical, even "hygienic." It must guard against propagating mysterious entities whose sole value is to mask our ignorance of the real mechanisms of our mind. Moreover, thanks to the behaviorists, the study of laboratory animals has led to the refinement of many techniques still used by modern experimental psychology. But it is clear that the mechanisms they invoked were inadequate to explain human behaviors in all their complexity, whether language, reasoning, discovery, or social relationships. Men and women are not toads or pigeons. We must therefore take seriously the existence of subjective mental states and admit that they number among the causes of our behavior. The human being can represent situations, but he or she can also abstract relationships and, most remarkably, make representations of representations. It is precisely this whole gamut that modern psychology must explain, in the mechanistic manner of the behaviorists, but without saddling itself with their overly simplistic principles. Which brings us back to our original question: how can we study human mental capacities scientifically?

Some might be tempted to give a pessimistic answer. For, on the one hand, it is impossible to account for the most simple human behaviors without invoking subjective mental states. On the other hand, mental terms are poorly defined, do not refer to observable realities, and may lead to pseudo-explanations. Therefore, human behavior cannot be studied. This is an exaggerated point of view. In fact, it is not because a theoretical term does not correspond to a directly observable reality that it is not scientific. That is just a positivist prejudice that haunted the behaviorists in their anxiety to bring psychology closer to the "exact" sciences. All science is driven to postulate primary theoretical terms that are not explained and refer to entities that are not directly observable. For example, in Newtonian physics, the concept of force acting at a distance remains unexplained. The fundamental principle of the mechanism ($f = ma$) is stipulated and given no justification whatsoever. Similarly, elementary particles are postulated and observable only through rather indirect inferences. Nevertheless, theoretical physics is a valid, fertile science. For once a relatively limited number of laws and primary terms are accepted, it is possible to explain a great many phenomena. Nothing prevents the same from being true for the study of mental faculties.

Commonsense psychology is unproductive because it postulates *too many* theoretical terms: *all* mental terms are assumed to be primary. Consequently, it can explain nothing. On the other hand, the failure of behaviorism is actually due not to an overly mechanistic conception of the workings of the mind, but to the excessive privilege accorded *too few* primary terms. Association, conditioning, and the stimulus-response connection are such rudimentary, weak mechanisms that they cannot account for even the most simple human behaviors. But between behaviorism and commonsense psychology, is there not a whole world of possibilities left for us to explore?

The objection will be made that human beings are unpredictable, and that it is impossible in a given situation to anticipate their reactions. What value, then, would a theory have that claimed to be scientific, but was incapable of prediction? However, just because a behavior is hard to predict does not mean it is utterly random. Meteorologists are still unable to forecast the weather a week in advance, but they do know that the movement of air masses is strictly determined by the laws of fluid dynamics. The weather system obeys these laws; it is not arbitrary, chaotic, or random. It is simply that these laws interact in ways too complex to be fully understood as yet. To forecast the weather, one would in fact have to know the position of every molecule of air at a given time, and of all the solid masses moving about in our biosphere.

Similarly, the ways in which humans react depend not only on the present situation, but also on all their past interactions with the environment. This does not mean that we cannot understand the principles governing their behavior. Their reactions are, in fact, far from random. They are strictly determined by subjective mental states, the contents of their memories, and their intentions. The example of computers shows this clearly. If you enter a series of commands into several computers of the same make, you will get different responses. One of them will reproduce what you have typed, another will display an incomprehensible series of characters, and a third will emit rumblings of explosion. The action of the environment therefore is not enough to explain the machine's behavior. But that does not mean it is in itself incomprehensible. Quite the contrary. The functioning of the machine is in fact determined by the way it has been programmed: the environment triggers different responses according to whether a data-processing, graphics, or chess-playing program is in its memory. Certain physical systems thus develop behaviors strongly influenced by their interior state. They seem erratic and random only if we are ignorant of the rules and principles that govern them.

In psychology, then, we can envisage formulating a theory comprising primary mental terms that would be the equivalent of the signs and symbols used in computer-programming languages. Such an analogy is extremely promising and has contributed to a renewal of interest in the study of superior mental faculties such as language, mental imagery, and reasoning, which had been abandoned by the behaviorists. Of course, the example of computers could not progress beyond the stage of a rather vague metaphor unless we had other means of empirically determining the nature of internal representations and the transformations to which they are subject in human beings. But how to go about this study? For a long time, it was thought that the learning process would give us the key to the problem.

Learning to Be Human?

How can we study the mental representations that underlie our behavior? What primary givens, what "atoms of thought" combine and recombine to form the flow of our inner life? These questions have often seemed insoluble. However, a solution has been proposed: by understanding how an aptitude is acquired, we might be able to determine its nature. Instead of directly studying the diversity of mental representations in the adult, we would have to focus our attention on their progressive stabilization during the course of development. We would then, of course, discover that this involves a relatively uniform operation: the *learning process*. Studying the ways mental aptitudes are developed in the child would help us to understand the cognitive mechanism in the adult. However, strictly speaking, it would be in perpetual evolution, moving from one stage to the next, and never standing still.

The impact of this approach has been enormous. From Piaget's genetic epistemology, to Engels, Wallon, and Sartre, all have assigned a leading role to the learning process. Thus, for Piaget,

> the nature of a living reality is revealed neither by its initial stages alone, nor by its terminal stages, but by the very process of its transformations. The initial stages actually only take on meaning in terms of the state of equilibrium toward which they aim, but, conversely, the equilibrium achieved can only be understood in terms of the successive constructions that led to it. In the case of a concept or of a body of intellectual operations, it is therefore not just the starting point that matters, always inaccessible as a real first departure in any event, or the final equilibrium, about whose actual finality we are never sure either: it is the law of progressive constitution, or the operative system in its progressive constitution. . . . It is thus only through a sort of shuttling back and forth

between the genesis and the final equilibrium (the terms genesis and final being merely relative one to the other and having no absolute meaning in themselves) that we can hope to learn the secret of the acquisition of knowledge, that is, of the elaboration of scientific thought.[21]

It is our goal, then, to define the law of progressive constitution according to which we acquire mental aptitudes such as language, reasoning, etc.

The Chicken or the Egg

In its most radical form, this thesis implies that the mental life of the organism depends exclusively on the environment. Nothing would be innate in humans except a few general principles enabling them to learn, and a baby would enter the world utterly devoid of any mental structure or a priori knowledge. Its mind would be empty, comparable to a blank piece of paper on which the culture, the sociocultural environment, and its teachers would write. Language, perception, thought, and memory would, therefore, be just so many aptitudes intimately linked to the culture and determined by the environment.

Learning by instruction is the mechanism that would allow structures present in the environment to be transposed into an organism. The fact, for example, that newborns are plunged into a macroscopic universe with three spatial dimensions and one temporal dimension would imply the organization of their perceptual mechanisms around three-dimensional objects that retain stability in space and time. In the same way, it would be because they live in the midst of a linguistically rich environment that they can integrate that structure and become capable of producing speech.

But how would this learning process be possible? The idea seems interesting, but how do we get beyond the intuition stage to arrive at a theory that can be tested? Piaget criticized this overly simplistic vision and attempted to postulate a more precise conception of the learning mechanism. According to him, it is not the environment as such that determines what the organism learns, but its own actions. By observing that certain actions produce the same results and by internalizing these regularities, the child succeeds in elaborating increasingly abstract representations of her environment. For example, it would be by making movements in one direction and then reversing the sequence only to find herself back where she started, that the child would become aware that objects retain their shape and position. She would then internalize the abstract concepts of identity and reversible process.

In fact, despite its sophistication, this approach is as imprecise as the idea of learning by instruction. We fail to see how this internalization mechanism would actually function, nor do we have a better understanding of how abstract representations could construct themselves purely on the basis of actions. As a result, the concept of the learning process considered as a transfer from the exterior to the interior is not very useful unless it also incorporates a precise description of the transfer mechanism itself.

Furthermore, cases where an organism learns by transfer of information seem extremely limited among natural species. Konrad Lorenz demonstrated, for example, that the duckling learns to recognize and follow its mother by a fixation mechanism or *imprinting*. Contrary to how things work in other species, the minute a duckling leaves the egg the image of the first object it sees is imprinted on it as if on a photographic plate, and for the duckling this is the image of its "mother." Under normal ecological conditions, the object is indeed its mother, but Konrad Lorenz demonstrated that, under other conditions, a man or even an electric train can just as well fill the bill.[22] This imprinting can only take place a very short time after birth. In this case, information present in the environment is indeed actually transferred to the psychological mechanism.

In humans, we see a similar phenomenon in the "flashbulb memory." It may happen that certain exceptional situations are etched in our memories, so that years later we can still describe them in the minutest detail. However, it was proved that this sort of phenomenon is extremely rare and limited to emotionally charged events. Such mechanisms cannot, therefore, account for all human mental aptitudes.

While we can clearly see how the transfer of sensory information to a "flashbulb" memory could take place, we perceive more dimly how abstract concepts like those of three-dimensional space, language, or rational thought could be transferred from the exterior to the interior. As teachers know only too well, students are not blackboards on which they can write at will. Knowledge, like luck, cannot be transmitted. Each student has his or her own ideas and understands what he or she chooses to understand.

As computer science demonstrates, a transfer from the exterior to the interior is only possible if the system already contains an initial internal structure that allows it to represent and process external information. The duckling's imprint is only possible insofar as it possesses a visual

Figure 1.6   When the ducklings were born, Konrad Lorenz was the first moving shape they saw. They followed him as if he were their mother.

system that allows it to represent objects from a three-dimensional world and another system that compares new data with the "image of mother" preserved in its memory. These initial structures, or preexisting cognitive systems, cannot themselves by acquired by instruction. So the question we must ask ourselves consists precisely in wondering, for example, to what specific mechanisms we owe our representation of space, or the foundations that make the acquisition of concepts possible. Learning by instruction obviously does not explain them to us.

This idea assumes an initially empty organism which, little by little, is filled through contact with the milieu. In fact, it contains a paradox like the one Plato denounced in his early dialogues, leading him to support theses of a rationalist nature. Even the knowledge of a simple fact like "chickens lay eggs" presupposes other facts. They, in turn, refer to others, and so on, ad infinitum. How then can children learn things if to do so they need to already possess a vast body of knowledge that includes the things they are supposed to learn? And how can they learn if they know nothing? In other words, the concept of learning by instruction, to be explanatory, must first of all be explained. This is why it has lost a great deal of its appeal for researchers today, many of whom have turned to a more realistic model.

From Chaos to Order

The idea of *learning by selection* is the exact opposite of learning by instruction. It assumes, in effect, that individuals are so rich in possibilities that they are incapacitated. To become functional, they must select possibilities that are compatible with the environment and eliminate the rest. The impoverishment of the cognitive potential thus permits an improvement in its efficacy. This point of view, adopted by many scientists from William James to Jean-Pierre Changeux, by way of Darwin, Thorndike, Skinner, and Simon, has the advantage of sidestepping the logical paradox pointed out by Plato. Contrary to learning by instruction, it actually gives the specificity of the organism an important role, endowing it with two fundamental mechanisms. First of all, an *internal generator of diversity* – completely blind, capable of producing mental representations compatible with our psychological machinery and independent of exterior stimulations – which Jean-Pierre Changeux calls "pre-representations."[23] Secondly, a *mechanism of selection* that compares internal representations with those coming from the environment and selects those that are compatible.

The innate component of behaviors is thus well safe-guarded in this schema, which is more precise than the one furnished in the learning by instruction account. However, such a schema remains general and of little use as long as it fails to specify in detail the workings of the two mechanisms it assumes: the generator of diversity and the mechanism of selection. According to which writer you read, one or the other has been emphasized, although most researchers, influenced by behaviorism, stressed the role of the process of stabilization over the generating mechanism.

The tabula chaotica   Skinner forged a selectionist theory in which the generator of diversity was not specific. For him, the organism is initially equipotential and acts in a random manner. Only reinforced behaviors are preserved. Thus he replaces the empirical *tabula rasa* by what one might call a *tabula chaotica*. Furthermore, for Skinner, and in accordance with behaviorist principles, selection is not based on representations but on behaviors. From this perspective, the learning process is, therefore, reduced to a blind groping: the organism tests things randomly and learns, as it were, from its mistakes. Positive reinforcement fixes one behavior and discards others. However, this theory runs into a number of obstacles.

According to this view, the learning process resembles the evolution of species. In the beginning, the world was a chaos of matter from which, gradually, the first cell was formed. It then combined with other cells to create multicellular organisms, and so forth. In the same fashion, the baby's mind would at first be a chaos. Then, starting with its first sensations, it would gradually elaborate complex and abstract representations.

If evolution were the model accounting for human psychological development, the learning process would accelerate with time. The first stages would be long and difficult, and then would succeed one another with increasing ease and rapidity. Thus, it took hundreds of millions of years for the first cell to appear, and one-tenth that time for the first vertebrates to appear. Starting from nothing and creating a structure by trial and error is very arduous. In contrast, the richer the structure at our disposal, the easier it is to obtain new organisms by minor modifications. It follows, according to this model, that a ninety-year-old man would be able to learn Javanese in a few hours and that a fifty-year-old woman could learn to sing operas in the space of a few minutes. But, as we all know, age is not accompanied by increased intellectual versatility. On the contrary, the ability to learn decreases markedly with the years. We cannot, therefore, say that humans have an unlimited capacity for adaptation and amelioration. Our sad world seems made in such a way that young organisms learn faster and forget less than their elders. There seems to be a time for learning new things and a time for using what we have learned.

Furthermore, what the infant must learn before having all the normal human aptitudes at its disposal can seem colossal. It must, for example, learn that the world is made up of objects, that the space surrounding it has three dimensions, that all objects have a spatial and temporal permanence, that they can be counted, that the same causes produce the same effects, that animate beings exist which are divided into species, that the infant itself must have behaviors peculiar to the "human" species, and so forth. It must learn so many things in such a short time that we may well wonder how humans ever manage to acquire all the knowledge they have as adults. Furthermore, as we have seen, abilities like speech or space perception involve more than a simple selection of appropriate behaviors. They are, rather, internal states that are selected.

Even if many researchers concede this point today, they still postulate, like Skinner, a rather general and non-specific generator of diversity. Yet it is hardly likely that the accomplishments of the human baby are attained through a blind process of trial and error. If such were the case, learning to talk would be quite impossible. Suppose that a baby, hearing the word "chocolate" spoken each time she is offered a piece of a certain brown substance, formulates the hypothesis that this group of sounds refers to that substance. How could it extend its discovery to liquid chocolate, powdered chocolate, or white chocolate? And why would it formulate the hypothesis that "chocolate" just refers to the brown substance and not, for example, to the brown substance *plus* the hand that holds it or the substance *plus* the aluminum foil in which it is wrapped? If the baby were not already governed by certain prior awarenesses, by certain structures, all learning would be impossible.

To emphasize the study of the stabilization of aptitudes without ever making reference to their specificity is therefore not tenable. Certain aptitudes are found in one species but not in another, like language in humans, echo location in bats and dolphins, sensitivity to polarized light in bees and to the earth's magnetic field in birds, and even the use of the nose as a grasping organ in elephants. The child, unlike the chimpanzee, produces pre-representations that allow him to acquire language. But the chimpanzee has a representation of three-dimensionality that allows it to jump from branch to branch without making errors in judgment that would have catastrophic consequences for the survival of the species. Better a chimpanzee than a college student when it comes to such crucial matters!

Selectionism, therefore, in its radical form, leaves unanswered the question of why all members of a species, regardless of the environment, converge on characteristic aptitudes. We must, therefore, now look to genetic endowment.

Everyone a Potential Mozart?   Ethology shows that organisms make very specific acquisitions. The generator of variability is not equipotential. On the contrary, it is regulated to produce certain "pre-representations" adapted to the species. For instance, young birds have an opportunity to learn many songs. But it is in relation to a determined environment that they take up a particular "dialect." The bird initially has a whole repertory of acoustic contrasts at its disposal, of "syllables" and possible sound sequences that allow it to encode the sounds coming to it from the environment. Its acquisitions are therefore limited to sounds it can represent in this manner, that is, to sounds appropriate to its species. Upon contact with the songs of its milieu, a young bird selects the most frequent contrasts and sequences and disregards those that are not relevant. After a critical period, the bird begins to produce a rigid subgroup of possible vocalizations which is compatible with the songs heard during the learning period and which respect the genetic requirements of the species.[24] Here the environment plays only a limited role: at best it serves to release or select the potentialities defined within a genetic envelope.

J. B. Watson, the founder of behaviorism, wrote:

> Give me a dozen healthy infants . . . and my own specified world to bring them up in and I'll guarantee to take any one at random and train him to become any type of specialist I might select – doctor, lawyer, artists, merchant-chief and yes, even beggar-man and thief, regardless of his talents, penchants, tendencies, abilities, vocations, and race of his ancestors.[25]

And yet, from the evidence, we owe neither Mozart nor Einstein to this type of procedure. It is not because children live in very different environments that they evolve in divergent directions. The sensory environment of children raised in the Sahara Desert, in contact with nature, has little in common with the surroundings of those who grow up in our large cities. Yet they all develop fairly similar basic psychological aptitudes.

The acquisition of language no doubt provides the most striking example. It is well established today that the human brain possesses an innate disposition to acquire language in radically different environments. The American linguist Noam Chomsky furnished the best arguments in favor of this thesis.

> No one would take seriously a proposal that the human organism learns through experience to have arms rather than wings or that the basic structure of particular organs results from accidental experience. Rather, it is taken for granted that the physical structure of the organism is genetically determined, though of course variation along such dimensions as size, rate of development and so forth will depend in part on external factors. From embryo to mature organism, a certain pattern of development is predetermined, with certain stages, such as the onset of puberty or the termination of growth, delayed by many years. Variety within these fixed patterns may be of great importance for human life, but the basic questions of scientific interest have to do with the fundamental, genetically determined, scheme of growth and development that is a characteristic of the species and that gives rise to structures of marvelous intricacy. . . . But human cognitive systems, when seriously investigated, prove to be no less marvelous and intricate than the physical structures that develop in the life of the organism. Why, then, should we not study the acquisition of a cognitive structure such as language more or less as we study some complex bodily organ?[26]

As the baby grows and begins to master her mother tongue, we note a succession of stages that seem to depend more on a "biological clock" than on the environment. At the very beginning, the baby babbles, and then she engages in syllabic games that soon lead to the production of words, and then of sentences. These are short at first, one or two words, and then become progressively longer and longer. As figure 1.7 indicates, the number of words produced by the infant begins to grow exponentially at about two and a half years. This is what we call the *lexical explosion*.

On the whole, parents are the passive and surprised witnesses to the way their children manage to master language. Of course, anxious mothers and fathers try to arrange things so that their children can learn more easily and quickly, but this type of effort is never crowned

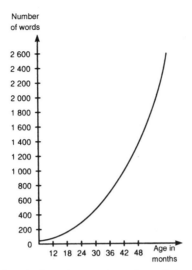

Figure 1.7   The lexical explosion: the number of words increases in a dizzying fashion at about two years. For the next six years, the child acquires a word an hour.

with success. We know today that, no matter how many hours parents spend speaking to their children, they all learn to talk at approximately the same age. We can of course improve certain performances, for example by pushing the child to acquire a richer vocabulary. But this sort of training only improves his linguistic abilities marginally, and gives him the air of a trained seal more than anything else.

The fairly regular calendar stages that the acquisition of language follows correspond to changes in other behaviors. The overall view of the child's progress suggests a maturation process that is both motor and linguistic at the same time. And yet language does not develop through maturation alone. How the environment induces the child to learn to speak the language of those around it remains to be explained, and has proved to be one of the most exciting areas of research in the field of cognitive science. Progress has been possible because we have recognized the important role the organism's innate predispositions play in the learning process, and because considerable effort has been expended on the empirical investigation of the generator of variability, also called *universal grammar*, that makes the acquisition of language possible.

Babies, as we have seen, walk when they should walk and talk when they should talk, as if a "biological clock" controlled when each of these aptitudes should click into place. Naturally, the environment plays an indispensable active role: it can trigger, select, and regulate various preexisting mechanisms. But in no case can the environment modify what has been defined by the organism's genetic program. The child, actually without the slightest difficulty, acquires certain aptitudes like language and walking, but she will never be able to fly like a canary or find her way in the dark like a bat. Of course, under conditions of great privation, language difficulties appear, just as a tree lacking earth cannot grow. But under normal conditions, the tree grows, and it is not the composition of the soil that induces it to produce bananas rather than coconuts.

The Innate and the Acquired   In *Biological Foundations of Language,* Eric Lennenberg argued for a naturalistic conception of language.[27] He was one of the rare researchers in the 1960s to understand that language rests on a biological foundation and to maintain that, while it is not fully specified in the genetic code, it is not fully learned either. In order to evaluate the roles played by genetic endowment and the environment in the acquisition of aptitudes, he proposed certain criteria. One of them, the presence or absence in all members of the species of the aptitude in question, provides a first clue. Thus, a minority of people know the Morse code. It would be absurd to say that mastery of the Morse code is a universal innate ability. Conversely, the fact that all humans speak a language suggests that linguistic aptitude could be a consequence of our genetic inheritance.

Another criterion, the existence of an organ which is the seat of the aptitude in question, suggests that it is genetically determined. Thus, certain aptitudes like an upright posture depend on specialized neurological structures dedicated to that task. We cannot be taught to grow a cerebellum or a eustachian tube no matter how hard we try. A final criterion concerns the history of an aptitude. Writing has a history. It took millennia to elaborate systems of notation that were ideographic at first, then syllabic and orthographic, an evolution that perhaps is not over yet. But regarding *spoken* language, there is no trace of an evolution of this sort. Of course, languages change and certain ones disappear, but we find no trace of a progression from a "primitive" language to an "evolved" language as such.

The acquisition of all physical or mental abilities is not, of course, entirely determined by the genotype. Besides the aptitudes appropriate to our species, we can develop particular skills, like mastering a musical instrument, riding a bicycle, or hang gliding. We can learn to write, do mathematical calculations, and build bridges. But these skills are based on the existence of universal aptitudes that remain within the limits defined by the genetic baggage of the species. There are "skills" that no human being could ever acquire. Paradoxically, we can therefore say that the fact that a large part of what we know depends on the learning process actually proves that not everything is learned. We still must know how to learn . . .

The Innate in the Evolutionary Chain   A rather widespread assumption has it that the higher we climb on the evolutionary chain, the more the innate disappears in favor of the acquired. The behavior of primitive animals like the sponge, the wasp, or the toad would be totally determined, while vertebrates would possess some faculties of adaptation and mammals would be able to learn rudimentary behaviors. At the very top of the chain, humans would be capable of adapting to any situation and would no longer be determined by any genetic restrictions. This position, in fact, owes more to ideology than to the natural sciences.

On the contrary, we could assert that the more evolved an organism, the more innate specialized aptitudes it possesses. In fact, we had to wait until the second half of this century for this issue to be tackled with the necessary seriousness and rigor, particularly in the experimental study of newborns. These studies revealed to us that the innate baggage of humans is actually far more important than we had thought.

One of the first significant studies in this field dates from the 1960s.[28] It showed that, from the earliest months, babies possess a sufficiently detailed perception of space to recognize depth and to avoid falling off the edges of things. The children were placed on a transparent sheet of Plexiglas resting on a flat surface covered with a checkerboard pattern. At a certain point, the patterned surface dropped down a yard below the Plexiglas sheet. The monitors observed that the child would move readily across the flat surface, but would stop at the edge of the "cliff," as we can see in figure 1.8.

This study caused a considerable change in our perspective: it contributed to a renewed dynamism and interest in the study of the infant, who could no longer be thought of simply as a blank page upon which the environment writes at will. It now seemed that the child does not have to learn everything after all.

Skinner's brand of selectionism therefore failed for two reasons. First, it limited the elements susceptible of selection to behaviors only.

Figure 1.8   The "visual cliff": in Walk and Gibson's experiment, the baby stops where the checkerboard drops off (Gleitman, 1981).

Secondly, it postulated a nonspecific, equipotential generator of variability. The more modern versions of selectionism, on the other hand, vigorously reject the first of these premises. Thus J.-P. Changeux and S. Dehaene are advocates of "mental Darwinism," a theoretical framework within which mental representations (considered as states of activation in brain cells) are the basic elements whose dynamic is explained by the following two mechanisms: "(a) the spontaneous productions of transient, dynamic, and coherent but fleeting activity states referred to as pre-representations, which would be analogs of the Darwinian variations; (b) the selection and stabilization of some of these pre-representations by matching percepts arising from external and semantic internal stimuli."[29]

According to this view, the learning process is more like the formulation and testing of hypotheses than like the pigeon's erratic pecking in its cage. It has a considerable advantage over Skinner's theory. However, for this framework to describe the acquisition of knowledge by humans, we cannot content ourselves with a nonspecific generator of diversity. Nor can we allow it to be indeterminate. It becomes, on the contrary, very important to specify the characteristics peculiar to each of the mental aptitudes. To do this, it is necessary to conduct an empirical study of their operation in the healthy adult, and also in the infant which has as yet had very little contact with its environment. By comparing the descriptions obtained from each of these extremes, we will arrive at a clear understanding of the "generator of pre-representations" or fixed bases specific to this or that aptitude. Only at a later stage will it become possible to examine the progressive unfolding of these acquisitions in the course of development and to attempt to explain them with the help of the mechanism of selection.

The appeal exerted by the concept of learning is linked to the fact that the mechanisms of acquisition were thought to be simpler, and more rudimentary, than the mental aptitudes observed in adults. But nothing of the sort is true. The existence of a simple, uniform learning mechanism, which would function in the same way for language, reasoning, the perception of faces and of music, is being seriously challenged. Also, the idea that the study of the progressive stabilization of aptitudes is the sole means of exploring mental functions is no longer accepted unquestioningly. The idea of learning by selection has the virtue of placing the emphasis on the innate foundations of behavior. But in so doing, it shifts the focus of study away from the progressive stabilization of mental faculties in the course of development, and toward the organization and workings of the different structures that make a particular accomplishment possible.

From Newborn to Human Nature

The human brain undergoes perpetual modification, interacting with the environment from birth. However, beyond these modifications and exchanges with the outside world, certain *invariants* must exist which explain why all human beings, despite the great diversity of environments in which they live, develop similar aptitudes. We can label as the *initial state* the body of invariant psychological characteristics that guides acquisitions and assures their convergence toward the *stable state* that is found in adults. It is the study of this initial state that will occupy the following chapters. But how can we explore it empirically? By observing newborns. They have had, by definition, such minimal contact with the environment that all behaviors observed from birth could reasonably be considered innate.

One precaution, however. Just because a behavior is not observed in the initial stage does not mean that we must conclude that it is necessarily learned. Certain structures can perfectly well be put in place by *functional maturation* at two to four months, at about eighteen months, or even at about seven years. There is a strong possibility that the observation of newborns in fact leads us to underestimate the *initial state* of the human species. All the same, this method can contribute to clarifying the origins of our aptitudes.

Atavistic Reflexes or Precursory Behaviors?

Newborns are far from totally amorphous. Pediatricians' observations have revealed that they have an impressive panoply of highly complex behaviors at their disposal.[30] Holding a newborn so that its feet are touching a surface triggers behavior that strongly resembles walking. When an infant is stimulated on one side of its mouth, it turns its head in that direction. When we shake its head, it spreads its forearms while opening its hands and extending its fingers. If, while it is lying on its back, we turn its head to the left, its right hand will touch its head while its right leg flexes toward the arm. It can also hang from a cord or hold its breath underwater.

We have generally minimized the importance of these behaviors, taking them for simple "primary," "atavistic," that is, "archaic" reflexes that reproduce those of other animal species. The reflexes of palmar and plantar prehension are often used to illustrate the postural resemblances at birth between infants and animals like the sloth.

However, this analogy has never seriously been developed, and we simply invoke the term "archaic reflexes." But a term explains nothing in itself, especially if it is also markedly inappropriate. How, in fact, can we explain the resemblance between some of these so-called reflexes and adult behaviors?

Instead of assuming, for lack of explaining them, that these reflexes are "archaic," shouldn't we instead study them as evidence of the initial stage of our specific abilities and as precursors of our adult aptitudes? Along the same lines, there are two possible approaches to explaining the

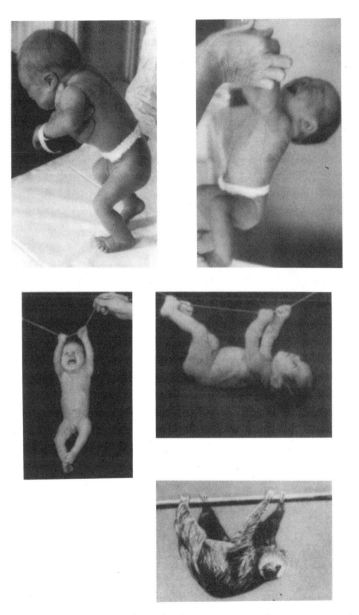

Figure 1.9   Some atavistic reflexes in the newborn, as they were presented by Peiper and Amiel-Tison. Photograph of a sloth in a natural position (Peiper, 1963).

successive appearance of two sets of human teeth. One involves claiming that they result from two very different mechanisms. For example, milk teeth would be archaic and closer to the dentition of inferior animal species than to adult human teeth. But we could also assume that milk teeth and adult teeth are only successive versions of each other. This proposition opens up wider prospects. The smaller milk teeth are well adapted to a child's head, but would not fit the adult jaw. Since dental matter is rigid and solid, replacing the milk teeth by other, larger ones once the diameter of the head has been established would be a convenient solution. Early behaviors might be explained by similar mechanisms.

The walking "reflex" disappears almost completely at about the eighth week. Is it archaic, or is it actually a precursor of "real" walking? If we give newborns a daily workout, we can prolong the period during which the reflex is active.[31] These children will stand and walk before the rest. However, premature walking often leads to problems with bones and joints. It seems, therefore, that the early behavior and its adult form are closely linked. If the reflex is inhibited during a large part of the first year, it is because the infant's bones do not yet have sufficient rigidity. A safety device thus keeps the child from walking until his whole body is ready. Rather than archaic reflexes, we should therefore call them precursory behaviors. The same principle undoubtedly also applies to mental aptitudes.

Modern cognitive science, then, must undertake a systematic exploration of the early behaviors of the newborn. In this way it can bring to light the invariable abilities unique to humans in general and elevate itself to the rank of a *science of human nature*. To do this, it must base itself on a rigorous experimental foundation.

Observing the Newborn

We could, like the average parents, settle for direct observation in everyday situations. But this simple approach is extremely limited and depends on generally unreliable intuitions. Our cognitive equipment makes poor judgments. Besides, if its evaluations were at all trustworthy, a universal psychological theory would have been in place for ages. Our mind jumps to conclusions, erasing aspects of reality that conflict with our preconceptions and exaggerating the importance of isolated events. These limitations, typical of *circumstantial observation*, are further aggravated by the fact that parental observers are notoriously prejudiced and actually deserve to be studied themselves.

But popular wisdom can indeed contain some truth. Boys are rowdier than girls, aren't they? And the second child learns to talk more slowly than the first even though it's brighter, right? And all little babies love music, don't they? Actually, these observations remain to be proved. One mother may think that her child is nothing but a kind of vegetable subject to the influences of the environment, and another that he or she has a distinct personality at birth. Which one is right? To decide, we would have to place identical twins in the same environment and vary their parents' attitude towards them, the relationship between the parents themselves, and so forth. This experiment is obviously impossible to perform: we cannot evaluate and control all the factors in the natural environment that influence a child. Observations made in the bosom of the family therefore cannot be conclusive.

Eager to overcome the limitations of circumstantial observation, determined yet modest psychologists therefore abandon ambitious, unverifiable questions and settle for those that seem simpler and that are, for that very reason, easier to control. They devise experimental protocols that allow them to control with precision all the variables and undesirable effects that might falsify their interpretations. To do this, it is essential to place the child in a simplified and constant experimental environment in order to reduce and standardize exchanges with it as much as possible. For example, the person conducting the experiment must not know in advance what the newborn is supposed to do, so as to avoid influencing the outcome, even unconsciously. Finally, psychologists assign the rating of performances to automatic equipment and repeat their experiments as often as possible.

But how do they formulate the questions they want to ask babies about what they see and hear, and how they perceive physical events, inanimate objects, living creatures, humans, faces, language? This can seem as daunting as trying to communicate with an animal or even an extraterrestrial. Fortunately, a universal nonverbal language exists: the language of behaviors as we perceive them with the help of experimental equipment.

Newborns are not amorphous or impervious to changes in their environment. They can be sleeping or waking. The alternation of these phases depends on the coming of day and night, as well as on mealtimes. When babies are awake, their moods can also change abruptly: speak to them softly and they will open their eyes, stare at you, and perhaps smile. Frighten them with a sudden gesture and they will start to cry.

We've known for a long time that respiration, cardiac rhythm, and other physiological data reflect the baby's waking state fairly accurately. But one of the best devices for evaluating infants is furnished by the sucking reflex. The sucking rate, that is the number of "sucks" per unit of time, as well as their volume, is closely correlated to other physiological data that reflect the waking state. The more babies suck, the more alert they are and the more attentive to their surroundings. In experiments, using a procedure called *non-nutritive sucking*, we place in the baby's mouth a blind nipple connected to a pressure gauge that measures the volume and number of sucks per unit of time. This gauge allows us to evaluate the interest babies have in a particular stimulus. Thus we can exploit their spontaneous tendency to be interested in what is new. But, like everyone else, babies get bored if we repeatedly present them with the same stimulus. This is what we call *habituation*. The song "The Yellow Brick Road," fresh and delightful at first, grows tiresome when played fifty times. Similarly, a baby hearing her father repeat "coochie-coochie-coo" over and over again, eventually loses interest in this charming stimulus. We can exploit this phenomenon in order to ask babies very precise questions about their abilities.[32]

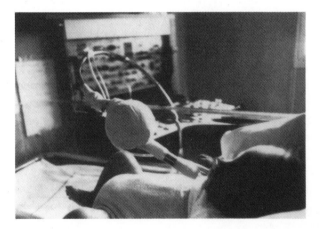

Figure 1.10   Measuring the rate of non-nutritive sucking in a newborn.

Suppose we want to know, for example, if newborns are capable of distinguishing two very similar stimuli, like two shades of red. We begin by presenting them with one of the shades for a certain length of time, called the *period of habituation*. They gradually get used to it and their level of activation drops progressively: they lose interest in the stimulus. Once their degree of alertness has fallen below a certain pre-established level (called the *criterion of habituation*), we change the stimulus and present them, for example, with a red of a slightly different shade for a certain time, called the *test period*. If all the newborns are stimulated by the change, that is, if they start to suck harder, we can deduce that they have perceived the difference between the two stimuli, and that the second one is "new" to them: this what we term *dishabituation*. On the other hand, if they have not perceived the change, their degree of alertness continues to drop. To evaluate the performances of newborns quantitatively, we generally measure, as indicated in figure 1.11, the difference between the two last minutes of the period of habituation and the first two minutes of the test period.

We must be certain that the revival of activity we have recorded is indeed due to the change in stimuli, and not to some other factor. For

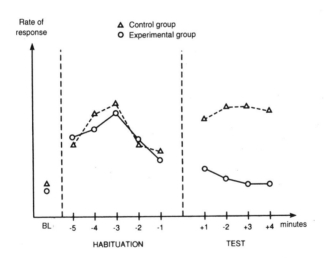

Figure 1.11   Schematic reconstruction of an experiment in habituation in the newborn: The babies are placed at random in the control group or the experimental group. From a base line (LB), we measure their spontaneous response rates. During the habituation phase, these responses trigger an auditory or visual reinforcement. The period of habituation ends when the baby reaches the criterion: a drop in the response rate. During the test phase, only the experimental group receives a different reinforcement. We then compare the results of the control group and the experimental group during the test phase. If the groups differ, this shows that the experimental group detected the change.

example, sometimes babies doze off and then wake up, and their sucking rate increases spontaneously, without a change in stimulus. We therefore conduct the experiment with a first group, called the *experimental group*, for which the stimulus is changed after habituation, and a second group, called the *control group*, which continues to receive the original stimulus even after having attained the criterion of habituation. We then compare the level of activation in both groups right after the change. If that of the experimental group is clearly higher than that of the control group, the change really was noticed, since it is the only difference between the two groups.

The principles of operant conditioning allow us to go even further. We can teach babies an arbitrary connection between a behavior (sucking or visual fixation) and the presentation of a stimulus. For example, we project a visual stimulus onto a screen placed before the infants. If they do not stare at it, the stimulus disappears. If they stare at it, it remains illuminated as long as they keep their eyes on it. When they look away, the stimulus disappears for a certain time, and then the sequence starts over. Thus, the babies can control the length of the presentation with their eyes. We can apply the same idea to non-nutritive sucking: then the newborns trigger the presentation of a stimulus only if they produce sucking responses of sufficient volume.

When this connection has been learned, we note that babies become habituated to it, and that after a certain time they produce the behavior that triggers the presentation of the stimulus less and less frequently. When the criterion of habituation has been reached, we change the stimulus for the experimental group and leave it unchanged for the control group. Once again, if there is a revival of the triggering behavior in the first group, we can conclude that the babies have noticed the change.

The methods of visual fixation also allow us to measure babies' *preferences*. The preceding experiments tested their reaction to the presentation of a single stimulus each time there was reinforcement. But we can proceed differently and present two stimuli at the same time, leaving the choice open as to which will attract the babies' attention.

We present the babies with two images side by side and measure how many times they stare at each one.[33] An experimenter invisible to the infants notes the duration of the visual fixation on each stimulus. In general, we arrange it so that the experimenters do not know which stimuli are being presented: for example, they look through a hole located in the center of the projection screen. Thus, the babies can only see the stimuli, while the experimenters can only see the babies and the direction of their gaze. In certain cases, babies tend to look first, and for a longer time, at one stimulus rather than another, no matter which side it is presented on. We speak then of preference. Of course, the images are only presented when the babies are looking at the middle of the screen.

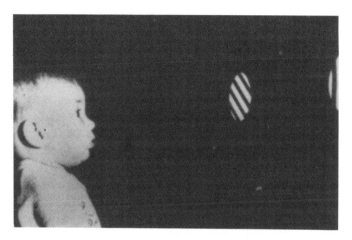

Figure 1.12   Experiment in visual preference (Held's laboratory): the baby sees two images simultaneously and the experimenter calculates the image he or she stares at preferentially.

This method, whose value has been widely demonstrated, is one of the principal means of studying the infant's visual world. But it can also be adapted to measure auditory preferences. We present the babies with two red blinking lights. If they look at one side, they hear one sound; if they look at the other side, they hear another. After a certain time, they learn this connection and succeed in indicating their preference by triggering through their own visual fixations the presentation of a particular stimulus.

These experimental methods constitute the nonverbal language through which psychologists can interact with very young children, and ask them all sorts of questions about the world they live in. Almost as precise and rigorous as their psychophysical equivalents currently used with adults, they have allowed us to catalogue the smallest physical differences the newborn is capable of noticing and evaluating. Armed with these rudiments of experimental technology, we can now tackle our problem head-on.

2

Seeing and Hearing

The reader may be surprised by the relatively modest number and recent vintage of works devoted to the newborn. In fact, though tiny babies take up all their parents' attention, they have only interested scientists for a very short while, as the conflicting beliefs and myths about them propagated over the centuries can attest to. In certain cultures different from our own, the baby was thought of as the repository of a soul that had already lived before, and therefore as possessed of all the faculties utilized by adults. Closer to us, generations of parents believed, on the contrary, that their children were born deaf and blind and that they remained in this condition for weeks, even months. The notion that the newborn was about as competent as a potted plant and that it had to learn to see, hear, memorize, and categorize, was extremely influential in Western thought. It proceeds directly from the British empiricist tradition, which permeated all the humanities from psychology to linguistics, by way of sociology and history. It is, therefore, necessary to begin logically at the beginning. The exploration of the capacities of newborns must first answer the question of whether or not they can hear and see, whether they perceive a chaos of moving, changing stimulations, or a stable world made up of coherent, structured forms, already close to the perceptual world of normal adults.

Is the Newborn Blind?

At the end of the 1960s, Held and his collaborators studied the visual capacities of the infant during the first year of life. The procedure they utilized is ingenious and simple. It consists of presenting two discs of identical moderate luminous intensity side by side, one white striped with vertical, horizontal, or oblique black lines, and the other gray. We can easily distinguish these two discs providing we are close enough, and the stripes wide enough; if the stripes are very narrow, the two discs look identical. The width of the stripes at which the two discs become indistinguishable defines the *threshold of visual acuity*. Infants prefer looking at a disc that is not uniform. As long as this preference is apparent, we can conclude that they perceive a difference and therefore that the threshold of visual acuity has not been reached. On the other hand, if they show no particular preference, it means that no difference has been perceived.[1] Thanks to this method, Held and his collaborators demonstrated that the visual acuity of babies increases gradually during the first year, by the end of which it has almost reached its upper limit.

These results have been confirmed on numerous occasions. For example, the visual acuity of babies was studied at the ages of one, three, and five months. Using the habituation/dishabituation method and checkered instead of striped discs, the conclusions were almost identical to Held's.[2] This method was also used on premature babies born after thirty-four to thirty-seven weeks of gestation.[3] Once again, the results concurred with extrapolations from Held's work.

From the study of visual acuity we can conclude that babies are technically blind at birth. Often myopic and somewhat astigmatic, they see everything beyond twenty centimeters as a blur. This is due, among other things, to the fact that the fovea centralis of the retina, the point of sharpest vision, only matures slowly during the first few years. Not until at least the age of one year do babies see with the distinctness of adults. Still, we cannot conclude that they have to learn how to see. Indeed, when we show them shapes close up enough, their vision has characteristics similar to those of adults, as the following example indicates.

Adult visual acuity is less efficient for certain directions than for others. We have more difficulty distinguishing oblique stripes than vertical or horizontal ones. This is what we call the *oblique effect*. For a long time, it was thought that this phenomenon was the result of our urban environment, in which precise horizontal and vertical lines predominate.[4] Today this notion may make us smile, but it was once taken quite seriously. To support it, certain observations were even cited by ethnologists who claimed to have noted among people living in the jungle that horizontal and vertical directions enjoyed no privileged status. Others contested these observations and a lengthy controversy ensued, for the simple reason that it is difficult to reproduce a psychophysical experiment in the middle of the jungle. The question has only recently been settled, thanks to a series of experiments conducted by Held and his team.

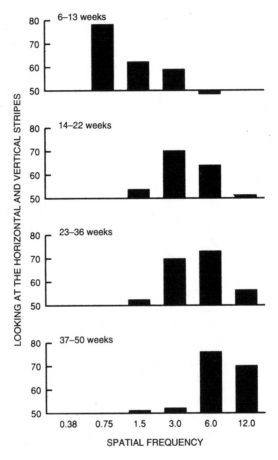

Figure 2.1 This figure shows the width of the stripes babies prefer to look at on a disk that is horizontally or vertically striped rather than obliquely. We see that at each age, this width varies. At six weeks, for example, the stripes must be very wide, or else both disks look gray to the babies. A few weeks later, the preference for the horizontal and the vertical is observed only for medium stripes. This is because babies can see wide stripes in any orientation, but if the stripes are narrower, they only see two gray disks. Therefore their preference is correlated with the development of their visual acuity.

Their study concentrated on children aged six weeks to one year. As in the preceding experiments, they presented the babies with two striped discs whose lines, of the same width, were in one case horizontal or vertical, and in the other oblique. If the child is experiencing the oblique effect, a stripe width must exist at which he or she can distinguish vertical or horizontal stripes but not oblique ones, which are perceived as a uniformly gray field. At this width, and at this width only, the child should prefer to look at the vertical or horizontal stripes. At any other width, they should either all be discernible or all indiscernible. This is precisely what Held and his collaborators observed. Of course, the critical value of the width of the stripes diminishes with age, as visual acuity increases. But no matter what the age tested, the oblique effect exists: our visual acuity is less efficient for oblique lines than for vertical or horizontal ones.

All the experimental results effectively demonstrate that visual acuity improves during the first year. Likewise the ability to discriminate between lights of varying intensity also improves during that time.[5] But this improvement is not due to instructions the child has received from the environment: it can be explained, rather, by the maturation of the visual system. This process can perhaps be accelerated, but the environment is not able to alter its progress to any great extent.

Is the Newborn Deaf?

Newborns may be myopic, but their hearing is excellent. They are whizzes at auditory perception, recognition, and memorization. From their first moments and, according to certain studies, even during the last weeks of pregnancy, their auditory equipment is in perfect order.

In a series of truly seminal experiments, Thomas and his collaborators showed that babies can hear and recognize quite complex stimuli.[6] During their first pediatric examinations, babies will turn their heads toward a sound source. Thomas also ascertained that they are sensitive to their mothers' voice. These phenomena were rediscovered twenty-five years later and subjected to a more rigorous experimental study.

Many studies also showed that the absolute auditory thresholds of newborns and adults are approximately identical. Children distinguish high-frequency sounds particularly well.[7] Low and middle frequencies are slightly better perceived by adults, but infants improve rapidly with

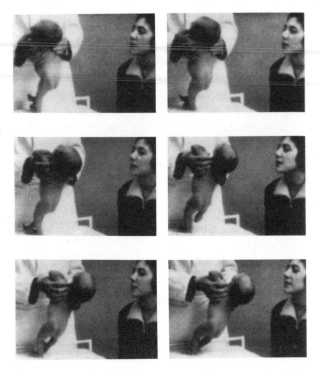

Figure 2.2 André-Thomas observes how newborns turn toward their mother when she speaks to them.

age in this regard.[8] From all this research, it emerges that children are capable of discerning very subtle variations in the intensity or frequency of pure tones. As Eisenberg said:

> Taken as a whole, however, these findings on intensity effects have further implications for our thinking on developmental auditory processes. First, the neuronal mechanisms for processing intensity may be fully operational at birth. Secondly, it seems possible that loudness and other so-called 'natural dimensions of sound,' (Flangan, 1965) have their roots in preadapted mechanisms referable to species history.[9]

The difference observed between vision and hearing in the newborn coincides with the neuro-anatomical data: we know that at birth the visual nerve paths are less developed than the auditory ones.[10] For this reason, the auditory modality predominates in children up until the age of ten months. Confronted with two events, one auditory and the other visual, an infant under ten months pays more attention to the auditory stimulus, while later, as with the adult, it is the visual stimulus that dominates.[11] Of course, while newborns are neither deaf nor blind, this does not mean that they see and hear like us. Are they activated only by a change in their sensations in a world that looks to them like a kaleidoscope of shifting impressions? Or can they already separate the visual world into tangible qualities, into shapes, colors, and relationships? In short, is their perceptual world similar to ours?

Categories

Our perceptual mechanism is not content to discern an infinite variety of tangible givens more or less clearly. It also organizes them by means of a system of *categories*, necessarily limited in number. Thus physical dimensions such as wavelengths are continuous, while the psychological representation we have of them is discontinuous: if, for example, we vary the wavelength of a luminous source, what we perceive is a change of color. Wavelengths change in a continuous manner, but our perceptual mechanism separates the stimulations into distinct color categories. We are perfectly capable of perceiving all sorts of stimuli that correspond to Prussian blue, sky blue, methylene blue or turquoise blue. But we group all these shades under a single category, the "color blue," even though the wavelength of a certain blue may be closer to that of a green than that of another blue.

This process of *categorization*, essential to our perception, is also found not only in vision, but also in hearing and taste. But where do these elementary perceptual categories themselves come from? Aren't they arbitrarily defined conventions, imposed by our environment and more precisely by our linguistic milieu?

Colors

Linguistic Relativism   It is commonly thought that elementary perceptual categories are arbitrary and that they are imposed on us by the milieu in which we live. According to this idea, we organize and perceive the world with the help of conventions that are transmitted by our parents and teachers. Society forms and transforms our representations of the world as the sun changes the color of our skin. The great American linguist and anthropologist Benjamin Lee Whorf provided the most coherent formulation of this point of view:

The categories and types that we isolate from the world of phenomena
we do not find there because they stare every observer in the face; on the
contrary the world is presented in a kaleidoscopic flux of impressions
which has to be organized in our minds – and that means largely by the
linguistic system in our minds. We carve nature up, organize it into concepts, and ascribe significances as we do, largely because we are partners
to an agreement to organize it this way – an agreement that holds
throughout our speech community and is codified in the patterns of our
language.[12]

It follows that because Eskimos live surrounded by snow all year,
their vocabulary, unlike ours, contains at least twenty expressions designating different qualities of snow. Similarly, astronauts, philatelists,
sailors, and scientists have their specialized vocabularies. It is quite obvious that our vocabulary depends on our communication needs. But
Whorf does not stop at this observation. For him, Bushmen and Eskimos not only have different vocabularies, but they also *perceive* the
world differently and to a certain extent live in different worlds. In his
view, then, babies could not naturally possess perceptual categories.

The study of color is an ideal field for evaluating this thesis. When we
examine human languages, we note the existence of all sorts of vocabularies for color: the Danis divide the spectrum into two categories, the
Hanunoo into four, and other cultures into three, five, or more. These
classifications are so varied that one gets the impression that anything
goes in this area, and that languages can divide the spectrum in a totally
arbitrary fashion. Even today, some psychology and linguistics text-
books make this claim.

At the end of the 1960s, however, certain discoveries cast grave doubt
on the thesis of linguistic relativism. An anthropologist and a linguist
became interested in the systems of color classification used in different
languages.[13] Underlying the apparent diversity of classifications, the
authors discovered a deeper pattern: color categories were actually limited in number and the vocabulary used to designate them was, in fact,
governed by very strict rules.

In their findings, languages that use four color categories always reit-
erate the same ones, red, blue, green, and yellow. Similarly, classifications of two or three colors draw their boundaries at certain very precise
and restricted locations in the color spectrum. Thus, these cultures use
the same word to designate several colors, providing they are similar. It
has never been observed that the same word designated yellow and
blue, or green and red.

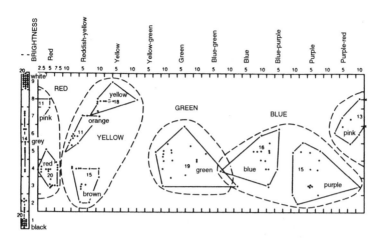

Figure 2.3   On a Munsell color chart, the way in which individuals from twenty different cultures characterize basic colors (Bornstein, 1985).

It seems, therefore, that the boundaries between categories are not arbitrary and that the thesis of linguistic relativism was false. A limited number of *natural* categories seem, on the contrary, to govern color classification. The cultural and linguistic environment can at most select certain of these categories while respecting the universal rules.

The Natural Categories   The concept of categories is actually much more complex than one might think. In fact, it behooves us to distinguish between *perceptual* categories and *linguistic* categories. The former determine the range of the possible and the latter result from a choice made among the various possibilities. While the chromatic qualities of perceptions are identical in all humans, each person best retains those to which their linguistic system draws their attention. Next we must differentiate between *natural* categories and *technical* categories. Natural categories are the first to be mastered by children, without our having to teach them. They are also the only ones that are taken into account by young children when they learn to talk, that occur in the vocabularies of all the languages in the world, and that can be learned despite serious sensory handicaps.

On the other hand, technical categories are acquired relatively late by the child: they depend on his or her knowledge of the world and must be the object of a specific learning process. Furthermore, all languages, quite obviously, do not possess the same technical vocabulary. We can

invent technical terms without taking into account the types of constraints that govern the constitution of natural categories. We could
thus decide to call the aggregate of all greens and pinks "grink." Once
this category had been created, an adult would be able to classify stimuli according to whether they were or were not "grink." However, the
learning process for these artificial categories resembles the training of
a circus animal. In the same way, it is perfectly possible to train an elephant to walk on two legs, but that does not prove that this involves a
specific natural ability.

Some scientists have stressed another important difference between
natural and technical categories: the first form our perception of the
world, but not the latter.[14] Thus Ibos, Hanunoos, and Inuits actually
perceive the world in an identical way. Yet if they have to communicate
what they see, they use their own language along with the names of natural and technical categories that it provides. The arbitrariness of technical categories thus does not affect the natural categories, which are
invariant, but only the terms used to designate and communicate them,
thereby creating the illusion that we perceive different worlds.

Whorf's linguistic relativism is therefore not entirely wrong. But he
confuses different cognitive functions: perception, memorization, and
communication. The linguistic code we use unquestionably influences
communication and memorization, but we have never been able to establish that it influences perception.

It seems, then, that we must admit that the perception of colors is
essentially the same in all humans, though the vocabulary that describes them varies from one language to another, within the limits of
certain universal constraints. The problem remains, however, of knowing whether newborns, who have no vocabulary for colors, perceive
them as adults do.

The Colors of the Newborn   Does the newborn under the age of four
months classify colors in perceptual categories? To find out, certain researchers repeatedly presented infants a color which adults apprehend
as blue (480 nm wavelength).[15] After habituation, they presented another blue (450 nm wavelength), or a color adults think of as green
(wavelength of 510 nm). Both colors were of equal distance from the
original stimulus that the infants had been habituated to. The infants
had a much stronger reaction when the color went from blue to green
(480 to 510) than when it stayed blue (480 to 450). This indicates that,

like adults, infants perceived a qualitative change in the first case, but not in the second.

Following this same method and running the gamut of colors in the spectrum, all the spontaneous groupings of the babies were studied. Thus it was possible to establish that they distinguish green from yellow (boundary at 600–620 nm). Therefore, like the adult, the child divides the color spectrum into four principal categories corresponding to green, red, yellow, and blue. As the comparison of results obtained from babies and adults shows (fig. 2.5), the babies' categories seem larger than those of the adults, but on the whole they cover comparable areas of the spectrum. The acquisition of colors is, therefore, not related to the cultural milieu or based on a learning process: it rests on natural foundations constant from one individual to another, one culture to another, one age to another.

While natural, the categories governing color perception are also very *specific*. In fact, many animals other than humans perceive colors and divide up the spectrum. But the number and location of categories vary from one species to another: bees use three, as do pigeons, as opposed to four for most vertebrates like monkeys and humans. With the monkey, it has been possible to show which cells respond specifically to a given category and to establish the cerebral map of chromatic categories.

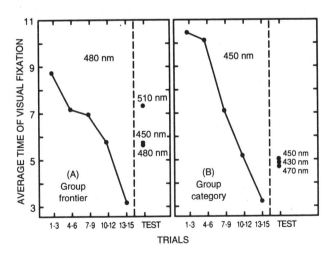

Figure 2.4   How babies habituated to a chromatic category of 480 nm or 450 nm react when we present them with different stimuli (Bornstein, 1985).

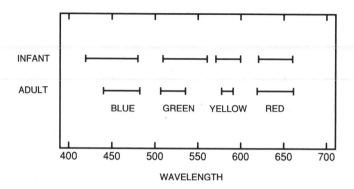

Figure 2.5   The baby's categories are similar to the adult's (Bornstein, 1980).

Contrary to Whorf's ideas, the newborn therefore already possesses a
system of perceptual categories. But what is their influence on the lexical categories?

The Vocabulary of Colors   What is the link between the ability to categorize colors and the acquisition of the vocabulary that describes them?
Actually, children have trouble naming colors before the age of four,
although they are capable of using adjectives like "big," "little,"
"good," or "bad" long before that age, and, at around three and a half,
they succeed in mastering terms that designate shapes.[16] How do we
explain this difficulty since we know from elsewhere that the perception
of colors is fully functional in the first weeks of life?

This difficulty has been likened to the syndrome called color anomia.[17] People suffering from it are incapable of retaining or recognizing
the names of colors, even though they are able to perceive them. This
ailment is due to a break in the nerve connections linking the structures
of the cerebral cortex that underlie visual functions with those that facilitate language. To explain the belated acquisition of color terms in
children, it was hypothesized that the development of these cortical
structures is slow and that they only mature at around the age of four,
which would explain the similar performances of young children and of
adults suffering from color anomia.

Although it would be advisable to support this hypothesis with further behavioral and neurological studies, we can at this point envision
linking in a general way cognitive functions with particular cortical
structures and thereby fully demonstrating their natural character.

Thus the distinction of categories that are actually perceptual or only linguistic and those that are natural or technical, opens up entirely new perspectives. Research in visual acuity has led us to believe that the visual perception of the newborn is relatively defective. Yet studies on the categorization of colors show that at birth the visual system, despite its lack of maturity, is already classifying colors in categories similar to those adults spontaneously use, no matter what their culture.

Orientation

Our perceptual system arranges stimuli according to categories. This is true of colors and, as we shall see later, of shapes. More surprising is the categorization of orientations into three groups: vertical, horizontal, and oblique. Neurophysiological studies of vision have demonstrated the existence of orientation detectors in the visual system of vertebrates. Most languages have words that designate these three orientations even though they do not in general possess adjectives to distinguish the different kinds of obliques.

It seems that babies can discriminate between any two orientations with a fair degree of precision. But what representations and categories do they use for coding directions? When we test their memories by letting three minutes elapse between habituation and the test, they cannot distinguish between several types of obliques, but still can tell the difference between an oblique and a vertical.[18] This proves that the infant classifies stimuli in at least two categories: verticals and obliques. But it is a good bet that a class also exists for horizontals, although to our knowledge this has never been tested. With infants of two to four months, the boundary between two categories, verticals and obliques, can be observed.[19] At first it is fairly crude (8 degrees), but it becomes more refined with age. Here again, the category of verticality is not acquired but given. It is, therefore, very tempting to say, countering the champions of linguistic relativism, that it is the processes of cognition and perception that determine the vocabulary permitting the representation of stimuli.

In fact, babies at birth not only possess natural categories of orientation, but certain of these even have a privileged status. Thus it has been shown that infants are capable of distinguishing a symmetrical shape from an asymmetrical one, if the symmetry is vertical.[20] Yet they are incapable of this if the symmetry is horizontal. Other experiments have produced similar results.[21] Shapes which are presented to the baby during the habituation phase are shown in figure 2.6. The babies' interest in group 1 (the control) diminishes when, during the test, they are presented with the same shape. Interest increases for groups 2 and 3 when we change the orientation. Group 4, on the contrary, reacts like the control group: the babies see no difference at all between the shape to which they first became habituated and its mirror image. However, this result is valid only if the symmetry between the two shapes is vertical. This predominance of the vertical axis may be due to the environment.[22] But we can just as well think that the predominance of the vertical is an innate characteristic of the perceptual mechanism which will greatly help the young child to discern pertinent visual properties in a world dominated by gravity.

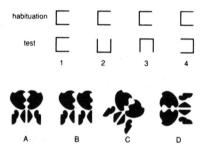

Figure 2.6   In the upper sequence, babies react to the presentation of the control (1) or of a vertical reflected image (4) in the same fashion. In lower sequence, babies are habituated more rapidly to A than to B, C, or D (Bornstein & Krinsky, 1985).

Forms

Do babies spontaneously perceive circles, triangles, and squares, like adults? Or must they learn to construct and stabilize this type of perception from its basic parts? For centuries, philosophers and psychologists have agonized over the question of knowing how the child can see objects before it has had sufficient experience of the external world.

In 1890 the German scientist von Ehrenfels formulated the hypothesis that humans perceive *form-qualities*, that is, complex forms corresponding to what he called *pure forms* (circle, square, triangle), without having to identify the basic lines that constitute them.[23] Similar pure forms also exist in the auditory field. According to him, a melody exists independently of the specific tones which it is composed of. Thus, if we transposed a given melody, that is, if we changed the absolute pitch of the tones while respecting their relative pitch, we would always hear the same melody. Our sensitivity to shapes and melodies shows that the cortex is capable of discerning the relationship between elements while disregarding their absolute value. The newborns' potential sensitivity to melodies or forms attests to the existence of capacities that are the result neither of a learning process nor of physical necessity. Recent studies have shown that birds can tolerate only very minor variations of frequency in the songs peculiar to their species.[24] But for humans the absolute tonality counts less than the relationship between tones. Whether temporal or spatial, it is these relationships that cause a global configuration, or gestalt, to emerge. Gestalt psychologists adopted and enlarged upon these ideas, some of them maintaining that form-qualities are innate.[25]

For them the separation of an image into a *figure* and a *background* constituted one of the fundamental aspects of visual perception. Thus the famous Rubin vase (fig. 2.7) can be seen as the profiles of two people gazing at each other, or as a vase, depending on whether we perceive the white part as the figure or the background. Furthermore, when one part is seen as the figure, it looks closer to us than the background. These organizations and reorganizations seem natural and spontaneous. Based on examples of this kind, Gestalt psychologists supported the idea that the light hitting the retina is organized into coherent objects by the laws of the perceptual dynamic.

Our perceptual machinery spontaneously seeks to construct forms and detach them from the background. As we have seen (fig. 1.5), the presentation of four incomplete octagons produces a powerful and striking illusion. Does our perceptual mechanism construct these subjective contours because we have wide experience with triangles, squares, and circles? Does the infant, whose experience is infinitely more limited, perceive these subjective contours as well as we do? Certain researchers tried to answer this question through experimentation.[26] According to them, babies become capable of perceiving subjective contours between five and seven months and their sensitivity to optical illusions improves with age. While these results are interesting, they do not allow us to determine if these age-related changes are due to maturation or to the fact that it takes a certain amount of experience before the baby begins to discern geometric forms in its environment. This question has still not been answered definitively. However,

Figure 2.7 The Rubin vase shows the organization of our perceptions into "figure" and "background." One can either see a white vase or two black silhouettes looking at each other. The figure which emerges is always perceived as being closer (Bornstein, Gross, and Wolf, 1978).

other experiments suggest that babies are sensitive to gestalts well before five months.

How can we know if forms, rather than simple optical parameters, play a role in the newborn's perceptual representations? To test this, we can use the constancy of forms when we subject them to spatial transformations such as rotation. Certain researchers are attempting to answer this question.[27] During the habituation period, they presented two figures, for example, a cross *above* a square. The arrangement was presented at different places within a fixed framework. After habituation, the experimental group was shown the cross *below* the square, that is, the same elements presented in a different configuration, while the control group received the original stimuli in a new spatial position. The newborns, all less than four days old, reacted more intensely to the new configuration than to the old stimulus placed in a different position. They therefore seemed to be able to retain a configuration in memory and distinguish it from another made up of the same elements, but by disregarding the variations in its spatial position. In other words, newborns can retain what we call *relative* or object-centered spatial representations as opposed to *absolute* spatial representations.

Elsewhere an attempt was made to evaluate more directly whether infants aged one to three months were sensitive to pure forms.[28] To do

this, figures were presented (circles or squares) made up of discontinuous lines, and the visual fixations on different parts of the figure were
recorded. Once the infants had carefully examined a figure, other very
similar ones were presented, certain of them containing a change of
orientation in one of the lines that disturbed the harmony of the figure.
In such cases, the babies' gaze was attracted by the changed line.
Yet they did not react to a change if the lines did not constitute a
"pure" form.

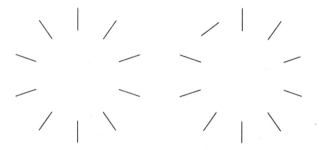

Figure 2.8   Shift a single line in a regular form to which babies are habituated,
and they will focus their gaze on it (van Giffen and Haith, 1984).

Another method was also used, based on non-nutritive sucking:[29]
three dots forming either a triangle or a line were presented to the babies. Then, after the period of habituation, either another figure was
presented, or the stimulus was not changed. All the results agreed that
three-month-old infants have a significant tendency to look at the element that has been modified and that they are sensitive to pure forms,
in agreement with Gestalt principles.

But does this apply to newborns? We do not yet know for certain. The
experimental difficulties are enormous, since we must take into account
their poor visual acuity as well as the skewed perceptions peculiar to the
period immediately following birth. A team of researchers nevertheless
studied this question with three-day-old infants.[30] During the period of
habituation, they presented either circles, crosses, or triangles. During
the test, they changed the figure. Newborns were sensitive to this modification. In a similar experiment, babies were habituated to a series of
triangles or crosses of different thicknesses, variously misshapen. During the course of the test, they were shown a pure form different from
what they had been habituated to or else the same form from a different

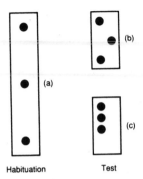

Habituation   Test

Figure 2.9   If babies are habituated to a shape like (a), they will be more interested in a shift like (b) which modifies it than by (c), which respects the general shape but changes its size (Milewski, 1979).

Figure 2.10   Misshapen crosses and triangles are represented as prototypes by the very young baby (Slater et al., 1983).

angle. They noticed the overall change of form, but did not see the difference between a pure form and its altered versions. Moreover, the newborns seemed to reconstruct a prototype or schematic perception rather than an image absolutely faithful to the stimulus. When newborns see a slightly misshapen cross, they classify it in the category "cross" and only retain the prototypical appearance which characterizes the category.

Since babies are capable of picturing pure forms, we are justified in wondering if, when we show them a partially hidden figure they use the principle of *pure continuation* to complete the appearance of the figure.

When we show newborns a partially occluded figure they have never seen, do they picture it in its totality? In a series of now famous experiments,[31] Bower studied this question and asserted that the newborn confronted with a configuration like that of figure 3.7 on page 86 pictures a complete triangle from the elements that project beyond either side of the block. It was subsequently proved that the baby pictures a triangle in this situation if, and only if, its elements move in unison behind the block.[32]

The exploration of the perceptual capacities of the newborn is in its early stages. The studies we have presented raise more questions than they answer. We can, nevertheless, say that the newborn shows a certain sensitivity to the relationships between elements. We also see that in certain cases movement is necessary for the baby to show a sensitivity to the principles of Gestalt. However, it remains to be determined whether this limitation is due to the experimental methods used, or to differences in the newborn's perceptual mechanism as compared with the adult's. While the ideas of Gestalt psychologists cannot be considered as substantiated at the present time, they can at least serve as points of departure for further research.

The Part and the Whole   The newborn's visual environment is far from a logical arrangement of simple geometric figures, of circles, squares, and triangles with clearly defined contours. It is, on the contrary, an incredible maze of partially overlapping forms, none of them truly regular or geometrically simple. How does the newborn perceive such complex forms? What happens the first time an infant is confronted with a complex form made up of diversely oriented parts, of varying brightness and color? What does he or she think when confronted with a complex noise like that produced by a crowd or even by an individual's speech?

Two possible theories are debated by researchers. According to the first (which goes back to the atomists), visual perception starts with elementary features like dots, lines and angles, orientations, or hues which are then organized into increasingly complex forms. Thus, confronted with a dog, the newborn will first notice its fur or details like the pads of its paws, its ears, or mouth, before perceiving an overall shape. According to an opposing view, closer to Gestalt principles, a baby first notices the overall shape and disregards the details. Thus, like adults, he recognizes his mother as an entity before noticing that she has changed her hairdo or makeup.

It is difficult to approach the problem of the perception of complex objects head-on. Researchers therefore asked the simpler question of how babies analyze images that comprise two levels of detail, how they perceive, for example, a simple geometric figure that encloses another, smaller, geometric figure. During the habituation period, they presented babies with a triangle inside a circle or a square inside a diamond. During the test, they presented another stimulus that differed from the first, either in the internal figure or the external figure, and noted that at the age of one month, a reaction only occurred with a change in the external figure.[33] This phenomenon, the *externality effect*, suggests that newborns pay more attention to the overall shape of a figure than to its details. This is not because of their poor visual acuity: if we present the two figures not one inside the another but side by side, they discern all the changes, in the larger as well as the smaller figure. The externality effect therefore seems more linked to attention than to visual acuity. Newborns are attracted by the overall shape of an image and have trouble focusing their attention on its details. But this is not insurmountable. We can, for example, attract their attention by making the interior figure flicker.[34] In this case, the baby becomes capable of discerning changes in the internal figure. This process must be taken into account when we evaluate newborns' ability to recognize faces: it is probable that only the larger contours, plus a very overall configuration, are initially retained by babies when we show them photographs of faces. On the other hand, when they see real faces with mobile features, they pay much more attention to details.

The externality effect disappears around the end of the third month: at that point babies become capable of reacting to changes in the internal figure as well as the external one.

In the course of a recent experiment,[35] figures were presented in which one can distinguish an external form, or macrostructure, and internal forms which constitute its texture or microstructure. It was thus demonstrated that three- to four-month-old babies react more to changes in the macrostructure than in the microstructure, although they can detect the two types of changes. During the processing of forms, the babies' attention is first drawn by the overall properties and only in the course of later development to the finer points. In fact, the perception of forms, like attention, moves from the whole (global perception) to the parts (analytical perception) rather than the reverse. The emergence of analytical capacities at around the fourth month is surely not an accident. It corresponds to an important phase in the development of the cortical areas that sustain cognitive functions.

An empiricist would respond to these experiments by saying that they have shown only that infants at first have at their disposal such basic elements as shape, orientation, and color; that complex objects are at first depicted and memorized as a collection of these basic elements; and that it is only progressively and by successive generalizations that infants can arrive at a more overall and more abstract representation of the objects around them.

A Gestalt psychologist, shocked, would then take the floor to insist that babies first perceive the overall shape of objects and not their basic elements, that they perceive a chair as an indivisible object and only later progressively analyze its internal structure, for example, by comparing the color of the chair with the color of a table. The empiricist and the Gestalt theorist would quarrel like this indefinitely, throwing the same arguments and presuppositions in each other's face over and over again.

Only further experimentation will settle this argument. While the tiny human's encephalon has not yet reached maturity at birth, neither is it as incompetent as one might think. The myelination[36] of the nerve axons continues beyond the first year. It will take many months for the connections between the different areas of the cortex to stabilize. The physiological maturation of the organ does not imply, however, that its function is entirely learned. Newborns, on the contrary, seem to possess astonishing perceptual capacities and nothing warrants the assertion that they must construct overall properties from elementary data. The Gestaltists thus seem to have the edge over the atomists.

Melodies   From the moment they leave their mother's womb, newborns attach the utmost importance to their acoustical environment. This is no doubt what enables them to master the spoken language in an incredibly short time. The adult attaches more importance to melodies, groupings, and rhythms, than to the elements that make them up. We are, therefore, justified in wondering if newborns must learn the principles governing the grouping of sounds into melodies and rhythms, or if these flow naturally from the structure of their auditory systems.

Several teams of researchers have studied the perception of temporal rhythms in newborns.[37] In Mehler and Bertoncini's experiment, melodies of three notes were played to the babies. The first and third notes were always separated by the same interval of time. When we varied the interval separating the middle note from its two neighbors, we obtained different subjective groupings (fig. 2.11). In case (a), we heard a pair of notes, followed by an isolated note. In case (b), we heard an isolated note, followed by a pair. The goal of this experiment was to determine if babies discern these configurations and if their rhythmic perceptions shift abruptly from one organization to the other. Thus it was shown that babies group sounds rhythmically in the same way as adults.

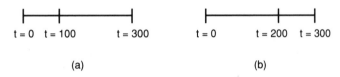

(a)   (b)

Figure 2.11   The lines indicate the times at which sounds are emitted. On the left, one hears two sounds and later one, on the right, one sound and later two.

This is true with three or four notes. But what happens in the case of a multitude of simultaneous sounds? We adults have a tendency to group them into several distinct "voices." This explains why, when we listen to a fugue or a motet, we do not hear a cacophony, but a structured ensemble of "sound streams." Demany specifically wondered if babies also spontaneously organized their acoustical environment as adults do. To understand the approach Demany took, we must refer to figure 2.12, a simplified schematization of some very ingenious research.

In panel (a), four notes that repeat in time are represented. In this situation, listeners hear one stream repeating the sound "x" over and over, but they also hear another stream repeating the sounds "do me re." Once they have become habituated to this sequence, they will easily notice the difference when it is played backwards. Of course, they will still hear a stream repeating "x" over and over, but now the sequence "do me re" in the other stream will sound like "re mi do." In panel (b), we hear two voices composed of two notes. We are incapable of noticing a change when the tape of these notes is played backwards: after a few seconds, "do re do re do re" is identical to "re do re do

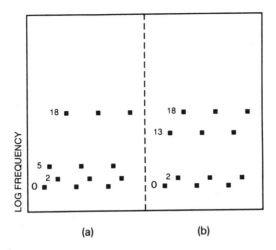

Figure 2.12 Simplified diagram of Demany's experiment (Demany et al., 1970).

re do." Babies habituated to a situation like the one in panel (a) react to its reversal, while they are not sensitive to the reversal of configuration (b). This result is only comprehensible if, just like adults, they organize acoustical material into distinct sound streams or "voices."

We can, therefore, conclude more generally that humans organize their auditory experience in a manner that is not arbitrary and that is not determined uniquely by a learning process. The laws of grouping into voices seem, on the contrary, to depend on the structure of their perceptual mechanism.

To understand better the perceptual world of the newborn, we must next examine some of its most essential properties. Do tiny babies perceive a two-dimensional or three-dimensional world? Do they perceive objects? What properties do they attribute to them? Are these learned or are they inborn, specific givens that determine the structure of the objects occupying the world around them?

3

The World and Its Objects

When we look around us, we see mainly objects, not merely shapes and colors. We have a three-dimensional representation of space in which we place objects that seem to us to preserve their integrity whatever the distance separating us, or the angle from which we view them. We can estimate with precision the size, distance, or speed of faraway objects. Moreover, objects seem solid to us, weighty, substantial, and we can anticipate the physical consequences of an event, like the fall of a glass of water, the collision of two billiard balls, or the trajectory of a football. The world we perceive is thus filled with concrete, solid objects, both moving and stationary: it is not a senseless, jumbled picture churning with chaotic shadows.

How is this possible? How do we make the leap from a multitude of diverse sensory data to an ordered, coherent, relatively stable *world*?

We adults benefit from many years of commerce with physical reality. We could, then, assume that during this time we have learned how to process our environment in order to construct representations and develop extraordinarily complex cognitive processes in ourselves whose origins must be sought in experience. According to Berkeley and the British empiricists, newborns must even learn how to see and hear. But how would they learn? Helmholtz was one of the first to notice the formal analogy between visual perception and the activity of the astronomer seeking to determine the position of the planets: in both cases what is involved is relying on fragmentary data to infer the properties of distant objects. With this difference: the astronomer's inferences are conscious, while those of our visual mechanism do not reach our consciousness. For Helmholtz, such unconscious inferences are learned by the child upon contact with the three-dimensional world. He joined the British empiricists in this belief, and he was later followed by Piaget.

For Piaget, "the initial universe is a world without objects consisting only of shifting, insubstantial images which appear and then are completely reabsorbed, either never to return, or returning in a modified or analogous form."[1] The physical interaction of the child with the surrounding world would explain the emergence of perception and thought from the original chaos. According to the nativists, on the contrary, and particularly the Gestalt psychologists, the object is primary: the world appears to us directly and naturally as a whole made up of objects, and not as a chaos of atomic sense-data which we must learn how to structure. But for objects to appear to us, we need a representation of three-dimensional space in which to place them. This is why we must first ask how babies conceive the space around them.

Space

Our retina transmits a flat, two-dimensional image to our brain. But the world we have the impression of seeing is a three-dimensional one. How then do we move from these retinal images to three-dimensional representations?

As people who make robots know only too well, this is a very difficult problem. Strictly speaking, it is actually insoluble. Every retinal image is in fact ambiguous: an image of a chair can correspond just as well to a real chair as to a distorted chair or a collection of disconnected segments. And yet our perceptual system, confronted with such a stimulus, tends to come up with the representation of an ordinary chair and not that of a "fragmented chair." Similarly, when we hold a coin at arm's length and look at it with only one eye, we see a circle, but we see a circle even if it is spinning, at which time its retinal projection resembles more or less flattened ellipses.

It therefore seems that among our cognitive dispositions are biases that allow us to choose a plausible interpretation for a flat image. For example, our perceptual system favors connected objects, regular forms, and symmetrical contours. These biases certainly are not infallible, but most of the time they allow us to reconstruct the third dimension. The question arises, then, of whether they must be learned by babies or whether they have been permanently programmed and are part of the genetic endowment of the species.

For many writers on the subject, the structure of the space in which we live is contingent. Babies have no particular predispositions for extracting three-dimensional representations and would do just as well if they were thrust at birth into a two- or four-dimensional world. We must recognize, however, that such speculations can hardly be tested, and, above all, that they do not take seriously enough the fact that visual perception cannot be independent of the organ of vision itself. For our sensory organs have a specific structure and organization that are very dependent on the structure of the physical world itself. How then is the perception of space possible?

Depth

Binocular Factors   The truth is that most vertebrates have two eyes and that, apart from tragic birth defects, cyclops are purely fictional. According to the empiricist philosopher Berkeley, depth perception results specifically from the fact that our eyes converge when we look at a nearby object, while remaining almost parallel when we look into the distance. Almost two hundred years later, Wheatstone described another parameter that would explain depth: it is *binocular disparity*, or the fact that our two eyes never receive quite the same retinal image. We can test this ourselves by staring at a distant point while holding a pencil close to and then further from our face. It looks double. Thus, when both lines of vision are parallel, as is the case when we look into the distance, the projection of nearby objects is displaced to noncorresponding positions on each retina. Conversely, when we are viewing a landscape through a dirty windowpane, if we make our eyes converge in order to examine a piece of dirt, the landscape in the background appears to split in two. This phenomenon of splitting is so common that we pay no attention to it in everyday life, unless the retinal disparity is great (fifteen minutes of the visual angle).

In most cases, we do not see a double image, but rather a single object in depth: this phenomenon is called *stereoscopy*. Wheatstone built the first stereoscope and demonstrated that two images of the same scene, presented to each eye from a slightly different viewpoint, give rise to a sensation of depth, that is, of a single scene in space. On the other hand, if we reverse the two images, what was "convex" becomes "concave."

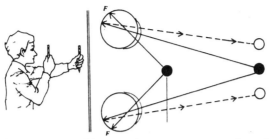

Figure 3.1   If you hold one object up close to your eyes and another object at a little distance, and stare at the nearest object, you will see its image clearly while the farther one will appear split in two.

Slight differences in the images received by both eyes, in the absence of any other factor, suffice then for depth perception and the construction of the space in which the objects appear to us. Everything happens, therefore, as if our perceptual mechanism, supported by the binocular mechanisms of depth perception, makes certain unconscious inferences which, more often than not, are correct. Just as an astronomer calculates the position of the stars, our perceptual system calculates the position of objects from two retinal images. It therefore makes geometric calculations, too.

What about newborns? Are they also budding astronomers at birth, or must they first familiarize themselves with the spatial and geometric characteristics of the world in which they live?

As we already mentioned on page 37, Walk and Gibson were among the first to indicate that babies organize the world according to a three-dimensional framework very early on and that by the time they can crawl, they are generally able to avoid pitfalls. The steep "precipice" they created in a laboratory with a Plexiglas sheet on a flat checkerboard surface is shown in figure 1.8. Adults could see the sudden drop, but what about six-month-old babies? Once placed on the glass, if their mothers waved at them to come closer and were on the other side of the "precipice," few babies dared to move forward, despite the reassuring tactile sensations of the transparent Plexiglas sheet (which bridged the "abyss").

Many researchers have been surprised by this relatively precocious performance. In fact, most of them thought at the time that the child was nothing but a tabula rasa until the age of two. Since then, numerous experiments have facilitated the study of even younger babies, the

clarification of the origins of depth perception, and a better understanding of how the perceptual system develops.

By means of the method of visual fixation, it has been possible to analyze how children four to five months old exploit binocular disparity.
R. Held used two discs with black stripes on a white background presented on either side of a fixation point. Under normal lighting conditions, they seem flat. But, in the experiment, the babies looked at the
discs through polarized lenses, so that one of the discs then appeared to
be three-dimensional. Between ten and seventeen weeks, this made no
difference. It was only after twenty weeks that the three-dimensional
image began to be gazed at more.[2]

Similarly, a study of infants' visual pursuit of moving objects was
made by presenting them with an image composed of random dots animated by movement.[3] In monocular vision, the images are nothing but
a fog, without structure or coherent movement. However, in stereoscopic vision, adults are able to make the connections between the images presented to each eye and can perceive an object endowed with
depth and animated by a movement from right to left. But babies do
not seem to be inclined to follow this "object" before five months.

The net results obtained on depth perception in babies all lead to the
same conclusion. A very young baby cannot utilize retinal disparity and

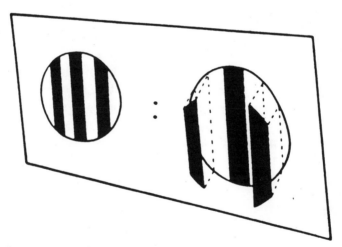

Figure 3.2   Stimuli used by Held, Birch, and Gwiazda for studying stereoacuity
in the infant. Stereoscopy is achieved when the infant wears polarized glasses
(Held et al., 1980).

stereoscopy. Fortunately, the latter is not the only useful factor in constructing the third dimension.

Pictorial Factors   A certain number of researchers, among them the American psychologist J. J. Gibson,[4] maintained that stereoscopy was far from the only explanation of depth perception, that it in fact depended on a number of other factors present in natural visual stimuli.

Actually, these stimuli are extremely rich and permit us to make do without binocular vision. When we close one of our eyes, our perceptual world is not thereby flattened out. *Monocular factors*, then, furnish us with information about depth, even when only one retina is stimulated.

Among them, we first find *pictorial factors*, which allow us to reconstitute depth from static images. Nearby objects block out distant objects, while the reverse is not possible. This relationship of superposition can reveal the distance between objects and their relative positions in three-dimensional space just as size and perspective can, which implies that nearby objects look bigger than distant objects. Similarly, light and shadow, extensively used by painters since the Renaissance, give depth to a two-dimensional image. Finally, the gradient of texture, the fact that texture made visible by subtle surface details becomes denser as the distance of the object increases, can be exploited by the visual system.

The question arises of whether babies can get an idea of depth from monocular and pictographic factors only, before they are able to use their binocular equipment.

One of the first experiments carried out to investigate this question used the Ames window[5] (a distorted window one of whose sides is larger than the other). When six-month-old infants see a window of this type with only one eye, they reach out to touch the side that appears to be closest to them. This gesture cannot be explained by a preference for the larger object, for, confronted by two sticks of identical size, no preference is manifested. Furthermore, when the window is presented under normal binocular visual conditions, their preference for the larger side disappears.

The experiments which have just been described, along with others, show that monocular factors are not functional before binocular factors are in place, that is, between the fourth and seventh month. Binocular factors could serve to get the organization of space started and thus make possible the discernment of secondary factors. Under such a hy-

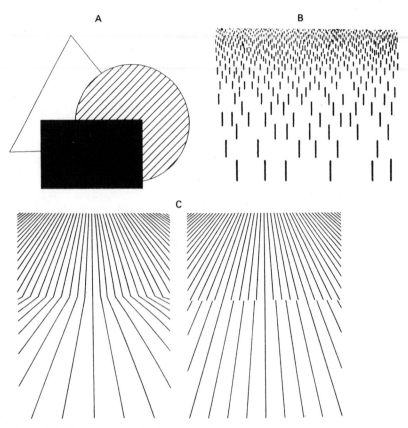

Figure 3.3　Some monocular factors:
A. The rectangle appears to be in the foreground since it is not intercepted by another figure and partially occludes the circle. Similarly, the triangle appears to be in the background because it is partially obscured by the two other figures.
B. A gradient of texture: the bars are closer together at the top of the illustration, which makes us think that this part of the drawing is farther away.
C. Sudden changes of texture can give the impression of a shift in incline on the left, and of a step or a drop on the right.

pothesis, the infant would, therefore, be unable to perceive space in three dimensions until after the fifth month. Note, however, that almost all the results about monocular factors are taken from experiments in which babies had to grasp an object. But voluntary prehension takes several months to become smooth and efficient. It therefore cannot be ruled out that the infant's ability to exploit monocular factors and represent objects has been underestimated.

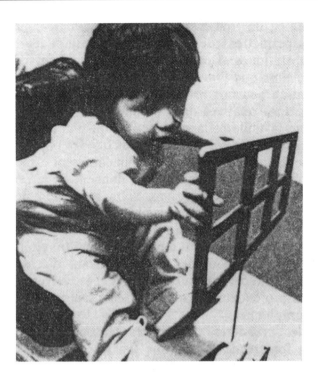

Figure 3.4 Yonas and Granrud's experiment allows us to evaluate the exploitation of monocular factors in babies. When they wear a patch over one eye, if they are over six months old they have a tendency to grasp the larger side of the Ames window, but not when aged five months or less (Yonas & Granrud, 1985).

But why should it take five months before babies can form spatial representations from the sense-data they receive? Although plausible, the empiricist hypothesis, that this delay can be explained by the neonate's need to learn to structure its perceptions, is now hotly contested. Many experiments have, in fact, led to a preference for the maturation of the visual cortex as an explanation for the baby's cognitive development.

Thus Held, in 1980, noticed that improvement in visual acuity is slow and progressive, while the emergence of stereoacuity is extremely rapid and that once the system of stereoacuity is in place, at about six months, the baby is able to discern differences in depth as subtle as a margin of three millimeters seen from a distance of seventy centimeters.[6] The two functions depend, according to him, on different nervous structures.

Visual acuity grows with the size of the retinal fovea, while improvement in stereoacuity depends on changes in more central structures, linked in particular to the visual cortex.[7]

Studies conducted on cats and monkeys show that stereoacuity appears abruptly in these animals between the third and fifth week.[8] The remarkable fact is that the age at which the ability to structure the world three-dimensionally crystalizes, coincides with the time when the fourth layer of the visual cortex is organized into columns of "ocular dominance," or distinct groups of neurons which separately receive the data coming from each eye. It would therefore seem that it is specifically this division into columns that facilitates the exploitation of binocular factors.

Thus, the emergence of stereoscopy would not be learned by the organism on contact with the environment; it would result from the structure of the visual cortex. However, stereoscopic vision is not a "given" at birth, not because a functional learning process takes over, but because the brain has not yet reached the required degree of maturity. The organ, in a sense, creates the function, in its own good time.

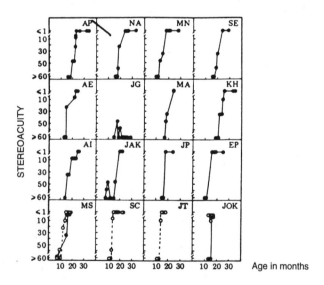

Figure 3.5   The emergence of stereoacuity in sixteen subjects tested between ten and thirty weeks: in each one, with the exception of JG, stereoacuity appears suddenly right before the twentieth week . . . JG suffered from a deficiency in precisely this area (Held et al., 1980).

Kinetic Factors   Besides binocular disparity and several monocular factors, certain elements of movement play an important role in the construction of space. We can discern them in flat images in motion. If we close one eye and look at a scene, slight head movements enable us to have an immediate impression of depth: this is the parallax of motion. When we are moving at a certain speed, for example, looking through the window of a moving train, nearby objects go past faster than distant objects: this is the gradient of speed or optic flow. Furthermore, nearby objects necessarily pass in front of distant objects; this is the principle of accretion and obliteration of contour.

In the 1960s, Bower and his associates maintained that six-day-old neonates were sensitive to visual animations that suggested an object approaching them at great speed: they would open their eyes, raise their heads, and try to protect themselves from this "thing" that seemed to them to be about to strike them.[9]

Bower's results have not been duplicated, at least with newborns. Under more rigorous experimental conditions with a larger number of subjects,[10] it appeared that infants from one to two months were not sensitive to expanding objects that seemed about to crash into them. They merely followed the trajectory of these objects with their eyes, but made no move whatsoever to protect themselves, contrary to what Bower thought. Similarly, an animation that suggested an imminent collision, but whose upper portion remained immobile in relation to the baby's line of vision, provoked no reaction. Finally, even when a real object, like a polystyrene cube, was thrown at two-month-old babies, they displayed no protective reaction or sign of distress. This kind of alleged "reflex" cannot therefore be invoked as a factor enabling newborns to construct depth.

The importance of kinetic factors to depth perception has barely been studied in detail thus far. The question therefore still arises of whether, before stereoscopy is in place, the baby possesses a three-dimensional representation of visual space. Whatever the case, since the maturation of hearing is more precocious than that of vision, babies perhaps can localize objects in three-dimensional space with the help of acoustic data.

Auditory Factors   When we hear complex sounds, our perceptual mechanism extracts their most important components. For example, you are at a lecture. The woman sitting on your left coughs while your neighbors on the right talk and one of them drops his camera. Out in the street, a bus pulls away, and a car honks its horn. A latecomer slams the door. Quite a challenge for the poor lecturer, but also for you! If the speaker knows how to hold your interest, you probably won't be bothered by all this racket. You will only hear the modulations of his or her voice, and the succession of sentences that so fascinate you. Thus, while all sounds are mixed in the ear into complex signals, perception itself is clear and organized. We distinctly hear the bus outside, the speaker, and the camera falling to our right. But we organize these sounds according to their qualities and their sources in the surrounding space.

Certain researchers have studied how our perceptual mechanism reconstitutes this whole scenario and transforms the complex stimuli into organized and relatively distinct sound waves. Frequency, timbre, the time sequence, among other factors, play a central role in the organization of the acoustic milieu. But the cognitive mechanism also constructs a three-dimensional space in which acoustic sounds are distributed. How do babies organize their auditory stimuli when they have had very little experience in correlating visual and auditory data?

Infants only a few hours old will purse their lips in the direction of a human voice.[11] But do they already associate a position in space with a sound? Month-old babies show signs of anxiety if they see their mother in one place while her voice is coming from another.[12] Their perceptual space, therefore, already seems to be organized into a unified representation of the environment where different stimulations converge giving data on the position and movement of exterior objects. This would explain why the dissociation of visual and auditory data is disturbing.

For a long time it had been noted that newborns turn toward their mother when she starts to talk. Experiments in 1971 supposedly discovered that infants in general turn their heads in the direction of any sound.[13] Teams of researchers subsequently labored to reproduce these observations.[14] In vain until, in 1979, they succeeded in developing a conclusive experiment involving numerous controls and calling for extreme care, as parents who try to observe orientation mechanisms in their own babies know only too well.[15]

The assistant observing the infant must not know where the sound comes from and must give the infant twelve seconds to respond, while in previous experiments the infants had had to respond in too short a time for their abilities. The duration of the sound can vary from one to twenty seconds and its nature is of little importance. Generally, the sound of a toy rattle was used. Finally, the babies must be kept in a position that allows them to turn their heads.

This experimental protocol showed that the babies' responses correlate with the side from which the sound comes. On average, they turn more often to the correct than to the wrong side, but they do not respond in every instance. It is necessary, therefore, to test large groups to establish whether newborns behave as if they localized sounds in space. The orientation behavior disappears at around two months, and reappears at around four months, under voluntary control.[16] We still do not understand the mechanism or the links between this precocious behavior and adult performances.

With an adult, the same sound presented in each ear, but slightly delayed in time, seems to come from one side, the one from which it was first heard. This precedence effect is not observed in the baby until the fourth month. It requires, in effect, an interhemispheric collaboration that is not possible before a relatively advanced stage of cortical maturity.[17] Conversely, the localization of sounds in a vertical direction seems to improve in a much more gradual manner.

As with stereoscopy, it seems that the ability to locate sounds in space in an adult manner only appears at about four months. However, a precursor of this behavior is already in place at birth. Much research is still necessary before its exact characteristics can be determined. We need to learn, for example, whether newborns can localize sounds coming from the same side, and if they are sensitive to more subtle differences than right and left, high and low.

It seems incontestable, then, that at about four months a veritable perceptual revolution occurs. At that age, in effect, a complex cortical reorganization enables the baby to exploit stereoscopic factors, to distill depth from flat images like photographs, and to locate sounds in space with precision. But what happens before four months? Do newborns live in a flat world, or can they represent the third dimension by utilizing other factors? The question is still up in the air. But one thing is certain: if it is true that infants do not perceive depth, an object should change size for them according to its distance, and shape according to its orientation. At under four months, they should not grasp perceptual constancies, and the world for them should be a chaos full of unformed, moving objects.

Perceptual Constancies

When someone approaches or moves away from us, we do not have the impression that their size changes. And yet their retinal image either grows or diminishes. When we look at ourselves in the morning in our bathroom mirror, we have the impression that our image is exactly the same size as our "real" face. However, if we trace its outlines in the condensation on the glass, we see that our image in the mirror is in fact ridiculously small. The perceived size of objects thus remains constant, except under extreme conditions. Even when objects seem small to us, our brain does not strictly reflect their retinal size.

Perception thus poses the classic question of how the perceptual mechanism succeeds in attributing a constant size and shape to objects despite their movements and ours. On this subject Berkeley wrote in 1709 that "the estimate we make of the distance of objects considerably remote is rather an act of judgment grounded on experience than on sense."[18] According to this view, it is therefore the confrontation with the solid objects occupying their immediate environment that allows infants to understand that visual appearances are deceiving and that teaches them to correctly judge the size of objects in relation to their distance. As Piaget thought, they internalize the sensory-motor regularities that allow them to organize their environment and to make representations of objects so that the construction of the object and of space go hand in hand.

Not very competent in the utilization of monocular or binocular factors, babies under four months should then be just as inept at preserving perceptual constancies. But are they, in fact?

Relatively few experiments have been conducted with such young subjects. The existing experiments were all constructed on the following model: two objects of different sizes are presented, but at distances at which they project the same retinal image, or else two objects of the same size are presented at two different distances, thereby projecting different retinal images. We can thus evaluate whether the babies react to the real size of objects or only to their retinal projection.

This is how McKenzie and her associates studied visual size constancy in six- to eight-month-old babies. The researchers presented babies with a model head at a certain distance and tested whether they would distinguish it from a larger head (identical except for size) placed at a longer distance in such a way that the retinal image would be the same.

And, indeed, the babies reacted to a change in object even when the retinal image was kept constant, whereas they did not react to a change in location of the same object. Beyond sixty centimeters, the results of the experiment are less clear. Four-month-old babies also display visual size constancy, but only if they are tested with shorter distances.

Figure 3.6   When we look at the person seated in the middle ground, we think that she is the same size as the one in front of her. But when we place both figures in the foreground, we see that this is based on visual size constancy rather than on retinal images (McKenzie et al., 1980).

Very recently, two research teams obtained results which suggest that visual size constancy is already present at birth.

What happens, still at four months, but this time with perceptual shape constancy? If we confront babies with photographs of cubes whose orientation we modify, they react as if they were seeing different shapes.[21] With the cubes themselves and not their photographs, infants view all these different orientations as if they were seeing the same objects. Similar results were reproduced in three-month-old infants using squares or trapezoids presented from different orientations.[22] Studies even exist which report the same results in newborns.[23]

While some of the works mentioned need to be replicated or elaborated upon, perceptual shape constancy seems to be accessible at a very early age, or well before four months. We are, therefore, faced here with an apparent paradox: on the one hand, studies on depth perception seem to indicate that infants cannot avail themselves of binocular and monocular factors before the age of four to four and a half months; and on the other hand, it seems that well before this age, they are capable of recognizing an object presented from different orientations as being the same object. How is this possible if they live in a flat perceptual world?

It is still too early to give a clear-cut answer to this question. Nevertheless, it seems quite probable that the ability to perceive depth in infants less than four months old has been underestimated. In particular, it is possible that in the absence of stereoscopic vision, the third dimension can be constructed from kinetic factors. In fact, in babies of that age, we generally observe good performances when the objects used in the experiments are presented close up: then a mere nod of the head is enough to provoke a significant parallax. On the other hand, when we present objects at a distance or in photographs, the performances deteriorate. It is only after the fourth month that depth perception of fixed images (monocular or binocular) becomes possible. If this hypothesis is proved correct, perception at birth would be similar to an adult's. Despite their still poorly developed sensory equipment and the lack of maturity of the cortical centers, the visual world of newborns would be nothing like the "blooming, buzzing confusion" of which William James speaks. It would quite simply be, like ours, a world filled with objects.

Objects

Let us suppose that by precociously exploiting kinetic factors to estimate the "real" size and "real" shape of stimuli furnished by their environment, infants postulate objects in a three-dimensional world. Would they actually attribute the same properties to them as adults? And furthermore, do all humans assign the same properties to objects? Do they see not only the same space, but more generally, the same world?

For you, dear reader, it is inconceivable for the same object to be simultaneously in Paris and in New York. Clinton cannot be in Little Rock and in Washington at the same moment. Similarly, the statue sculpted four hundred years ago which you contemplated at length in the museum yesterday cannot have ceased to exist between that era and today. The *Mona Lisa* we see in the Louvre, if it is authentic, is the same picture Leonardo da Vinci painted. We are absolutely sure of this. But why? Why does any other hypothesis seem like a fantasy to us, the product of a deranged mind?

Our primary perceptual and conceptual system provides us in this respect with unshakable convictions. They are not affected by what the sciences may say about the physical properties of particles, quanta, and so forth. The way in which we construe the properties of the objects around us is therefore not the fruit of what we are taught in school. We do not need the physical sciences in order to see the world. It seems, rather, that the mind to some degree has its own way of functioning, allowing it, for example, to attribute continuity and solidity to objects it perceives. Where does it get this?

Why Do Objects Remain What They Are for Us?

When we are sitting on the terrace of a cafe, our visual field is crowded with autonomous objects separated one from the other. Each of them is made up of interconnected parts, as leaves are attached to branches and branches to the trunk, together constituting the object called tree. Each part moves with the other parts so that the whole keeps its shape.

Furthermore, two objects can never occupy precisely the same space. Their retinal projection is partly hidden by that of objects interposing themselves in our line of vision. Thus, the cafe wall is obstructed by a lot of furniture and posters, the entrance door cut into thin slices by the rungs of a chair, and one of the chair's feet is hidden by a corner of the table. The passers-by on the sidewalk mutually obstruct one another, a foot appears here, an arm disappears there . . . But spectators sitting on the cafe terrace do not see things as mutilated, broken, cut in half, or in continual transformation. For them, each thing retains its own unity.

But how can our perceptual system convert this incomplete, fractured data into integrated objects? Perhaps we were taught that moving objects generally retain their shape? Perhaps, from contact with actually continuous things, we learned to reconstruct their unity from fragmented images? But perhaps this reconstruction process is inherent and to some extent natural to our perceptual mechanism? From this perspective, the baby very early on could perceive a world organized into homogeneous, constant objects and not a chaos of atomized impressions, as the empiricists would have it.

As we stressed in the preceding chapter, Bower began to try to answer this question experimentally in 1967. He asked himself what happens when the center of a simple shape like a triangle is occluded by a strip of paper that exposes its base and apex (fig. 3.7). Do babies who have never before seen a complete triangle infer one, or do they accept with equal facility all the images, simple or complex, that might have existed behind the occlusion? For Bower, it would seem that one-

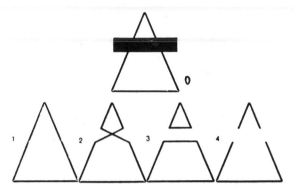

Figure 3.7 The adult perceives figure 0 as a triangle partially covered by a crosspiece: he or she "sees" 1, and not 2, 3, or 4. Bower maintained that the baby does likewise (Bower et al., 1972).

Figure 3.8 When we look at this figure, we should see a Dalmatian (Gregory, 1987).

month-old infants tend to complete partially occluded figures according to the laws of pure form, even though their experience of the world is scant. It was later shown that these early experiments, while motivated by great theoretical daring and ingenuity, were conducted with insufficient concern for precision and experimental rigor. Since then we have learned to be extremely careful and to exert the strictest controls. Now Bower's ideas, tested with greater precision, have been confirmed, at least in part.

This is how certain researchers, for example, became interested in the principles of pure correct continuation in young children.[24] For their experiments, they used a vertical rod that moved from left to right and was partly occluded so that only its extremities showed. What happens at four and a half months? Once babies were habituated to this configuration, the occlusion was removed and they were presented either the entire rod, or its two disjointed extremities. They reacted much more intensely in the second case, which indicates that they perceived the initial stimulus as an occluded whole rod and not as two disjointed objects, as we can see in figure 3.9. Bower's interpretation must therefore be made more explicit by saying that the presentation of a pure form, like a triangle, partially occluded by a strip of paper, does not suffice. It is the congruence of the movement of the exposed parts that allows the infant, despite the occlusion, to reconstruct the unity of the whole. The fact that the results obtained by Bower were not reproduced with an immobile figure clearly show this. We can therefore conclude with Spelke[25] that

> the infant's perception is guided by a conception of physical objects. Infants may group together surfaces that touch and move together because they conceive of the world as consisting of units that are internally cohesive and separately movable. Infants may fail to group together surfaces that form units with smooth contours and a homogeneous color, because they do not conceive of the world as consisting of units that are regular in shape and coloring.[26]

For certain researchers, this conclusion may be valid for most objects, but not for a partially occluded human face. At five months, faces are perceived as unities.[27] However that may be, and contrary to what the alleged empiricists might lead one to believe, newborns are not lost the minute something around them moves. Quite the contrary, movements are essential in order for them to be able to grasp the properties of objects surrounding them.

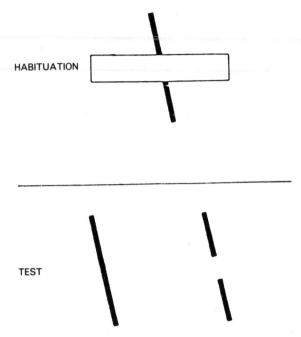

Figure 3.9   Stimuli used by Kellman and Spelke (1983). For the baby to be able to clearly "see" the bar represented below on the left, and not two segments, the two segments visible above and below the occlusion must move in concert.

Objects as We See Them

In any case, an object is not just an organized, constant form. It is also something dense and material. This is why we cannot conceive, except in some other world, of two objects being able to occupy the same space at the same time. Materiality, an essential property of our object conception, could result, in young children, from a difficult apprenticeship in the principle of reality. After bumping into things and trying in vain to go through walls, they would somehow end up accepting the real in all its solid, homogeneous materiality. In 1966 Piaget explained that

> nothing proves that direct perception is at first a perception of "objects.". . . As for the immobile thing, it is only gradually that an appropriate spatial structure would allow [the child] to attribute to it the relief, shape, and depth characteristic of its objective identity. As for the thing in motion, nothing authorizes the child at first to differentiate changes in position from changes in condition and thus to endow perceptions with the quality of geometric "groups," and consequently of objects. Quite

the contrary, at first lacking the ability to situate itself in space, and to conceive an absolute relativity between the movements of the outside world and its own, the child would in the beginning be unable to construct either "groups" or objects, and could perfectly well consider alterations in its image of the world as both real and ceaselessly engendered by its own actions.

Piaget was meticulous in describing this progress toward the principle of reality. But, despite his fascinating observations, we can no longer accept his point of view. For the infant, objects are endowed with intrinsic properties that in no way derive from its own actions. Simple experiments prove this.

We have seen that infants naturally have very abstract and elaborate concepts that allow them to organize the world they perceive. But do they have to learn that objects are permanent in time and space, that they exist even when we no longer see them, that they are solid, and that two volumes cannot occupy the same space? In short, are they completely naive and innocent, or is the inborn representation of certain physical properties part of their genetic heritage as it has been fashioned by millennia of evolution?

For Bower, babies have a concept of the object that is independent of their own actions and, in particular, of the direction of their gaze. Infants wait for an object that has disappeared behind a barrier as long as it has a fairly regular trajectory that allows them to infer its exit point.[28] At about two months, they try to grasp an object in the dark that they saw before the light went out.[29] At around the fifth month, they seem very surprised when an object that has disappeared behind a barrier reappears a different color. How can we explain this surprise if, as Piaget maintained, an object has no permanent existence for a baby outside of the various occasions when he or she is actually looking at it? When the object reappears, a new representation would then have to emerge, with no link to the preceding one, in a way with no past or future. But this is not the case.

Who is right, Bower or Piaget? For the infant, all else being equal, are objects conceived as dense and substantial, or can one solid object pass through another? An experiment was devoted to this question.[30] Two situations were presented to the infant. In the first sequence, a yellow cube decorated with red stars was gradually hidden by a wooden screen. The screen rose, then descended to its original position. In the second sequence, the screen passed through the cube, as it were. This material impossibility can be created in a laboratory with optical devices.

During the habituation phase, four-month-old infants were familiarized with the screen moving as in the impossible sequence, but in the absence of the cube. They next looked at the possible sequence during three trials, and the impossible one during three trials. Half the infants saw the possible sequence first, and the other half the impossible one. During the presentation of the impossible sequence, the babies' attention increased markedly, while the possible sequence failed to heighten their curiosity.

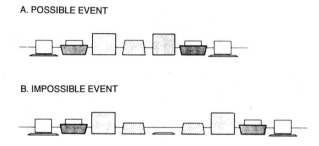

Figure 3.10   Experiment conducted by Baillargeon, Spelke, and Wassermann (1985) to evaluate babies' representations of objects. In the possible situation, they see in the foreground a wooden board that rises from a horizontal position until it touches a cube in the background. In the impossible situation, the board continues its movement through the cube, as if the object had disappeared. Babies accept the possible situation, but are surprised by the impossible situation.

How to explain this? The experimenters checked to see if the movement of the screen alone could explain the results obtained. In one case, the screen follows its course to the end, while in the other it stops at 120 degrees. However, with just these movements and in the absence of the cube, the babies showed no reaction. The movement alone, therefore, could not explain the difference in the groups tested. We must instead invoke the principle of substantiality.

Object conception was also studied in five-month-old babies observing a toy stuffed rabbit in motion.[31] The rabbit passed behind a wall with a window in it. Two different animals were used during the experiment, one tall and one short. The short one cannot be seen through the window, while normally the tall one should be visible. If the tall one does not appear, adults are surprised, just as they are if the short one does appear. We can verify that the same is true for five-month-old babies. They show little interest in the normal progress of the rabbits, while those who watch the impossible scenarios are surprised and even agitated. Recently, Baillargeon obtained similar results with fourteen-week-old babies.

Before five months, babies therefore already conceive of objects as dense, material entities. They are surprised by situations that contradict the principle of substantiality. The empiricist theory as well as the constructionist position espoused by Piaget must be rejected and replaced by a theory of rationalist inspiration which looks to biological heredity for the explanation of the behavior and representations of the infant.

But didn't Piaget and hundreds of psychologists after him prove that babies do not search for an object that interests them, their full bottle, for example, when we hide it under a napkin placed right in front of them? Strange behavior indeed. Adults, for their part, clearly see a bottlelike shape through the napkin, and babies too, no doubt. Why, then, don't they even try to find it? With a smile, the wily Piaget would answer that what babies cannot see ceases to exist for them. In most languages, sayings like "out of sight, out of mind" describe this be-

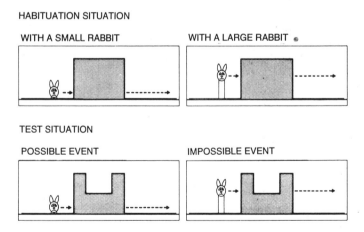

Figure 3.11   Babies are habituated to seeing the little or the big rabbit dissapear behind the screen and emerge on the other side. . . . They are then tested with a possible situation, the one on the left, or an impossible situation, the one on the right, in which the big rabbit's head does not appear in the window when it moves from left to right (Baillargeon, 1987).

havior. How can we explain these deviations and these contradictory observations?

The phenomenon set forth by Piaget is simple. When we hide an object babies desire, they make no effort at all to find it. Does this mean that they do not have the concept of the permanence of the object? Experimental results, on this point, are fairly disturbing. When babies are a few months older, they will start to look for the object right where the experimenter has hidden it. But despite this, they cannot have understood what is going on since another phenomenon, just as strange, now appears. If the experimenter changes the hiding place, babies then have a strong tendency still to turn to where the object was concealed earlier, providing the delay separating the first and second responses is short enough. Persevering this way in a response that is no longer pertinent seems to be due to an inability to inhibit the movement produced earlier.[32] Certain experiments conducted with monkeys and with patients suffering from a lesion of the frontal lobe show the same behaviors. They suggest that the difficulties the babies encounter might be due to the immaturity of their frontal lobes. Their inappropriate behavior could better be explained by problems linked with response management than by a conceptual insufficiency.

This can also be demonstrated with chimpanzees by means of a Plexiglas box open on one side in which we can hide an object. When the open side is oriented laterally, the chimpanzee with a frontal lobe lesion still tries to put its hand through the closed side, as if its movement were under the strict control of the object. Chimpanzees who have had, in addition, both hemispheres surgically separated behave in just as aberrant a manner: the hand controlled by the hemisphere that has undergone a frontal lesion tries to penetrate the closed side, while the other hand searches for the lateral opening. These pathological data confirm that, inversely, the frontal lobes permit healthy individuals to plan their behavior in a reasonably autonomous fashion in relation to the last stimulus received, rather than to a habit.

Why is this not the case with newborns? They conceive objects in a manner that conforms on the whole to reality and is fairly close to that of adults. But their behavior is not yet under the strict control of the cortex. Once again we must evoke the necessary biological maturity of the neurological substratum to explain the progressive development of the cognitive faculties. This in no way means that these faculties are "learned." They increase with age according to a preset biological clock and a master plan specific to the species which owes little to acquired experience, the environment, or to learning processes. Babies' minds therefore are not "tabulae rasae"; written on them are their own laws of development, if nothing else. While babies do not possess all the cognitive skills of "normal" adults, at least we can say that they will inevitably develop them. But, happily for them, babies are already quite competent. In fact, they have a concept of other physical properties peculiar to the object.

Amodal Representations

When we look at the world, we see objects that are immobile or in motion, and hear sounds that emerge from the background noise. We smell odors and detect multiple tactile and kinetic stimulations. How can this crowd of varied data give rise to the representation of a stable, unified world? How can these sensory minutiae, so tenuous, so fragmentary, in themselves so empty of meaning, which Kant called "the diversity of sensory impressions," how can they be unified and coordinated in a coherent fashion?

We can hypothesize that our senses are unified at birth and there is no need to teach them to collaborate. This is Gibson's thesis. For him, when the infant perceives a sound or an image, it encodes it in an abstract representation by means of which it reconstructs objects as well as visual, auditory, tactile, etc., effects. The infant thus possesses a body of *amodal representations* (independent of any one particular sense), a mental model which provides them with connections between the different senses. For a Piaget, on the contrary, visual and auditory sensations are not at first linked. Synthesis comes later, with experience. What is the reality? What does the most recent research on babies teach us?

In the 1970s, it was observed that, faced with objects whose three-dimensional appearance resulted from optical illusions, week-old infants made motions which seemed to reveal their desire to grasp them.[33] A striking result emerged: when infants have before them a holographic image of a virtual object, they show signs of agitation if, for example, their hand passes through the apparent object. It is exactly as if they were upset by the contradiction between their visual sensation, which lead them to expect a solid object, and their tactile sensation. One type of sensation induces the infants to infer another in advance and to expect a sensory confirmation. This betrayal and frustration of their calculations and expectations would disconcert them. Unfortunately, this observation has never been published in detail, so we cannot make too much of it for the moment. It has been confirmed in part, however, by similar signs of agitation observed for other types of contradictory sensations.[34] Must we not postulate, though with some reservation, that it is abstract representations that allow babies to unify sensory data?

The ability to learn the arbitrary relationships between sensory modalities has been studied in four-month-old infants.[35] These experiments use two objects, stuffed animals that jump. Sounds are synchronized with each of them. Thus the teddy bear always jumps to the first sound and the duck to the second. Once the infant is familiarized with this relationship, we make both animals jump at the same time and accompany their movements with only one of the two sounds. We then note that the infant's gaze goes preferably to the object that corresponds to the sound heard.

Similar results have been obtained with two films, one showing a drum which someone is beating and the other the face of a woman talking. Without the sound, they both attract the babies' attention equally. If we accompany the projection with a soundtrack corresponding to one of them (the drum beats or the woman's words), the babies' eyes turn unfailingly to the side where the image and the sound agree.[36]

What about the correspondence between faces and voices? An experiment was conducted using babies and their parents.[37] The parents remained seated on either side of their child throughout the entire experiment. A central loudspeaker broadcast one of their voices. It was noted that between three and a half months and seven and a half months, the babies looked more often at the parent whose voice they were hearing. It could be that upon hearing his or her own voice, the parent in question had a tendency to attract the child's attention. However, after analyzing the film of this experiment, a group of independent judges concluded that there was no evidence that would cast doubt on the results obtained and that, as the authors of the experiment suggested, "the children used their knowledge of the visual and auditory characteristics of their parents to direct their gaze."[38]

However, this type of connection-making seems to depend on the stylization of the stimulation employed. With checkerboards whose squares light up at different rhythms while synchronized auditory signals go off, at four months no trace of an attempt to interrelate the data from the different senses was observed.[39] For that, we must wait until the age of six to eight months. However, the difference between these two series of experiments could stem from the abstract and stylized character of the squares, less natural than stuffed animals or human beings.

In any case, it seems that the same interrelating mechanisms can be reproduced, in this case between tactile and visual sensations. The tests used two pacifiers, one perfectly smooth and spherical, the other rough and studded with cylindrical knobs. During the habituation phase, one of the pacifiers was given to the infant, but without showing it to him or her. When pictures of the two pacifiers were projected onto a screen, the infant's gaze preferred the one it has been sucking. The representation formed by the baby during sucking therefore corresponds to the visual image, so that we might conclude that representations can be matched regardless of their sensory modality, thereby assuming previously existing abstract representations.[40] But while a relationship between the senses exists, we do not yet know its extent.

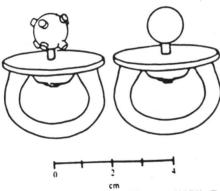

Figure 3.12   Stimuli used by Meltzoff and Borton (1979). Babies suck one of the pacifiers while they are shown the pictures: their gaze tends to go to the image that corresponds to what they have in their mouth.

Thus, for babies as for adults, the world is filled with objects. We do not have to learn to coordinate the various data from our senses in order, almost miraculously, to distill objects from them. The newborn's perceptual world is organized at birth, organized because it refers to abstract representations that are inherent and that somehow furnish schema that allow us to make connections between visual, auditory, or tactile stimuli.

All these connections are not equally acceptable to infants. The representations that help them to build a coherent world, function like preexisting norms that indicate possible or impossible sensory associations in advance. As a result, just like adults, newborns will not try to link the sound of a river with the image of a charging rhinoceros, for example, even if they have never seen either one.

Bahrick tried to substantiate this by using stimuli that the babies could not have previously experienced:[41] Plexiglas cylinders which contained either a big glass marble or millions of grains of sand. At three months, it was noted that the associations between sound and image are not arbitrary. For the babies, a big glass marble *must* produce a contact sound, and sand a hissing sound. It seems as if they refuse to learn aberrant connections. Sensory data therefore hold strong affinities for them, which they seem to identify spontaneously, as it were, in the absence of any experience or prior learning process.

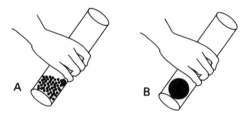

Figure 3.13   Images like those used by Bahrick (1988). A is a Plexiglas cylinder filled with grains of sand. B contains a big glass marble. At three months, babies act as if they know the sound of A and that of B. Bahrick was unable to teach them to match a sound with an image that did not correspond to it.

This confirms the existence of amodal representations. Abstract notions that convey an image of the physical world therefore predate the data of experience, and of interaction with the environment. In an abstract, amodal representation of the scenes and objects we are confronted with, the question of number often rises quite naturally. When babies see one teddy bear and three teddy bears, do they represent the same thing to themselves? Or do they distinguish between unity and plurality? While we are almost all able to learn to talk, only a few among us become mathematicians. However, we find rudimentary mathematical aptitudes even among inhabitants of the remotest parts of the globe. Our cognitive mechanism thus would be a natural mathematician and logician, as rationalists and philosophers of the "a priori" school have maintained since Plato's time.

Piaget, on the contrary, sought to show that for a young child the number of entities comprising a group of objects varies if we change their arrangement. The idea that the number is constant would be acquired, in this case, at about five or six years. However, certain more recent experiments indicate that the matter is far from resolved.

Certain researchers have shown that seven-month-old babies can distinguish groups that differ only in the number of their elements, at least with groups of two or three elements.[42] Of course, it was necessary to make sure the babies weren't relying on evidence such as the distance between objects or their density.[43] Once all the control tests were carried out, it seems that we can affirm that babies are actually capable of making a correct numerical evaluations for groups comprising less than four elements. Subsequent research has yielded similar results for babies a week old.[44]

Arithmetical competence, clearly, is difficult to study since number is an *abstract* concept. Certain researchers, however, have perfected a very clever experiment that works with this attribute.[45] They asked if babies can match auditory and visual sensations in relation to the number of events or objects in each category. They simultaneously presented two images: one displaying two objects, the other three. Then two drumbeats were heard, and the image the child looked at was observed. This was repeated then with three drumbeats. The babies tested looked more readily at the image corresponding to what they were hearing, which implies, in children under seven months, the ability to match acoustical stimuli correctly with visual data in relation to their arithmetical properties. To explain this, one would have to postulate a sufficient level of abstraction. Babies therefore seem sensitive to numbers, at least the most elementary numbers. More recently it has been shown that five-month-olds can also keep track of how many objects there are in a scene, and perform what looks like mental additions and subtractions, when very small quantities are involved.[46]

These data show that a baby is not only capable of processing visual and auditory data, but also possesses certain precursors of the more abstract operations around which human beings organize their rational life.

Imagine an irrational world in which a falling grain of sand landed with a horrendous crash, while a block of granite fell to earth with a barely perceptible swoosh. Imagine that we could knock on water like wood, and that satin creaked like a rusty hinge. More generally, imagine a multitude of contradictory perceptions which suddenly derail our expectations. Adults, confronting this strange world, would think they were having a nightmare or had been transported to a world of false, outlandish images. Everything to which they had become accustomed after long years of commerce with the "real" physical world, would suddenly be turned upside down. But babies only have a very restricted experience of what constitutes the world of adults. They have as yet "learned" almost nothing. And yet a change in the congruence of elementary perceptual data throws them just as much as it does adults. The world, to them, is therefore not an ambiguous, confused chaos where anything can happen and where they stand as innocents incapable even of surprise because they are without expectations. On the contrary, what they see and hear must respect certain laws that have nothing arbitrary about them, but are the cognitive expression of the genetic heritage proper to the human species.

We know that humankind is the result of a long process of evolution by adaptation. Perhaps it is by virtue of this very mechanism that people possess an image of the world. But this model is part of our heritage. It is therefore just as important to study the functions of the cognitive mechanism as the morphology, anatomy, and physiology of human beings. It is more valuable, in any case, than endlessly repeating, with the partisans of relativism, that nothing is innate, nothing is stable.

From space to objects, as we have seen, the baby seems to come equipped with a rich model of the world. We do not just perceive shapes, colors, or the directions of sounds, however. We live with other people and together we forge complex social bonds whose roots probably go very deep in us. Leave a newborn alone and he or she will not survive. The relationships we have with other people, with our own kind, are therefore essential to our survival. This is why it behooves us to pursue our quest by exploring what it is, in our genetic heritage, that allows us to recognize our own species from the very beginning.

4

Self and Others

Among the various stimulations they receive, can babies identify their own kind? Or is the concept of being human gradually developed through contact with the social environment? If this were the case, infants might well think of snakes, mice, larks, pine trees or – why not? – automobiles and computers as members of their own species. Do we have to learn to recognize our fellow humans? Or is this concept, rather, part of the genetic program that is uniquely ours, as is the case for many of the more evolved species? The latter hypothesis fails to receive unanimous endorsement among either scientists or philosophers, however. But the most recent research, on both humans and animals, now seems to allow us to come down on the side of a native predisposition that sees another person as another self, as a fellow human being. This capacity would rely on a certain number of physical and psychological characteristics that constitute the prototypical image of the human being.

It is hardly likely that the living slimes or magmas we see in science fiction films look to us like human beings. On the other hand, fictional characters like E.T., Golem (of Tolkien's *Hobbit*), or Mickey Mouse, despite their physical appearance, behave in ways that have something in common with humans. Physical appearance, therefore, does play a role in recognizing our fellow beings. But it is not the only criterion: a physically deformed person is a human to us, while we would never think of a statue or a robot as one of our own. What is it, then, that determines our faculty for recognizing our fellows? And how does this aptitude manifest itself in a baby?

The Body and Other Persons

It is undeniable that the physical appearance of human beings defines a prototype clearly distinct from that of mollusks or fish. It is just as true that we have a concept of this prototypical appearance, even if we are not skilled at drawing and are only able to render a crude likeness of it. Our spontaneous ability to imitate the gestures of others shows this. To mimic someone, we must associate the model's movements with our own musculature. We therefore really must have an abstract schema of the human body, for that is what makes the natural connection between vision and action possible. In order to learn about the innate bases of these representations, it is tempting to examine the newborn's capacity to imitate the people around her or him.

Imitation

Imitation is a behavior that is very widespread among the higher verte- brates. During the first half of the century, it was often invoked to ex- plain the learning process without having to postulate inherent dispositions in the organism. Certain behaviorists, in particular, saw in imitation one of the fundamental mechanisms that allows the child to learn to speak, by mimicking sounds emitted by its parents or songs heard in its environment. By extension, interacting with others and – why not? – reasoning then seemed possible to develop entirely through learning.

But imitation is not a simple behavior. It consists, in fact, of hooking sensory stimulations up to a motor program capable of producing movements corresponding to those perceived in a fellow human. It's hard to see how newborns, in the absence of all prior knowledge, could use it as a learning tool. How would they figure out what movements to execute to coordinate their bodies with what they see? Besides, in order to imitate, mustn't they already have the concept of the resemblance between their bodies and the bodies of other people? To be able to learn by imitating, they would therefore have to learn to imitate. Here we see the paradox the behaviorists ran up against. To escape this vicious cir- cle, shouldn't we, on the contrary, view the question from a differ- ent angle?

Imitation is relatively easy to study. For this reason, pediatric treatis- es dating back to the turn of the century have often described it in the newborn.[1] However, until recently, it was believed that babies were incapable of imitation before a relatively advanced age. It took the work of Maratos to shake up our assumptions.[2] Her studies, carried out on children aged one and a half to three months, in effect demonstrated that babies are capable of imitation at a very early age. Long before they were able to establish a visual correspondence between their face and the faces of adults, they were able to make certain grimaces that corresponded to adult expressions. Maratos also noted that these imitative reactions did not increase in the course of development. Instead they decreased, and disappeared at about the third month. It was at about the ninth month that a different form of imitation then began to appear: instead of being automatic, it now seemed to be under the child's voluntary control.

Many studies have tried to reproduce and expand these results, and have often failed.[3] They have, however, revealed an astonishing fact. While it is fairly easy to observe newborns imitating certain facial expressions, gestures involving other parts of the body provoke no reaction. Curiously, this tendency contrasts with the fact that newborns can see their own hands and legs, but not their mouths or eyes. How could a child who has never seen her own mouth imitate the movements of another person's mouth? To move one's leg like someone else's would seem more natural and simpler. The following experiment shows that this is not the case and that, contrary to what one might think, it is definitely facial expressions that are imitated first.[4]

A model placed near the baby assumes a particular expression every forty seconds. An experimenter who cannot see the model's expressions, carefully notes all the faces the baby makes. The baby becomes quite agitated: he sticks out his tongue, opens his mouth, waves his arms, and so forth. Nevertheless, more often than not the baby actually assumes an expression resembling that of the model.

Experiments on newborns require extreme finesse. It is not enough just to look at them and stick our tongues out to know if they are able to imitate various expressions.[5] But if what we observe really does involve imitative behavior, how do we explain the fact that newborns specifically imitate certain expressions and are disinclined to reproduce others, even though they are quite capable of doing so? Above all, we must ask ourselves if we are dealing here with actual imitation, or if we are simply in the presence of an "archaic" reflex, to resort to pediatric terminology? Can we be sure that this behavior really prefigures what will be imitation in the adult?

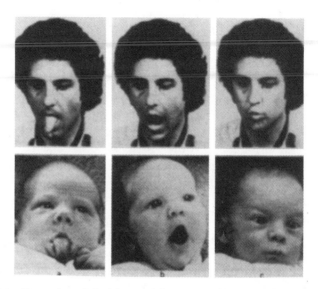

Figure 4.1 Examples of facial expressions and imitations by newborns, as presented in Meltzoff and Moore's experiment (1983).

To answer these questions, it seems that we must compare the data about children with those collected from animals. Tinbergen demonstrated that certain animals react with rigid behaviors to specific sensory stimulations.[6] For example, the baby seagull opens its beak as soon as a white cylinder with a red point appears in its visual field. Similarly, a fish like the stickleback reacts with a complex sequence of specific behaviors when confronted with another fish with a reddish belly. Is imitation in the newborn comparable to this?

The responses we have just described in animals are innate and rigid. But, more importantly, they do not necessarily resemble the stimulations that trigger them. Thus the baby gull opens its beak in the presence of a cylinder, but does not assume a cylindrical shape. The stickleback likewise does not turn reddish to resemble the approaching fish. The baby, on the other hand, reproduces the facial expression she perceives.

Piaget noticed informally that his young daughter mimicked the opening of a matchbox by opening and closing her mouth. But Bower challenges the generality of this observation and seems to be correct when he writes that the newborn "knows very well that no part of him corresponds to a matchbox. He would not map the opening and closing of a matchbox onto any part of his own body and so would hardly imitate it."[7]

However, while this remark seems pertinent, experimental data are not as clear-cut as one might believe. Certain results show, in fact, that precocious imitation could derive from a very simple reflex.[8] Schematic stimulations can indeed provoke a facial response. Thus, if we present babies with a circle through which we poke a pencil, they will stick out their tongues, and confronted with a cardboard cylinder whose mouth we distort, they will open and close their mouths. These are not, strictly speaking, forms of imitation, but rather instinctive and schematic reactions to certain specific stimulations. Thus, babies would not really have the ability to imitate at a very early age, but certain stimulating configurations could trigger responses in which, as if by chance, observers could then see a correspondence with the movements of the model.

Conversely, for other researchers, imitation in the newborn would actually consist of linking external stimulations with internal sensations, by means of a *body schema* that is innate.[9] This is how Meltzoff showed that the infant reacts even when we impose a certain delay before the response is possible. In this experiment, if we have the baby suck a pacifier while the model assumes a given expression. A short while later the model leaves and when we withdraw the pacifier, the baby imitates the model's expression in the absence of any stimulation. This observation would tend to show that the link between the stimulations and the body schema rests on abstract representations, contrary to what happens with animals.

In fact, the interpretation that postulates a body schema and the one that assumes innate releasing mechanisms are not as incompatible as they might seem. We can indeed imagine that imitation may be possible from birth by virtue of a simplified body schema that consists of a network of "prewired" connections between certain stimulant configurations and certain sequences of movements. It is only later, with the help of experience, that this mechanism would be taken over by more evolved centers like the cortex and would assume its adult form. Let us also note that, in the animal, rigid imitative behaviors involve vital functions (eating, copulating), while in the child they concern subjective interactions, or social relations with fellow humans.

Recognizing Faces

Do babies have to learn that their fellow humans have faces of a certain shape? Or do they have, at birth, a schema that orients them by preference toward their own kind? Must they learn that individuals of their species have bodies with arms rather than wings, and legs rather than flippers? Or do they know this in some way already? The study of the early forms of perception of the human face seem to furnish an answer. If, as we might think, imitation assumes an elementary body schema which is part of our genetic endowment, we can then ask whether human young have a tendency to recognize the human face.

In the course of a frequently cited experiment,[10] infants were presented a few minutes after birth with stylized faces, some more or less distorted, or else with blank ovals, as we can see in figure 4.2. All these designs had the same luminosity, were symmetrical, and had the same overall shape. The experiment consisted in having one of these images pass before the baby, from left to right, and in registering the movements of its head and eyes. The person holding the baby did not know the stimulus in advance, and could not see it. It was noted that new-

Figure 4.2   Stimuli similar to those used in experiments on the perception of faces in the newborn. A, contour of a face; B and C, distortions of faces; D, a schematic face (Dodwell et al., 1987).

borns were more apt to follow the stylized faces than either the deformed ones or the blank oval. This experiment suggests then that they possess a schema of the face of their fellow humans and that their attention is drawn to the corresponding stimuli.

As is often the case with experimental research, a short time after this discovery the substitution of a different method produced divergent results.[11] We might, in fact, have expected newborns to look by preference at the schematic faces, rather than at another design, when the stimuli were presented side by side. However, at about one month, they will stare with equal insistence at a distorted face as at a schematic face.[12] On the other hand, at two months, they are more inclined to direct their gaze toward the schematic faces. Thus, newborns have a greater tendency to look at a schematic human face moving in front of them than at distorted faces, but they show no preference when we present the face and the distortion side by side. The preference for static faces does not appear until two months.[13]

This observation prompted Morton and Johnson to propose that the recognition of faces depends on two mechanisms.[14] At birth, the infant is equipped with a mechanism that orients it toward human faces. Later, a second mechanism kicks in which, now based on data from the environment, permits the recognition of familiar faces. The first system would use dynamic data, often from peripheral vision, and would serve to draw the attention toward the zone in the visual field in which a face appears. Thus, for example, it was possible to observe on several occasions that a stylized face that appeared in a baby's visual field attracted his attention more often and for a longer period than a distorted face. This behavior of fixing and following schematic faces decreases between four and six weeks. According to the authors, it may be due to a retino-collicular mechanism which is part of our genetic heritage and constitutes one of the components of the apparatus that orients us toward our fellow humans. This mechanism, which helps the baby to place all the faces she meets at the center of her fovea, would play an important role in the emergence of the second mechanism that enters the picture at about two months and processes static data centered in the fovea. It is this second mechanism which would enable the baby to form a representation of the face of each person in his entourage so that at around the third month, as has been demonstrated, he can recognize a photograph of his mother from among other photographs.

In any case, we must note that some results do not conform to this model, at least at first glance. In fact, Morton and his colleagues think that the newborn is not able to recognize a face until the second mechanism is in place. However, certain experiments show that at less than a week, babies recognize their mothers' faces.[16] Newborns forty-eight hours old on average were seated thirty centimeters from a partition with two windows in it. Through them, they could see the face of their mother and that of another woman with the same hair color and facial contours. The mothers were to look the baby in the eye while keeping a neutral expression. The experimenters also sprayed perfume on the partition, to avoid recognition of the mother's scent. The newborns tended to look at their mother's face, no matter which side it was on. This ability to recognize his mother's face when the baby appears to be incapable of recognizing even a schematic face seems astonishing. There are several possible explanations for this paradox.

Babies less than two months old, as we have seen, have trouble focusing their attention on the interior of figures. They are more attracted by the overall shape. This is why they have trouble distinguishing a normal schematic face from a distorted one: they perceive, in effect, only an overall shape, that is, an oval. On the other hand, as soon as we animate the interior of a figure, or make it flicker, they are able to notice differences in the details of its features. This phenomenon can account for the differences we note in the recognition of living faces and of simple drawings of faces. It is very difficult for a person who has not practiced this to keep her face absolutely immobile, particularly not to blink her eyes or swallow. Confronted with a real face, it therefore could be that babies can focus their attention on its features and perceive the minor differences that distinguish two faces. Experiments made with fixed images underestimate the babies' capacities precisely because of the externality effect, which disappears at around four months, shortly after they are able to process stationary faces. But there are other differences between a flesh-and-bones face and a stylized drawing. For example, one is in relief while the drawing is flat. Although stereoscopic vision is not in place before the eighteenth week, the infant may be sensitive to depth factors, such as shadows and slight facial movements, which are specifically lacking in schematic drawings.

Be that as it may, the mechanism for the recognition of the mother's face seems to be well established at an early age, while the orientation toward stimulations resembling faces is in place at birth. It is only after two months that another mechanism appears which permits the creation of an album of familiar faces.

Newborns do not have to learn what a human face is. On the contrary, it is as if they already know this in advance since they seem equipped at birth with a schema corresponding to the prototype of the face of their fellow humans.

The Body Schema

Certain experiments have established that babies prefer the stylized face of a human being to a blank disk. In the same way, empirical exploration could help us to decide if they have any preferences for stimulations that evoke body characteristics like those of their fellow humans. Unfortunately, very little work has been done on this question of the recognition of the whole body. Experiments have been carried out which used a film showing a man walking or running in total darkness.[17] Eleven luminous diodes were attached to the eleven most characteristic joints in the human body, as we can see in figure 4.3. This film creates an interesting illusion in adults: not only do we see eleven points of light in motion, we also reconstruct the schematic image of a

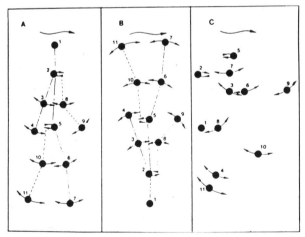

Figure 4.3   Stimuli used by Berthenthal, Proffitt, and Cutting (1984). A shows the animation of a human in motion obtained from eleven moving points. B: the same image as A, but presented upside down. C: the same points with the same motions, but occupying random positions on the screen. The experiment shows that points that coincide with a walking human are the only ones to be integrated into a figure.

man walking or running according to the cadence of the motion. When the gait changes, a striking qualitative difference between these two types of movement emerges.

This kind of motion perception in the adult could be explained by the learning process. It would then seem as if we had learned from watching humans running or walking to reconstruct mentally the skeleton of a moving man from just eleven animated points of light. However, it is also possible that we are born with a prototypical schema of the human body which permits us to reorganize images to make them correspond to a body, even an extremely simplified one.

Animations like those we have just described were presented to babies from three to five months old and they distinguished the configurations that were walking from those that were running. But weren't they just reacting to changes in the absolute speed of the luminous points? If we present the same eleven luminous points, but without having them correspond to a movement of the human body, adults obviously no longer recognize a coherent figure: they can no longer distinguish the "walk" from the "run." The test babies also seemed to no longer discern anything when we changed the stimulant configuration or when the image of a body produced by the luminous points was simply presented upside down. The change in the absolute speed of the configuration which takes place when we go from "walk" to "run" would therefore not suffice to release a discriminative response.

At three months, the baby therefore links the moving points into a unified dynamic representation that only emerges when the points are derived from a human figure moving right side up – unless we dream up some really far-fetched alternate interpretation. We must, therefore, assume the existence of a human body schema. Natural and absolute, it would be functional from the age of three months and would permit the control of movements and the recognition of the bodies of our fellow humans. This interpretation has the merit of raising new questions for the experimenter, particularly that of how the infant would react to animated representations of a chimpanzee or a galloping horse. We can also wonder if this behavior is observable in newborns too, or if it assumes a prior contact, however limited, with the biomechanical movements of nature.

Let us for the moment retain the hypothesis that human beings possess at birth a body schema that permits not only the control of their own bodies but also the recognition of their fellow humans. The repre-

sentations they make from it would be, at least in part, innate. Therefore, it would not be necessary for us to assimilate the facial and bodily
form of our fellow humans by a learning process: our heritage would
have programmed us in advance.

Nevertheless, the prototypical representation we have of the physical
appearance of other people is subject to modifications due to the variations we encounter in our daily experience. Research on the perception
of faces shows that, in order to formulate our mental album of familiar
faces, we use a prototypical face or "average face" and represent each
face as a deviation from this model. Faces belonging to another ethnic
group are so alien to our prototype that they all look the same to us, that
is, until we know enough members of this group to establish a new prototype and are thus able to appreciate the differences. The recognition
of faces, as we see, is a process at once versatile and complex, but it
would not be possible without the specialized mechanisms which are
part of our genetic heritage as a species.

But obviously our elementary representation of our peers does not
derive from physical characteristics alone. In all probability it relies just
as much, or even more, on psychological functions. Our fellow humans
must have a mental life comparable to our own. We have beliefs, desires, and intentions that determine our actions. For example, we want
to buy a car and don't have enough money. Believing that it's possible
to find a good deal, we check the classified ads in the newspapers and so
on. Our desires and needs, interacting with our beliefs, determine the
plan of action we put into effect. We are all familiar with this kind of
problem-solving, and we all attribute a similar modus operandi to our
adult peers. But it is harder to imagine how babies, deprived of language, or even animals, could also have such mastery of mental terms in
their dealings with others. Does the "theory of mind" we attribute to
others derive from our interactions with other people, or is it, too, part
of our genetic heritage?

The Thinking of Others

The renewal of interest in the study of the capacity to attribute mental
representations to others has come not from the study of human adults
or babies, but from that of the great apes. Psychologists studying these
animals have in fact noted some extremely curious behavior.

One psychologist, Dr H., was studying the ape's ability to learn. After weeks and months, he had finally established a friendly relationship with a female chimpanzee. Every morning, without fail, he gave his friend a present of dried fruit or nuts when he came in. She had gotten into the habit of anticipating this generous gesture and of leaving the other chimpanzees to come to the front of the cage and hold out her hand. This behavior had become a routine, as was the gift itself. But one morning, to Dr H.'s great surprise, it was not his "friend" who came toward him, but another chimpanzee. Since his "friend" remained motionless, sulking at the back of the cage and not responding to his calls, he finally gave the fruit to the "stranger." The next day, when Dr H. arrived at his laboratory, he saw his "friend" holding her hand out to him as usual. Confidently, he gave her the nut. She grabbed his wrist and, before anyone could intervene and despite his cries, tore off his fingernails.

David Premack, one of the greatest specialists in the cognitive capacities of the chimpanzee, told a similar story. The Premacks had been working for a while with a female who had gotten into the habit of taking objects they held out to her. They had drawn a white line around the cage to indicate how far the chimpanzee's arm could extend. One day, she dropped an object between this line and the cage. Anne Premack, in a friendly fashion, tried to give it back to her. But the chimpanzee grabbed her arm and bit it so badly that she still has the scar fifteen years later.

Dr H. saw what had happened to him as a mark of the chimpanzee's jealousy of him. The Premacks, for their part, interpreted Anne's misadventure as a sign of the chimpanzee's ability to formulate plans of action that take into account the behavior of others, be they human or animal. The chimpanzee in all probability disliked Mrs Premack. But, noting that she could get a response from her, she threw the object where she could easily grab her arm and bite it. Anticipating the behavior of others had thus allowed her to organize her own.

Several explanations for chimpanzee behavior are actually possible. We could say, for example, that the animals shift erratically from a friendly attitude to a fiercely aggressive one, for no rhyme or reason. Psychologists who work with animals admit, however, that one must never offend a chimpanzee. All Dr H.'s associates thus spoke of "jealousy," attributing complex social and psychological representations to the chimpanzee. This "jealousy" would assume that the chimpanzee was convinced that a tacit agreement linked her with Dr H. and that he had betrayed it. It is even possible to think that she stayed at the back of the cage to test the "faithfulness" of her "friend." This explanation endows the chimpanzee with feelings, desires, and intentions similar to those of humans.

For a behavior to be intentional, it must enable the satisfaction of a desire. The knowledge at our disposal must also be used to guide the behavior toward the satisfaction of the desire. If someone dangles the paw of a sleeping cat in front of a mouse eating a piece of cheese, it would be ridiculous to say that the cat's behavior is intentional. The cat obviously has no desire to catch the mouse, nor does it believe that dangling a paw could satisfy it! For us to able to speak of intentional behavior, there must be a causal chain relating an abstract mental state (the desire that P has) and the actual behavior (that results in P's being satisfied).

Attributing intentions to other people implies the capacity to formulate very complex mental representations. The young child and a fortiori the adult have a mental representation of reality that constitutes either a "naive theory" of the world or a veritable "mental world" in miniature, according to the point of view we adopt, From the latter perspective, an intention, desire, or goal can seem like a focal point of our "mental world" toward which our whole organism strives and in relation to which it organizes its actions. But our mental world becomes quite complex if we include in it other living beings who are also endowed with intentions. Attributing intentions to other people therefore comes down to being able to formulate representations . . . of representations. The picture gets even more complex if we assume that the other people can also attribute representations to other people. We then see mental representations begetting mental representations, one inside the next, like Russian dolls.

If this were the case, a behaviorist might retort, why couldn't we speak of annual tourist expeditions to explain bird migration or, to illuminate the labor of termites, say that they understand the value of teamwork? Psychology has always resisted these kinds of anthropomorphic excesses. The attribution of such complex representations to animals and young children has always roused a spirited resistance, particularly on the part of behaviorists, who saw a form of anthropomorphism in them. Today, when their theoretical authority is being seriously contested, we can beware of their philosophical prescriptions. But there is no dearth of reasons admonishing us to be just as vigilant as they about attributing subjective mental states to animals. Be that as it may, it nevertheless remains difficult to explain behaviors such as those we have just cited, without attributing subjective mental states and social and psychological representations to chimpanzees. It is useless to try to dodge the issue by invoking their rarity: that would be irresponsible. In any event, the difficulty is all the greater since in the preceding examples the chimpanzees seemed not only to have intentions, but also to anticipate the behavior of other people.

In any event, we cannot avoid noting that human beings, at least, have subjective mental states and attribute them to their fellow humans. This is why we strive, before acting, to understand or anticipate our peers. As we observe other people's behavior, we have two spontaneous explanations for it: on the one hand, we invoke internal causes, or subjective mental states, and on the other external reasons, which derive from physical events. Thus, when we see someone fall from a balcony, we explain his behavior by subjective mental states leading to a desire to commit suicide, or by physical circumstances such as an explosion or . . . another person who pushed him. We are thus all experts at explaining the behavior of others, and this is precisely what allows us to calculate what behavior we should adopt. If we did not assume the existence of mental states in other people, we would be incapable of making decisions and would be paralyzed by fear and indecision. Imagine for a moment a motorcyclist speeding down a crowded highway at 80 mph. This would be impossible if he or she thought all the other drivers were maniacs behind the wheel, apt to change lanes at any moment without signaling. Taking risks would therefore be out of the question unless we could rely on various assumptions about the behavior of others. Driving on a highway would be hell if we thought that anything could happen and that the other drivers wanted us dead and would swerve into our path to cause a head-on collision. On the contrary, we attribute to others subjective mental states resembling our own. When we drive our car or motorcycle, it is to get somewhere and not to kill, and everything leads us to believe that others are doing the same. Without this assumption, it would be completely insane to be member of a roped group on a mountain-climbing expedition, or to have confidence in an airplane pilot.[18] The very possibility of engaging in these and a host of other, even more basic types of behavior, depends therefore on our spontaneous understanding of our own subjective mental states and our tendency to attribute similar ones to our fellow humans.

David Premack maintains that humans have a naive psychological theory, analogous to the naive physical one that allows us all to anticipate certain physical events before we've even been to school. We can wonder what the laws of this naive psychology are and if it is shared by humans and chimpanzees or is specific to our species. Certain experiments have shown that interaction with chimpanzees sometimes leads us to attribute this kind of theory to them.[19] For example, confronted by someone who bullies or deceives them, chimpanzees sometimes adopt secretive behavior. On the other hand, faced with an open, friendly person, the quality of information shared with the experimenter is entirely different. Chimps therefore seem to be able to adapt their behavior to that of the experimenter, according to whether they see it as symptomatic of collaboration or of competition. As we clearly see from this example, we can hardly avoid postulating a "theory of mind" in chimpanzees, which they use for interacting with other beings.

However, whenever Premack, in his writings, applied this type of theory to creatures without language, he did so with great prudence. The question left unanswered is its source. Where do the abstract representations which permit such calculations come from? Must the chimpanzee learn all the subjective mental states of others, or is a primitive mode of understanding that is part of the genetic heritage of complex brains?

One thing is certain, apes are expert behaviorists. They know exactly how to adapt their behavior in relation to the reinforcement obtained. They know which stimuli release which responses in their fellow apes and even in humans and thus are remarkably adept at controlling the behavior of others. Much research is still necessary to determine more precisely the exact nature of the representations apes use in their commerce with others, but it is highly unlikely that they rest on mental representations like "She thinks that I think that she thinks . . .". Only humans, it seems, are especially talented at entertaining several representations of reality and at switching from one to the other in their dealings with other people.

This is why it is vital to shift the perspective to human young before they can even talk. Do babies have to learn that their fellow humans have subjective mental states and intentions, or do these ideas arise spontaneously in their minds from their evolved cortexes? Work done by psychologists on these questions should allow us to round out our knowledge about our concept of our fellow humans. Babies seem to manifest a natural tendency to orient themselves toward their own species. But does recognizing their appearance also imply the concept that they are already endowed with the psychological characteristics necessary for being accepted as humans? For newborns, the fact of spontaneously conferring subjective mental states on others would thus be part of the mode of recognizing their fellow humans. To understand this would be to understand one of the key elements of human nature and what disposes us to live in community with our peers.

The Concept of the Subjective Mental State in Young Childeren

The concept of other humans as our fellow beings rests on attributes that at first are physical, as we have said. But these characteristics are not enough. We can recognize our kinship with other humans only by endowing them with intentions, desires, and beliefs. This ability, which we share with other higher vertebrates, is so fundamental that even when we see a stationary object start to move of its own accord, we can't help endowing it with the intention of moving. But is this spontaneous tendency on the part of us adults the result of learning through contact with the people around us? Or do our predispositions, rather, enable us to see the people in our surroundings this way?

As we have just seen, the study of perception in the human baby has only made important progress quite recently. The general belief among psychologists that the newborn cannot attribute subjective mental states to others before the age of four has for a long time led to the neglect of this area of research. It is thus that the genetic epistemology of Jean Piaget, for example, presents the child as an egocentric being, hardly able to distinguish its point of view from that of others or of separating the physical cause of events from its own intentions – all this is suppose to obtain up to a fairly advanced age. No subjective mental state other than their own would by definition be accessible to them. While the notion of egocentricity was judged inadequate for explaining the behavior of young children, certain experiments illustrate the problem that can be encountered on the road to understanding mental functioning. Let us consider a particularly ingenious experiment, conducted in the early 1980s.[20]

A person, whom we'll call Mary, takes a child into a room containing some furniture and a researcher, John, for example. All three of them hide a doll in a drawer, and then Mary exits, leaving the child with John.

John, with the child's complicity, moves the doll and hides it in a box. He first makes sure that the child clearly remembers both the first and the second hiding places. Then he asks where Mary would look for the doll if she came back. In the box and not in the drawer, the child answers without hesitation. She knows perfectly well that Mary has not seen the change, but seems to think that beliefs are somehow reviewed and corrected spontaneously, without the need of additional information.

Numerous other experiments also suggest that the ability to understand subjective mental states appears between four and six years. Until that age, children perhaps might have some rudimentary notion of what intentions, desires, and beliefs are. But they would not understand the laws governing these subjective mental states, and would have to acquire the properties regulating them before they could anticipate behavior.

The experiments conducted along these lines are fairly close in method to the work done by Piaget and his associates, who thought that children under the age of four were incapable of most of the operations that facilitate adult thinking. For example, according to Piaget, a child under the age of four or five does not yet have at its disposal such fundamental operations as identity and reversibility. Before four, it cannot understand that moving a number of peas around on a plate with a fork does not change their quantity, or that the amount of soup left to eat remains the same regardless of the shape of the bowl it's in.

Piaget's influence during the larger part of this century was so great that all psychology found itself under his shadow and experiments of this kind seemed irrefutable. It was only in the 1960s that the grave problems posed by his theory became obvious and that his observations began to be examined more closely and with a cooler critical eye.[21] In particular, certain researchers pointed out that it is not always easy to interpret childrens' responses during the tasks Piaget conceived for his experiments.[22] According to whether or not the children had to give verbal answers, we in fact observe radically different behaviors.

Thus, quite recently, nonverbal tests were used to evaluate the conceptions children have about the beliefs of their playmates.[23] They were told a story and given masks with expressions like surprise, sorrow, or joy to choose from. In one version of the story, the character in question has a belief; in another, a desire. At the end, the belief can be confirmed or the desire fulfilled. The children had to give their opinion on the character's subjective mental state and, to do this, choose from among the various schematic faces the one whose expression best described this state. For the belief, they were presented with two expressions (neutrality and surprise) and for the desire three (satisfaction, sadness, and neutrality). This work showed that children, even three-year-olds, understand the difference between desire and belief. They can anticipate people's actions on the basis of desires and beliefs and coordinate the one with the other. At three, it is not difficult for them to know that it is necessary to take beliefs into consideration in order to explain how an organism satisfies its desires. In the course of other, more difficult experiments, the stories were written in such a way that the children could only infer the character's beliefs, which were not explicitly mentioned. Even then, three-year-old children had no problem.

But how can we explain the difference in behavior between the earlier experiments and those we have just described? Certain authors maintain that children fail when confronted with situations in which the character has false beliefs. They then encounter a conflict: they can understand that the character's beliefs are false, but they can also identify with his or her desires and give an answer that corresponds to their own belief, disregarding the character's. But even if this is the case, it still doesn't explain anything.

Can we not, however, imagine that the differences observed can be explained by the means used to evaluate the responses? When children must answer questions and say what they think about the behavior of others, their performances are not very good. On the other hand, when they must choose the mask that best describes the mood of the character according to how the story unfolds, their responses are much better. This is not a gratuitous hypothesis. For at least twenty years, actually, it has been observed that children's behavior becomes less clear when it is evaluated by the medium of language. For example, it was shown that a young child's performance seemed more advanced when it was assessed by a *behavior* rather than by answers to questions asked by the experimenter.[24] To verify this, a test made famous by Piaget was used which had been created to study number concept in the very young child (fig 4.4). When children see the two rows of marbles represented in (a), they say they contain the same number, which is correct. On the other hand, when we rearrange the configuration in one of the rows right in front of them, and without changing the number of marbles, as in (b), and then ask which row contains the most marbles, most of the time the children reply that the longest row contains the most marbles. We continue to observe incorrect answers even if we add another marble, right

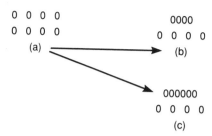

Figure 4.4   Configuration used by Mehler and Bever (1967) to evaluate numeration in very young infants. When we make the four marbles in the top row correspond to four identical ones below, children say there are the same number in each row. But in (b), they say there are more below (in the longest row). When we add two marbles to the shortest row, most children continue to say there are more marbles below. But when we replace the marbles with candies and propose that they eat one row or the other, they choose the row that contains the most candies.

in front of them, to the shortest row, as in (c). The youngest children continue to confuse length with cardinality, as we seem to have proved by using a great number of subjects in the experiment.

We repeated the experiment, replacing the marbles with candies. At first, the babies' responses seemed to be those described by Piaget and his associates. However, if we allow them to eat one of the rows and only one, their behavior changes radically. At every age and in a systematic fashion, the children chose the row containing the most candies rather than the longest one. Everything points, then, to the idea that young children know how to detect the greatest number of candies regardless of appearances – at least when they are looking out for their own interests, which here involve getting as many candies as possible to eat.

How can we explain why their behavior differs according to whether we ask their opinion or let them choose a row of candies? Mustn't we seek the answer in the children's spontaneous beliefs? When they fail in the classic tests of the conservation of number or of volume, it is generally because they are answering questions asked by the experimenter. But research has shown that such a failure does not occur under certain experimental conditions. For example,[25] what happens if, contrary to what takes place in the classic tests, it is no longer the experimenter who changes the arrangement of the rows of marbles, but a teddy bear that comes out of a box, a device conceived for the requirements of the experiment? From the child's point of view, a toy is now interfering with the experimenter's procedure. After the toy has messed up the arrangement he or she had put in place, the experimenter adopts an exasperated air and asks the child to help him or her determine which row contains the most marbles. In classic experiments, only 10 percent of the children answered correctly. But in this case, the proportion rose to 70 percent.

The authors of these experiments suggested that children questioned by adults cannot help wondering why the adults are asking questions when they should know the answers themselves. Children then tend to become wary, and suspect a trap. When the experimenter changes the length of one of the rows, it is probable that the child will factor this into its answer. When, on the other hand, the child views the request for information as legitimate since the teddy bear rearranged the marbles, apparently leaving the experimenter genuinely in the dark about which row now contains the most, he answers with no ulterior motive. It is clear that this interpretation assumes that we attribute a fairly complex cognitive system to children and, in particular, a preexisting theory of mind. Children think about the experimenters' questions as well as about the reasons they may have for asking them. This is why we observe different responses according to whether we question them or invite them to participate.

We can, therefore, legitimately suppose that, by about two and a half or three years, children already attribute subjective mental states to other people. In order to make decisions about behaviors and responses, they rely on conjectures about the subjective mental states of others. When language intervenes in the experiments, they show a precocious sensitivity to conversational and discursive evidence and use it to decide on an appropriate answer. Even very young children, then, are able to use the concepts of intention, desire, and belief to understand and anticipate behavior. Still, we shouldn't go overboard and think that three-year-olds understand every situation they find themselves in exactly as adults do. The processes of growth, maturation and data-collection are far from over.

We can, for that matter, indicate situations in which the child behaves entirely differently from the adult. The experiments we have just described demonstrate that young children encounter certain difficulties in tests of their concept of subjective mental states. These problems may derive not from false conceptions, but rather from the situations themselves in which the children are involved. The method of questioning, for example, can influence the nature of the answers given. Children would have to be a lot more sophisticated to avoid being influenced by the psychologists interrogating them. Actually, there are so many examples of adults letting themselves be taken in by fads, cults, rumors, and innuendos, that it is hard to expect anything else from children.

The evidence suggests that children, no matter how young, attribute subjective mental states to their fellow humans. However, a skeptical reader could point out that there is no evidence showing that they possess a naive psychology before the age of three or four. This is an important objection. But we could counter it by saying that the differences that exist between the newborn and the three-year-old are most probably not due to a learning process, but to growth. The argument bearing on the poverty of the environment applies better here than in any other area. Rather than assuming that families teach babies the concepts of desire, intention, and belief, which we have never succeeded in doing in the laboratory, it seems more practical to think that human beings, even at their youngest, naturally possess a concept of what a subjective mental state is, and that they use it to characterize themselves and others. Children's games confirm this by showing that they use theories that are natural and thus universal, rather than learned.[26]

Pretending

At a very tender age, all children play at make believe. They use a chair as a motorcycle or pretend to shoot a pistol. These familiar routines are called games of "pretense": children play "let's pretend." For example, they can pretend to be a doctor and try to convince you that they have a hypodermic needle and are going to give you a shot. Similarly, we have all seen children making a terrific racket pretending to be a plane or a car. In each case, they know perfectly well that they are not doctors or cars or planes, that they are really sitting on a chair and not a motorcycle.

We have all witnessed thousands of examples of this type of play in young children. But this does not mean that the cognitive aptitudes they imply have been elucidated. Why are these sorts of games so widespread? What psychological lessons can we learn from them? Couldn't they help us to clarify the young child's world of beliefs, and more generally the origins of the concept of subjective mental states she or he spontaneously elaborates?[27]

Being able to play this kind of game assumes very particular representations. Humans possess, as we have seen, abstract representations of reality that allow them to deal with the continually changing flow of sensory stimulations and to interpret them as objects endowed with certain properties and localized in space. But they are not enough to account for games of make believe. Actually, when children pretend that a banana is a telephone, they are not having hallucinations or optical illusions; they are in fact combining several representations: a "primary" image, which refers to existent sensory data (e.g., a red telephone), and a "secondary," indirect image (e.g., I am looking at a red telephone). The first is directly linked to the senses and to actions: confronted by a starving tiger, your perceptual mechanism identifies the object at hand and releases the appropriate reactions. Your adrenaline rises, you shake like a leaf, and look around desperately. On the other hand, if you imagine that your couch is a tiger, your reactions are quite different. Even if you have a good imagination and can picture the big cat's cold stare and "feel" its breath, you remain in perfect control of yourself. In other words, "dissociated" representations can be as precise and realistic as primary representations, but that doesn't make then any less fictitious.

For Alan Leslie, this ability to entertain fictitious representations of reality is not very different from the one that attributes subjective mental states to other people. Certain apes, like humans, can attribute internal states to those around them. If we are crossing a field and see a bull twenty yards away lowering its head and pawing the ground, we tend to attribute the inner state of "anger" to it and, more generally, a representation of reality in which we play the role of irritating target. Two representations of reality are in fact present: our own, which involves our panic, and the one we imagine in the bull. We can try to manipulate them: play dead in the hope of calming the bull, or hide behind a bush. Our behavior then seeks to modify the bull's mental world.

Here we see what the games we play and the ability to attribute subjective mental states to others have in common. In both cases we add to the primary representation given by our senses another representation which is dissociated. In the first case it is purely fictitious, while in the second it corresponds to the world seen from another's point of view. This ability to dissociate applies not only to others, but also to ourselves: we can build castles in the air and live in dream worlds of our own imagining.

It would seem that it is thanks to this ability to dissociate that children can play at pretending. This type of game implies a comprehension of subjective mental states that would admit of evaluation, but unfortunately this has not been fully exploited. While it is, in fact, perfectly possible that children possess a naive theory of the psychology of others long before they engage in such sophisticated games, the innate bases of these aptitudes, their precursors, and the stages of their development remain terra incognita.

We therefore need new experimental techniques that will throw a fuller and more direct light on the baby's "naive psychology." David Premack proposed a direction for research along these lines that might prove fruitful in the coming years.[28] According to him, our naive psychology is based on perceptual foundations. When we open our eyes, we classify the objects we see in two categories: inert objects and animated objects. The former are subject only to the laws of physics: we push them, they move. The latter can move by themselves: they are subject to an internal causality. For Premack, this distinction is as primitive and as fundamental as the concept of the object or of sensory properties. He therefore developed graphic animations consisting of different-colored balls moving on a screen. They give the impression either of inert objects colliding with one another, or of objects moving under their own power, so much so that spectators even attribute subjective mental states and intentions to them.

Our intuitions about the little balls could be the result of the habit we have of interpreting puppet shows and cartoons in an anthropomorphic manner. But Premack suggests that they could also be based on a universal capacity to attribute subjective mental states to objects in relation to certain characteristics of their behavior.

In any case, one thing is certain, it is unlikely that the understanding of mental states operant in very young children results purely and simply from a learning process. In fact, spontaneously we have no clear awareness of the dissociated nature of our psychological representations. Most parents, unless they have read certain philosophers, don't know the difference, then, between the truth or conditions for simple propositions and those which apply to someone's beliefs. We appreciate this difference in our daily lives, but we have not explicitly mastered it. How then could we teach it to our children? This argument should confirm our skepticism about an instructivist etiology. We must also add that it is impossible to instruct people who are not amenable and who do not already believe that the learning process can help them. How can we teach children about the properties of the mind unless they are able, in themselves, to imagine having subjective mental states, and more importantly, able to recognize such states in others?[29]

The learning process, then, does not explain everything. On the contrary, we must assume an innate disposition that experiences the learning process, an inborn structure that makes it possible. It is, if you will, a young child's naive psychological theory that underlies her progressive acquisitions. This naive psychology – rather than a magical learning process – is the precursor of the later refinement of her behavior and her reasoning about the conduct of others.

The concept of our kinship with other humans is, therefore, innate. This idea can, though, easily be modified by learning or by culture. We could certainly succeed in excluding Jews, Arabs, Blacks, or Swedes from our list of possible fellow humans. Even though the concept of "race" is a fabrication of ill-informed minds and even if its boundaries are often very hard to establish, it can be acquired. Do we not readily talk about "junk bonds," the "Star Wars" program, or "deconstructivism" without actually knowing what they are?

The data just presented permit us now to formulate certain hypotheses about the mind at birth.

The Mind at Birth

Babies perceive, classify, and recognize visual and auditory stimulations a few months after birth. They seem able to assign a spatial position to an acoustic source, to attribute a third dimension to visual scenes, and to correlate stimulations coming from several senses and attribute them to the same physical object.

Some of these behaviors are fairly primitive compared to their adult equivalents. A great many of them also disappear for a while before reappearing in a more mature form. How can we explain this? We could first assume that these behaviors are simple reflexes. But we could also surmise that they are linked to dispositions that characterize adults, a point of view that is unquestionably more promising for the analysis of cognitive faculties and their link with specific nervous structures.

How can we explain precocious faculties in young children? The data obtained from newborns allows us to assume that human beings do not come into the world as utter innocents. Their genetic baggage contains data and constraints that will determine their first acquisitions and preside over the emplacement of their entire cognitive machinery. It thus incorporates the general information and universal principles guiding the representation of the physical and social environment. For example, the concept of three-dimensional macroscopic space would be a given, just as that of the macroscopic object or certain basic properties such as position, speed, solidity, impenetrability, permanence in time, or causality.

All these data would emerge at precise moments in development in the form of specialized mechanisms like those that enable us to calculate the position of an object in space from visual or auditory data. Thus an abstract model of the environment would be built which would facilitate the representation of different objects, the linkage of certain data, and the making of certain inferences. A biologist would give this model an evolutionist coloration: the human species was stabilized by interiorizing a faithful map of the physical properties an individual meets during her or his lifetime. It would therefore not be the learning process that explains why everyone can produce these fundamental attributes, but genetic transmission. Newborns thus would have a physical model at their disposal, while the ability to measure and calculate would enable them to extract data from their environment. In this regard, they would resemble scientists more than sea sponges. And while they would learn, it would be more by deduction within an already established framework than by conditioning.

This model of the physical world is, nonetheless, naive and approximate. At the very heart of these genetically guided procedures, learning processes facilitate the acquisition of richer conceptual structures. Our logical abilities permit us to elaborate "working" hypotheses proper to the species, although clearly the theory of relativity and quantum mechanics are not innate. Furthermore, it is not necessary for this model to be fully functional at birth, any more than it is necessary for the bones, the cortex, or the organs to be definitively formed in the newborn. Thus it is perfectly possible, and even probable, that the model of the physical world only manifests itself in the newborn in the form of a few rather primitive mechanisms, similar to precursory behaviors. It will only emerge in its completed form with the maturation of the cortical structures in contact with the environment.

The initial data available to humans do not stop at the physical world in which we have been called upon to live. The concepts of our kinship with other humans and of the psychological mechanism are also part of our genetic heritage. They express themselves very early in newborns' ability to process human faces in a selective manner and to imitate certain facial expressions long before an explicit knowledge of their own bodies exists. At a later stage, it becomes possible for newborns to recognize individuals from still photos of their faces. It therefore seems that newborns carry in themselves not only a model of the physical world, but also a representation of their fellow humans which they use to process certain data received by their senses. In fact, the human prototype will permit them to assemble abstractly certain physical characteristics of the human body, to make a connection between perceived gestures and motor commands, to focus their attention on faces, and to create an album of familiar faces.

This model would also embody the psychological characteristics unique to humans. It would seem, indeed, as if normal children possessed a pre-comprehension of the mind that permitted them to attribute intentions, desires, and beliefs to others. Thus, babies recognize their fellow humans without having to engage in complex calculations to discover that the world is divided into various species one of which they belong to, that members of the same species tend to feel empathy for one another, and so forth. Physicists without diplomas, they would also be budding physiognomists, psychologists, and sociologists.

Thus it seems that babies come into the world with a heritage that defines their possible behaviors. Among these predispositions is the idea of humankind. We do not have to learn that we and others like us are of a common species. As we have seen, it is the innate capacity to recognize in others a collection of physical and mental characteristics similar to our own that enables us to distinguish, among the objects in our environment, those who actually are our fellow humans.[30]

As soon as we recognize another being as one of our own kind, the idea is born that we can communicate with him or her through *language*, and not just through gesticulations and mimicry. The ability to communicate according to a specific system is never in question. As Chomsky has demonstrated, the rules governing natural languages are so abstract and numerous that it is impossible that they must be rediscovered by each individual. We should instead consider that our genetic heritage specifies a universal grammar. It materializes in an environment and stabilizes itself in the grammar of a particular natural language, like French, English, or Bantu. The exact nature of this actualization is not yet completely known. However, it seems that we grant our peers a competence consistent with the demands of this universal grammar.

With no further delay, let us move one to on of the most advanced realms of the cognitive sciences: language. For it is thanks to linguistics, psycholinguistics, and neurolinguistics that considerable progress has been made in the cognitive sciences.

5

The Biological Foundations
of Language

And the Gileadites took the fords of the Jordan against the Ephraimites. And when any of the fugitives of Ephraim said, "Let me go over," the men of Gilead said to him, "Are you an Ephraimite?" When he said, "No," they said to him, "Then say Shibboleth," and he said, "Sibboleth," for he could not pronounce it right; then they seized him and slew him at the fords of the Jordan. And there fell at that time forty-two thousand of the Ephraimites. Judges 12.5–6

Before undergoing any kind of learning process, the newborn can identify objects in space and recognize his or her fellow humans. This aptitude is not particularly astonishing. Baby ducklings and very young apes can do as much. But what about mental aptitudes that are conventionally thought of as uniquely human? Are they also basically innate? Or do they only proceed from a general faculty for learning or an aptitude for imitating which, in humans, would be particularly developed? The question poses itself with special acuteness when it comes to language, the foundation of culture.

The history of psychology and linguistics is strewn with theories and hypotheses which claim to account for the origins of language, most of them fantastic and above all of the exuberant imaginations of their authors. They are no more valid, in the end, than the theory that language was revealed to humankind by a Babylonian deity. Luckily, we have gone beyond that point. It is now possible to envision seriously the biological foundations of language and to formulate interesting hypotheses that have an empirical basis.

The Chimpanzee That Babbled

If learning played a decisive role in the emergence of language, the linguistic capacity of a creature should correspond to its place in evolutionary history. The chimpanzee should learn language faster than the rhesus monkey, and the monkey faster than a rabbit or a squirrel. But this is not the case. A chimpanzee is no more capable of speech than a mouse. But is this not because until now learning conditions have not been favorable to the great apes? Since the mynah, the parrot, and the cockatoo can imitate words, shouldn't apes also, and even especially, be able to talk?

Before the First World War, particularly in the United States but also in the Soviet Union and Germany, attempts were made to develop the linguistic aptitude of the great apes.[1] But the most rigorous attempts really began with the efforts of an American couple, both psychologists, who adopted a female chimpanzee, Vicki, and raised her with their son.[2] For several years, the animal and the child were treated in the same way, with equal amounts of care and love. They slept together, ate and played together. The experimenters were scrupulous about talking to one as much as to the other, and the living conditions for the little chimp and the little human were therefore strictly similar.

However, when the child began to talk normally, the chimpanzee was left behind. Like a domestic dog, she was capable of recognizing a small number of words, but could speak not one. She was content to put her hand in front of her mouth and make a few sounds, but never used a system that even vaguely resembled a language. Much more refined experiments of this sort have been conducted since. Their results were always predictable, however, especially when we consider the abrupt fashion in which this experiment was terminated. While Vicki remained incapable of talking like a human, she did develop astonishing physical capacities which allowed her, like all members of her species, to climb trees. The boy, an indefatigable playmate, tried to follow as best he could. He was liable to fall and scientific curiosity had to give way in the face of impending danger to the child.

The limitations observed in Vicki discouraged researchers for a long time. However, one hypothesis seemed to open new avenues: Vicki had failed, but was it not because chimpanzees are incapable of controlling their vocal chords? It seemed necessary to make up for this handicap by using, for example,[3] some mechanism that would allow them to produce sounds and overcome their difficulties in articulation. Unfortunately, failure again was just as bitter, and the experiment had to be abandoned.

To resolve these problems, other researchers turned to a gestural language like that used by the deaf. Another psychologist couple, the Gardners,[4] thus raised Washoe, a male chimpanzee, never treating him like a laboratory animal and teaching him sign language as if he was a deaf child. Washoe became a full partner in an environment in which even humans used sign language to communicate. This experiment generated enthusiasm far beyond scientific circles and produced the passionate debates of the 1970s.

Washoe actually learned to recognize and use a rather impressive number of signs, several hundred according to certain publications. During the learning period, he made some very amusing mistakes. For example, he used the sign designating flower for perfume, and the one for a wound to indicate the navel of one of the experimenters who entered the lab in a bathing suit. But above all, he seemed to be able to combine certain signs to produce sentences. It seemed to the Gardners that Washoe used a syntax and semantics close to those underlying natural languages. Their interpretation, based on many touching anecdotes, finally convinced the scientific community that chimpanzees were capable of acquiring language providing they lived in favorable conditions under which certain physiological handicaps were circumvented. Never before had humans felt so close to their cousins, except perhaps just after Darwin formulated his theory of evolution.

Now that a few years have gone by, we are in a better position to evaluate these studies objectively. The anecdotes recounted by the Gardners, the films they took and showed, and the informal presentation they made of their experimental results contributed to the rapid and exaggerated support their work generated.[5] Without being aware of it, the Gardners in fact gave a distorted picture of the animal's behavior. While it seemed as if Washoe produced statements shaped like sentences in his gestural language, this was above all because the expurgated transcripts of her "sentences" led one to believe this. For example, Washoe produced disorderly sequences of signs like "You me banana me me banana you," which was transcribed as "you me banana," closer to human language. At best one could say that Washoe associated a few signs with certain objects in his environment when his behavior was reinforced. He had thus been introduced to communication in general rather than to language, strictly speaking. He had understood that the use of signs was validated by the experimenters, or, to put it another way, that playing with signs had a positive effect no matter what their real meaning was. His behavior reflected rather complicated strategies that might be formulated as follows: "Make a sign until the experimenter is satisfied and stops the test." Or, in a particular situation: "Make signs taken from a series associated as a whole with this circumstance." This behavior, as such, is interesting to study and reveals the animal's intelligence as well as his ability to socialize and communicate with humans, but it does not really involve language. For an ape to make signs actually does not imply that he understands their meaning. He knows how to manipulate them, because he was taught through reinforcement, but does he understand them?

Washoe's failure can seem surprising, however. In the sophisticated exchanges he had with the people in his entourage, he did, in fact, demonstrate a certain intelligence. How can we maintain that this obvious cognitive aptitude has no relation to any genuine linguistic aptitude? The Gardners' studies do not allow us to determine the precise nature of Washoe's limitations. Fortunately, research conducted by Premack on another chimpanzee, Sarah, is much more instructive in this regard.[6] It was based on very strict training. A psychologist sensitive to ecological issues might regret the rather high price paid to control Sarah's acquisitions, for it turned her, in effect, into a laboratory animal. Behaviorists have often claimed that poor chimpanzee performances could be explained by the poverty of the environment in which they were placed for learning. Still, it is easy to show that Sarah was able to learn a lot very quickly under her deprived, but strict, laboratory conditions.

To establish a system of communication with Sarah, David Premack used magnetized plastic figures which could be affixed to a metal panel. They designated objects or characteristics but had absolutely no relationship to them. For example, the figure designating the object "banana" could be a red triangle or a blue square, but not a yellow half-moon. Approximately forty words referred to objects, the others to attributes (colors, shapes, sizes), actions (taking, giving, putting, etc.), or abstract relationships (bigger than, equal to, different from, etc.).

The method was the following: Sarah was shown a banana, but, in order to get it, had to place the corresponding abstract figure, chosen from two, on the panel. Figure 5.1 shows a few sequences to which Sarah had to respond. Her training was facilitated by the fact that Sarah never had to study more than one word at a time and that the probability of her making the right choice was 50 percent. Once she was in possession of this basic vocabulary, she was trained to respond to the sequences of words the experimenter placed on the metal panel. It was thus that Sarah, little by little, learned to respond correctly to "sentences" containing more and more "words." We could translate them, for example, by *Sarah put banana plate apple pail* or *Sarah give banana Randy*.

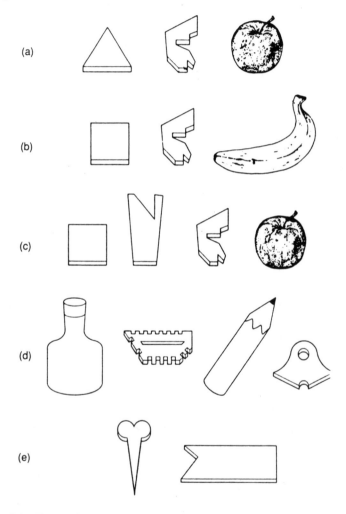

Figure 5.1   Types of sentences to which Sarah must respond: (a) corresponds to the phrase "The word 'apple' designates an apple"; (b) to "The word 'banana' designates a banana"; (c) to "The word 'banana' does not designate an apple"; (d) means "Is the bottle identical to the pencil?"; (e) "yes" or "no" (Premack, 1971).

But for all that, had she learned the language of humans? The best answer to this question, a jocular one, was given some years ago by a psychologist. During a seminar, he told the story of an imaginary laboratory where they were trying to teach chimpanzees to fly without the aid of a prosthesis. After years of hard labor, a scientist was assigned the task of determining if the experiment had succeeded. To reporters who were badgering him with questions he confided that the apes had not learned to fly but that they could jump like hell. Similarly, Sarah had not mastered the language. She showed an astonishing aptitude for learning, generalizing her knowledge, and applying it to new areas. But she was unable to use the system she shared with the experimenters spontaneously because, outside the experimental exchanges, the plastic figures were of no use or interest to her. This is why she never tried to create new phrases with the primitive "vocabulary" that the tests had introduced her to.

However, while Sarah did not learn to talk, she did enable us to learn a great deal. This is no doubt why David Premack was able to state that his work had above all contributed to the definition of language. Sarah could utilize words, combine symbols, and respond correctly to questions. What was missing from her acquisition of a linguistic system or at least a protolanguage? First of all, she should have shown interest in the shapes of the objects with which she worked, and asked her examiner questions like those he put to her. She should have tried new combinations. She should have understood that a linguistic system is as useful for obtaining information as for transmitting it, and that it consists of the primary terms and abstract laws of sentence structure. But nothing of the sort happened.

How, then, is it possible that creatures as intelligent as chimpanzees have so little linguistic competence and are unable to develop a culture of their own? This is no doubt due to what separates the human brain from the animal brain. Humans, even when their intelligence is diminished, often retain the ability to use language. Most retarded children can learn to talk. Since the acquisition of language is not totally connected to intelligence it is possible that it depends on a specific mechanism which is not necessarily affected by certain mental deficiencies.

Consequently, even though humans share many complex cognitive faculties with other animals, they are fundamentally differentiated by the aptitude, based on the emergence of a specific cortical mechanism, for acquiring language. The structure of the cortex determines which aptitudes humans and animals can employ.

Language and the Limitations of Perception

Another way to verify that the linguistic faculty depends more on our genetic heritage than on our capacity to learn consists in examining what happens to humans whose sensory link to language is deficient. If children learn to talk the way adults learn to play chess or recognize a good wine, they should in fact be very disadvantaged when certain data happen not to be available to them. It is impossible to tell a Margaux from a Saint-Estèphe if you have never tasted them or if you have lost your sense of taste. If learning a language resulted only from interaction with the environment, a child who was unable to hear what members of its family were saying, or see the surrounding world, should be unable to learn to talk. An environment diminished by limited perceptions, especially from birth, should prevent the child from talking.

Deaf Children

The congenitally deaf experience major problems acquiring the language used by their parents if the latter are not also deaf. While they see the lip movements, gestures, and facial expressions of others, the deaf cannot link them to their sounds. For them, the passing automobile and the raindrop splashing on an umbrella are no different in this regard. Events leave mnemonic traces that correspond to shapes, movements, colors, and textures, but never to sounds. Imagine the trouble we would have if we had to learn to speak a foreign language without acoustic data. Deaf people have even more problems because they must first understand that the lip movements perceived in others have auditory consequences that can convey information even to someone who is not looking at the speaker. And they must also understand that the sounds transmitted are words that refer to objects, feelings, ideas, and grammatical operations, that this system of correspondences is arbitrary, and that it is part of a learning process. Do these difficulties doom the deaf person to a life of solitude, silence, and total lack of communication?

This is a very widespread and very ancient belief. Aristotle wrote that the deaf were stupid and ignorant. In ancient Rome, they had no civil rights. For Condillac, they had no memory and thus were incapable of thought.

However, since Abbé de l'Epée, we know that the deaf, even if they have problems reading lips, readily learn that the "others" use a natural language produced by their vocal chords and decoded with the help of acoustic data. But more importantly, we recently discovered that they have no difficulty learning a language just as sophisticated and natural as that of hearing people, but which functions by another method: that of signs.[7]

There are two different types of systems based on signs. One of them, known by the name *finger spelling*, was devised by the hearing, while the other, *sign language*, is used spontaneously by the deaf. In finger spelling, the hands and fingers assume a distinct configuration for each letter of the alphabet. Words are formed from the total number of hand configurations for the different letters. But sentences can only be transmitted at a relatively slow speed. That, among other reasons yet to be determined, is why this system is far from helpful in the acquisition of language, and can even hinder the intellectual development of the congenitally deaf who actually have so much trouble mastering finger spelling that they are significantly held back. On the other hand, it is so convenient for the hearing that they have often adopted it for communicating with the deaf, whose problems with it were taken as signs of their impaired intellectual capacity. Finger spelling was taught for several centuries and it is only recently that the situation seems to have been reversed.

The second system is a natural language in its own right, like English or Chinese. As Abbé de l'Epée wrote, "the natural language of the deaf and the mute is sign language; their only teachers of it are nature and their diverse needs: As long as they have no other instructors, they will have no other language."[8] The path to follow in educating deaf-mutes was therefore clearly marked: since they cannot talk and vocal signs are arbitrary, they must be taught the sign language that offers them the same advantages as an oral means of communication.

Relying on his observation of the gestures spontaneously used by the deaf, Abbé de l'Epée established a system that became extremely popular in pre-revolutionary France and astonished the whole world. His work, as well as that of his follower Sicard, led specifically to the foundation of the Institute of Deaf-Mutes in Paris. Unfortunately, this success was fleeting, and it took two hundred years before his system was taken seriously once again.[9]

Sign Language

Among themselves, the congenitally deaf use a sign language similar to the one Abbé de l'Epée formalized. These signs combine three elements: the shape or configuration of the hand, the place where the sign is formed, and the movement made by the hand. Even though, contrary to what happens in verbal language, words are not made up of a sequence of phonemes, this system permits the creation of an infinite number of signs and the formation of complex sentences. Obviously, syntax and semantics depend on the linguistic community to which the speaker belongs: just as the concept of flower is designated by the words *fleur* in French, *Blume* in German, and *fiore* in Italian, the signs specific

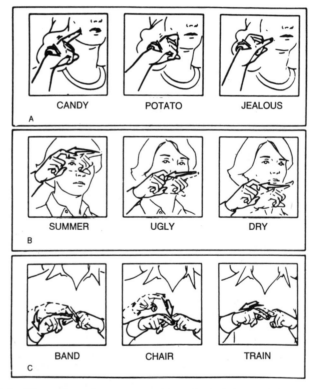

Figure 5.2 Nine signs that correspond to lexical items in American Sign Language described by Klima and Bellugi (1979). The three signs in the top row differ only in the configuration of the hand, those in the middle by the place of articulation. The three signs at the bottom differ only in the type of motions utilized.

to different gestural "languages" are themselves different. Like verbal signs, they have no "natural" rapport with what they designate. While perhaps at first they had their origins in imitation, they have since become arbitrary.

All languages combine elementary segments to form words which are then grouped into sentences. All have basic grammatical categories such as verb or noun; respect the differences between a preposition, a predicate, a subject, or an object; and distinguish a question from a statement or a command. These levels and distinctions enable us to create a nearly limitless number of well-formed sentences. Thus, a well-formed statement can be a component of a longer sentence: "The cat is eating the cake" can be included in "The fact that the cat is eating the cake displeases me." All these properties and many more also exist in sign language. In fact, other than the use of signs instead of sounds, no fundamental differences seem to exist between sign languages and other natural languages.

While the deaf clearly prefer sign language to finger spelling, we do, however, observe an important difference according to whether we are dealing with first- or second-generation deaf. Only the latter, themselves born to deaf parents and therefore exposed since birth to sign language, achieve a perfect mastery. First-generation signers usually have been exposed to sign language relatively late in life, and often have serious problems, using the system in rather the same way as the hearing speak a foreign language acquired late in life.

The stages of acquisition, for deaf children being exposed to sign language early enough, correspond to those of verbal language. The first attempts to sign appear at about the same time as the first babbles in hearing babies. Next come words, then sentences, increasingly long. We note that at each age the average number of words per expression is similar in the deaf child acquiring sign language and in the child learning French or English.[10]

Moreover, when deaf children are exposed to an impoverished linguistic input (pidgin sign language), they tend to regularize and enrich it in much the same way as hearing children create a creole when they are confronted with an unlinguistic mixture of language in their environment.

If we compare verbal language to sign language, we find many similarities. For example, when we talk, we sometimes make mistakes: a word like *six* might be mispronounced as *sex* or *sick*. For Freud, this type of "slip" illustrates the unconscious processes that influence our behavior. However, psychologists and neuropsychologists have shown that most errors of speech or memory follow fixed patterns. One very similar formal element is substituted for another. One phoneme, and not two or three, replaces a single phoneme. Similarly, "b" would substitute for "p" or "n" for "m", but never "c" for "u". Likewise, in sign language, errors can be attributed to the similarity of structure between the slip and the sign intended.

The different sign languages, therefore, are natural languages and can be viewed as simple variants of spoken languages. This shows that even with severely degraded sensory inputs, humans can still develop languages which are as rich and intricate as in the case of an intact sensory system. Hence the cause of the linguistic aptitude has to be sought within the structure of the human brain rather than in the outside environment, which merely enables the different preprogrammed stages of language development.

In short, higher vertebrates are not capable of learning anything and everything. We can easily acquire, though, what the programs specific to our species have destined us to learn. This is why babies deaf at birth learn to manipulate signs so easily: because this language corresponds to the genetic structures that govern language in general. Apes, on the other hand, no matter how much intensive training we subject them to, will never master the grammar that natural languages are based on.

Of course, humans are capable of learning an infinite number of things. They can master mathematics, biology, and astrophysics. They can build machines that allow them to fly higher and farther than any bird, navigate in the dark better than a bat, or dive deeper and faster than a walrus. But these possibilities are part of the culture we have succeeded in creating with the distinctive aptitudes of our species. Our capacity to radiate culture is indeed infinite, but it rests on well-defined, fixed structures which are peculiar to our species.

From this perspective, it therefore seems that "The very intricate simultaneous differentiation and integration that constitutes the evolution of the noun phrase is more reminiscent of the biological development of an embryo than it is of the acquisition of a conditional reflex."[11] The example of children who are born blind shows this as clearly as that of deaf children.

The Acquisition of Language in Blind Children

Blind children might appear to have even greater problems than children who are born deaf. The world seems extremely impoverished to them: they will never see houses, trees, rocks, cars, furniture, all the objects that make up our everyday world. They will never know the colors of the things they touch. Furthermore, while visual perception allows sighted children to comprehend several objects simultaneously, blind children only have the sense of touch to work with, which procures data in a sequential manner.

While the perceptual data of the deaf are far from perfect, at least they can see what the blind can only imagine. They can, for example, read the lips of those talking to them. The blind, then, should have more trouble accessing meanings than the deaf. But this is not the case: they acquire language as easily and rapidly as other children.

When we hear a mother telling her blind child: "I can still see the blue cube I hid behind the box," we have the impression the child understands this statement. How is this possible? How does he or she learn the difference between the word *cow* and the word *horse*, between *car* and *sedan*, or between *see* and *look* with no visual data at all? It is an astonishing accomplishment. However, believe it or not, the blind talk without the slightest difficulty and understand perfectly well what the sighted say to them, even when it refers to visual activities.

Psychologists had been convinced for such a long time that the blind were handicapped in acquiring language that it was only recently that work by a group of American psycholinguists established the facts,[12] which are fascinating in every respect, even for researchers convinced of the importance of biological factors.

One might think that children learn words from hearing them repeated in the presence of the objects they designate: parents would show them a dog and repeat the corresponding word until the association became clear. But why don't children think that the word *dog*, for example, refers to all furry-creatures-sitting-Wednesday-afternoon-at-the-end-of-the-garden-when-it's-sunny, if this was the case when their parents tried to teach them the word? Why don't they generalize or, inversely, unduly limit the word? The number of possibilities that could occur to children trying to learn the meaning of a word is considerable and is in no way diminished by the finger their mother points at the object in question. Each time I point to a dog, I point to a furry animal, an animal that breathes, an animal with a tail and paws, and so on. Or I might be pointing out its color or its four leggedness. Vision, therefore, does not seem to help crystallize the meanings of words, and might even confuse the issue if it were the only factor involved.

At around the end of their second year, children start producing words, one by one at first, then, over time, in increasingly large groups. Soon parents can no longer count the new words and expressions that emerge every day in their child's chatter. They soon stop marveling at each new utterance, the word of the month, the word of the day, and no longer pay attention to what has become an ordinary phenomenon. At the very most, they are amazed by some picturesque or particularly charming expression that appears out of the blue, soon to be over-whelmed by the rising tide of what their child is learning.

The rate at which words are acquired, up until the "lexical explosion" phase, varies a great deal whether we refer to children learning a prima-ry language or adults studying a foreign one. It is very difficult for the latter to acquire a new vocabulary. And yet they know a multitude of objects, whose nature and function they understand, which they can classify, and of which they have had frequent and precise visual experi-ence. Vision and more generally experience are, therefore, not crucial factors. They count, but are not the only factors involved.

Young blind children, for their part, behave like children learning a primary language and not like adults painfully trying to master a second one. They do not lag behind sighted children at all, and their vocabular-ies contain just as many abstract terms and precise expressions. Since the evolution of both groups is so similar, certainly sight is not decisive in acquiring language (fig. 5.3).

However, things are not identical in the two populations. For exam-ple, sighted children use auxiliary verbs correctly much faster and, at the age when they produce sentences like "I am eating a pizza" blind children are still saying "I eat pizza." This delay, described by several research groups, might lead us to believe, despite all that has just been said, that blind children really do have more problems learning to talk correctly than sighted ones. But nothing of the sort. This distortion must instead be attributed to the different linguistic behavior of the mothers: those with blind children actually have a tendency to stress words that have a meaning even outside a sentence, to the detriment of subordinate words. No doubt they think they are thereby making

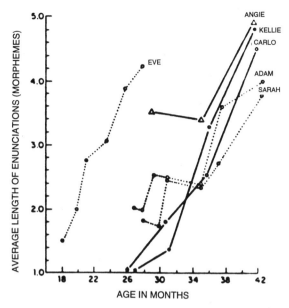

Figure 5.3   Curves indicating the acquisition of language in three blind children (Angie, Kelli, Carlo) compared to three sighted children (Eve, Adam, and Sarah) studied by Landau and Gleitman (1985) and Brown and Bellugi (1964) respectively. We observe that the acquisitions are completely comparable.

things easier for their children, but this is not necessarily the case. The fact remains that this emphasis diminishes the grammatical data of blind children by neglecting function words. However, this difference is only transitory and eventually they catch up with sighted children.

Certain psychologists were also interested in how blind children handled verbs of perception like "look." This term refers to the act of using the eyes to comprehend an object, landscape, or scene visually, but adds an idea of intentionality that is not contained in "see." We can use "see" to describe a factual state, while "look" always describes an action. When we think, for example, about these subtle distinctions, we can't help but be surprised by the young child's ability to acquire them at a very young age. An even more astonishing fact is that blind children have no more trouble with them than sighted children. They simply shift the nuance appropriate to the verb "look" from the visual modality to what, for them, has priority: the sense of touch. This is why we do not find in blind children's conversations expressions like "See the toy" or "See the rain," while sentences like "Look at the toy" or

"Look at the rain" are frequent, even if they sometimes say "I see the car" when their hand is resting on the hood.

They do not, however, confuse vision with touch and realize fully that other people can see. For example, if we ask them to show us the back of their pants, they turn around and shake the pants as if to attract our attention. When we ask them to show a sighted person a toy, they lift it up and hold it that way for a moment. On the other hand, if we ask them to let their mother touch the toy, they go over and hold it out to her.

But while blind children master verbs of visual perception well enough, how do they manage with colors? Do they understand what blue, red, and yellow are? It is only at about three or four years that sighted children use terms designating colors in a stable and consistent

Figure 5.4   Response of the blind child when his mother asks him to let her "see" the back of his pants (Landau and Gleitman, 1985).

Figure 5.5   Response of a blind child when asked "Show me the car" (A) and "Let me touch (see) the car" (B) (Landau and Gleitman, 1985).

fashion. This is precisely the moment when these terms disappear from blind children's speech. At most, we hear them asking for explanations about red, blue, and yellow. These facts suggest, then, that terms designating colors are generally used in a superficial and way by all children when they are very young, whether they are blind or not. At four, however, the semantic chromatic field stabilizes in sighted children, while blind children recognize their problems determining the meanings of the various words they realize refer to specific visual characteristics. For the blind, balloons, pencils, and dogs have a visual property they call color, even though they do not know what that property looks like.

While we obviously cannot deny that the blind are handicapped in this respect, at least we can say that since they understand what vision is they have an idea of color or rather of a specific visual property that applies to sensory objects. Their handicap, which only affects the content of terms whose use they understand, therefore does not interfere with the acquisition of language in general. It is a relatively circumscribed limitation from the cognitive point of view.

One day, a mother opened an envelope containing photos of one of her other children in front of her blind daughter. The little girl asked to look at them: she touched the slick surface of the paper, shook it, licked it, and smelled it. After a long period of intent examination, anxious comments, and questions, she said that the pieces of paper were of no interest because her eyes were "broken." Later, after many such frustrating experiences, she said that other people could see with their eyes, while she could only see with her hands. What could better illustrate the real meaning of the limitations specific to the blind? This little girl was just as intelligent as her brothers and sisters, despite her more reduced sensory experience of the world.

Toward New Hypotheses

Although incomplete, this study of the deaf and blind nevertheless allows us to reject certain hypotheses and models that were conceived to explain the emergence of language. Some authors, in effect, have maintained that we learn words by merely associating visual data and auditory stimuli. But today it is understood that blind children behave like sighted children. To develop their vocabularies, they rely on certain sensory data, but above all form hypotheses conditioned by specific cognitive structures and by the formal constraints of the language itself. Among these three parameters which aid us in acquiring a vocabulary, only sensory data depends on the environment and the functioning of the sensory mechanism; the other two are common to us all – deaf, blind, sighted, or hearing – or so it seems, provided we are human. It is precisely for this reason that apes, even though they see and hear to perfection, cannot acquire a real language. We cannot agree with an empiricist like Locke for whom ideas, being simple copies of sensory impressions, have their origin in the senses. The mind of the little blind or deaf child is not an empty box; it is rich in concepts and possibilities, just like everyone else's.

Language seems, therefore, to appear because of a genetic program that is a component of human nature and not because of an aptitude for learning which we have in common with certain animals but which, for mysterious reasons, is more developed in us. While the part played by learning is enormous in the acquisition of language, it is, in fact, a form of learning that characterizes us in our own right and that only certain specific cortical structures can activate. As a result, and to confirm this admittedly indirect hypothesis, we must now shed some light on the part of the brain responsible for grammar and vocabulary, and for the rules governing the production and comprehension of sentences: the very factor, as we have seen, that fails to appear in chimpanzees.

The Organ of Language

The Localization of Language

It was by chance that the relationship between the left hemisphere of the brain and the linguistic aptitude in humans was discovered, and by the second half of the nineteenth century the intellectual climate in Paris was clearly ripe for such a breakthrough. Since many hospitals were admitting patients whose lesions involved the loss of language, the concept of the cerebral localization of intellectual functions was coming under serious consideration. Gall and Dax had proposed it at the start of the century, but it was Broca who was the first to give it a clinical foundation.

In 1865, after many observations,[13] Broca announced to the scientific community that the loss of speech without articulatory paralysis and with no impairment of intelligence was linked to lesions in the third frontal convolution of the left hemisphere of the brain. The acquisition of certain aptitudes, therefore, would depend on and be controlled by specifically localized cerebral structures. Broca's position gained many followers in the medical world. After more than a hundred years of research, it is incontestable that the left hemisphere, and more particularly certain convolutions thereof, are the seat of language.

However, certain neurologists reported cases of aphasia after lesions to the right hemisphere in left-handed people. It was therefore assumed, erroneously, that Broca's theory was only valid for right-handed people. With left-handers, on the contrary, the right hemisphere would serve as the seat of language, so that language would have its origin in the hemisphere opposite the dominant hand. The great psychologist William James claimed that the lesion causing aphasia was located in the left hemisphere in right-handed patients and in the right hemisphere in left-handed ones.[14] Manual dominance was, for him, responsible for the lateralization of language. More recently, precise tests have shown that the split between right- and left-handedness is less rigid than it had seemed and that a good many people are in fact ambidextrous. For about 95 percent of right-handed people, the left hemisphere is responsible for language, while in left-handers the rate is about 75 percent.[15] It seems that, in accordance with Broca's affirmations, language actually is located in the left hemisphere in the great majority of cases.

Certain studies done on patients who had undergone commissurotomies amply confirmed and sharpened this view. This surgical procedure, used sometimes in the treatment of epilepsy, consists in severing the nerve fibers communicating between the two hemispheres of the brain. With these patients, we can be certain that the two hemispheres function separately and we can better evaluate the contribution specific to each. It thus appeared that it is always the left hemisphere that governs grammatical processing, while the right hemisphere plays a completely secondary role in linguistic production.[16]

Another method also allows us to evaluate the contribution of each hemisphere. It consists in injecting sodium amytal directly into the left or right carotid artery of patients about to undergo neurological surgery.[17] This selective anesthetic technique renders the patient incapable of using the corresponding cerebral hemisphere. It permits, then, a good evaluation of the aptitudes linked to each hemisphere and has confirmed the data obtained by the observation of lesions in aphasics. It was thus proved that the origin of language is in the left hemisphere in right-handed persons, and also, to a lesser degree, in left-handers;

the right hemisphere is the primary seat of language in only 4 percent of humans.

It was also noted that there are two types of left-handed people. A minority are left-handed through a genetic factor, but most become so following intrauterine accidents which, if they happen early in the pregnancy, can entail a reorganization of the neuronal connections. In the laboratory, lesions were produced in the fetuses of monkeys at different stages of gestation. The fetuses were then allowed to reach term. All had brains different from those of members of the same species who had no lesions.[18] But only those with early interventions could mitigate an eventual defect: a function normally handled by the injured side was partly taken over by its healthy counterpart. This process would explain why certain persons become left-handed while only a small proportion of them are natural left-handers, so to speak. With all the rest, the great majority, language would indeed have its seat in the left hemisphere, which would be the "organ of language."

The Fragmented Mind?

Franz Joseph Gall remains famous in the history of science for his theory of *phrenology*. Refuted today, it postulated that intellectual aptitudes, developing unequally according to the individual, determined not only the growth of the brain itself, but also the apparent morphology of the cranium. As a result, conclusions about a person's cognitive aptitudes could be drawn from the configuration of his or her cranium. These are the conclusions that science has refuted. But Gall was the precursor of a hypothesis that does seem pertinent. He thought of the mind not as a homogeneous entity but as a collection of faculties each one separate from the other. This principle made him one of the forerunners of the notion of *modularity of mind*, currently revived by Fodor among others.[19]

Gall's novel views drew the sharpest criticism from Jean-Pierre-Marie Flourens.[20] Along with arguments of an epistemological order directed against phrenology, Flourens also raised objections of a religious nature: for him the "soul" could not be fragmented. Opposing Gall's idea of localization, Flourens in effect set forth a globalist conception of the functioning of the brain.[21] This view was taken up again in the twentieth century by Lashley.[22] On the basis of ablations performed on rats, he reached the conclusion that the brain is *equipotential*, that is, that any one of its parts could take over the various cognitive aptitudes. No part, according to him, would be "specialized," which would explain why, in the case of a lesion to a portion of the cortex that assumed a certain function, the function could be taken over by an intact zone. Lashley dubbed this ability *vicariance of function*.

We know today that the experiments on which Lashley based his theory used behaviors that were *not* characteristic competences of the laboratory rats tested. In fact, the rats learned the behaviors for the occasion before undergoing an ablation of part of the cortex. It was as if, in order to measure and test the aptitudes of our species, we chose as our criteria bridge engineering or programming in FORTRAN, neither of which would have any value in understanding how aptitudes are located in the brain.

The discredit heaped on the theories of Flourens and Lashley coincided with Gall's return to the good graces of psychologists. His idea of localization, recast in terms of the localization of brain function, is now taken seriously by neuropsychologists. This is because their discipline, which studies the relationship between cognitive functions and the structures of the brain, has come a long way assuming that a given function has its basis in a particular cerebral region. Gall believed, in effect, that the faculties of the mind were organized into different "modules" specialized in the processing of certain types of data. From there, it is but a step to assume that they have very localized cerebral roots.

When we are listening to a symphony, looking at a painting or a landscape, doing a math problem, or reading a novel, our mind seems to be absorbed in a single activity, homogeneous and unified. But in fact, each of these operations brings a number of specialized systems into play.

This becomes obvious when we examine the effects that certain lesions of the parietal and temporal lobes can have on different human aptitudes. For instance, some patients who have undergone cortical lesions can read, watch movies, and see everything going on around them, but are unable to recognize the most familiar faces. They must rely on details of clothing or the sound of a voice to identify their nearest and dearest. These patients can easily recognize a bottle of Coca Cola or Perrier from a photograph, but a picture of George Bush or their grandmother leaves them clueless.[23]

The recognition of faces is not the only module that can be affected by a cortical lesion. For example, after an accident, a painter lost his color perception. His vision was normal in every way, but he saw the world in black and white.[24] Reds and greens looked black to him, while yellows and blues seemed almost white. As a painter, he "knew" how to describe precisely what shades Van Gogh or Rubens had used in various paintings, but he could not see them even in his imagination. We can scarcely conceive the problems he must have had relating to a world that now had nothing in common with what he had known before. Other people seemed to be "the color of rats," and food had a dull, unhealthy appearance. Even in his mind's eye tomatoes were black, salad dark gray, and lemons whitish. Gradually he came to eat only colorless foods like rice, and lived essentially at night. He took up sculpture and painting in black and white.

Comparable phenomena can affect the perception of movement. Mrs R could not see movement. For example, she had difficulty pouring herself a cup of tea: the liquid seemed congealed and she did not see the cup filling up. Similarly, she did not perceive the people around her in motion. "People appear suddenly here or there, without my seeing them move," she said. She avoided crowds and could not, for example, cross the street: she saw cars, but was unable to gauge their speed: "When I first see at a car, it looks very far away. But when I go to cross the street, it suddenly seems very close."

Thus we see that vision relies on differentiated mechanisms that can function separately. An autonomous sub-system deals with the perception of colors, for example, still another with the perception of movement.

Like vision, language also appears to us to be a whole. It even seems indissociable from the other higher faculties. But we have known for more than a century that certain cortical lesions localized particularly in the left hemisphere can have specific effects on linguistic capacity. Some patients lose the ability to understand language, while others lose the ability to produce sentences. Others, more seriously affected, lose both abilities. Neuropsychologists have been trying to link these symptoms with the affected areas of the cortex since the nineteenth century. Thus it was believed that anterior lesions in particular caused problems with production of speech, *Broca's aphasia*, and that lesions of the posterior parts of the cortex tended to create difficulties in language comprehension, *Wernicke's aphasia*. Today, thanks to a better description of these symptoms and deficiencies, this gross classification has proved to be of limited interest. On the other hand, a more specific description has permitted us to show how traumas can cause a loss that remains limited to a very specific component of the linguistic system. Thus, some patients experience difficulty identifying words, while others have problems with grammar, reading, or writing. Without enumerating all the different forms of aphasia, it is possible to say that clinical studies have facilitated the relatively precise description of the various stages of linguistic data processing. They seem to be specific and modular.

As Broca discovered, certain cerebral traumas can cause loss of language without affecting other faculties. Aphasics suffering from a serious lesion in the left hemisphere thus can still reason and calculate. However, one might think that since both language and music are auditory, patients who have a hard time understanding what is said to them would also have a problem recognizing a piece of music. But this is not true, as several celebrated cases demonstrate.

At the age of seventy-seven, a well-known composer and organist, who was blind, suffered a stroke. A cerebral lesion of the left hemisphere left him aphasic. He could no longer speak words or utter sentences. And yet his musical abilities were unaffected: he could still decipher scores by ear. But above all, and even more astonishingly, while he could read music in braille, the accident had left him almost unable to read braille texts. This discrepancy was all the more surprising since the symbols representing notes and letters are identical in braille. The nature of the system used was therefore not a factor. Musical ability would then be a function of the right hemisphere, while linguistic competence would be handled by the left one.[25]

Figure 5.6   A, a musical score; B, the same score in braille; C, a transcription of the braille score with the letters used. The patient can play the score presented in braille, but has great difficulty reading E, which represents the syntagma "le père" [the father]. He reads: "Le . . . Pa . . . le . . . ta . . . le frère [the brother] . . . la . . . le par . . . il y a [there is] pé." (Signoret et al., 1987)

The example of another patient, also a professional musician, bears out this theory. It concerns a right-handed conductor who had led the La Fenice orchestra in Venice and the La Scala orchestra in Milan for many years. At sixty-seven, a stroke injuring his left cerebral hemisphere caused the loss of all linguistic aptitude, and he was unable to speak for the next six years. On the other hand, his musical capacities remained almost intact. He was incapable of naming notes, but could sing or play them. He made such rapid progress that, despite his inability to communicate with an orchestra except by gestures, he continued to be a completely professional conductor capable of detecting the most subtle musical errors. His interpretation of Verdi's *Nabucco* was especially appreciated by critics.

The lesion resulting from his first stroke therefore affected only his left hemisphere, the seat of language. Six years later, a second vascular accident partly destroyed his right hemisphere. Unfortunately, this time he did not recover and his death prevented our testing his musical capacities. Other cases of lesions suppressing the aptitude for music confirm, however, that musical ability has its seat in the right hemisphere of the brain.[26]

As indicated above, commissurotomy cases illustrate the dissociation that exists between language and other mental functions, for in these patients we can present data to one hemisphere only. For example, we can arrange for the image of a word to reach the left hemisphere only.[27] Subjects can read it and even point to the corresponding object. But this is possible only if they use their right hand. This hand is directly linked to the left hemisphere, in other words, to the one that "saw" the word.

If, on the contrary, we present a word to the opposite hemisphere, subjects are unable to read it, and even claim not to have seen anything. However, they can locate the object, with their left hand. In these cases, the left hemisphere, which is responsible for language, has not "seen" the word presented, and subjects are therefore unable to formulate a verbal response.[28] To summarize, if we analyze the subjects' behavior in terms of what they perceive and produce with their right hemispheres, we conclude that they have a very diminished linguistic capacity similar to that of certain aphasics. Yet if we analyze their behavior in terms of what they control with their left hemisphere, we conclude that they are in full possession of their linguistic capacities.

How is this possible? How can one both be and not be aphasic? In fact, this discrepancy between mental faculties in the same person is only partial and manifests itself only in very specific experimental situations. Under normal conditions, both hemispheres function in a coherent fashion, for they have many means of communicating with one another. For example, eye movements permit the duplication of visual data in both hemispheres, and information can also circulate through the intermediary of motor activity. For instance, we have observed a subject give an incorrect verbal response, raise his eyebrows, and then immediately correct himself. No doubt the right hemisphere, which knew the correct answer, prompted the raised eyebrows, which informed the left hemisphere of its error and led him to change his response. It is also possible that such phenomena sometimes occur in healthy individuals.

Be that as it may, these surprising observations clearly show that it is counterproductive to see our mental faculties as an inseparable whole. In the light of neuropsychological studies, our psychological mechanism seems rather to be composed of independent and autonomous faculties like the perception of faces and of language. And language itself is not all of one piece either. Very specific afflictions illustrate this. Some patients, for example, lose the use of conjunctions but not of nouns and adjectives, or even the use of a whole semantic group like fruits and vegetables, or trees.[29] An apparently simple and homogeneous task therefore calls upon many distinct and specialized submechanisms, which can break down while the rest of the system continues to function normally.

Commonsense psychology, as we clearly see, cannot explain this type of phenomenon. Nor is the perspicacity forged by years of experience of any use. We therefore must assume that a part of our cognitive system is divided into functional units, or modules, which are responsible for a given aptitude and operate in an autonomous fashion oblivious to what is happening elsewhere in the system. The more research advances, the less our intelligence seems to resemble a whole with indistinct, equipotential parts, rather like a bowl of jello, and the more it seems to be subdivided into a great number of functions which have a certain autonomy. Gall's intuition has proven to be right. As we already mentioned, it was taken up again in more modern form by Jerry Fodor.[30]

According to Fodor's formulation, we can compare a function, or module, to a physical organ. Our body is made up organs which have their specific functions and which, through their interaction, contribute to the functioning of the whole. However, modules do not exchange fluids or energy, but information. Thus each module constitutes an abstract organ which we could describe, at least in a rough approximation, in terms of concepts borrowed from computer science (representation, structure of data, manipulation of symbols, etc.). In a sense, then, a module is closer to a computer program than to a heart or liver. However, like its physiological counterpart, it has a specific function: it only processes a fragment of the information circulating through the whole psychological mechanism and can only use rather restricted, predetermined channels of communication. Conscientious, but rather limited, it is an expert in its field. Furthermore, just as in the case of physical organs, the growth and organization of cognitive modules is guided by the genetic program specific to the species. And finally, as the example of language shows, a module is not distributed throughout the entire brain, but involves a specific nervous structure, circuit, and/or cortical area.

From this perspective, we can no longer imagine that our psyche is controlled by a central intelligence. The data used by each module are limited and its field of operation is restricted. A so-called superior intelligence is no longer necessary. It is the system as a whole that exhibits a behavior we can term intelligent, not its parts taken separately, and not just one part in particular.

How many modules are there? How are they organized? According to one of Fodor's hypotheses, there are many specialized systems which are consolidated into large modules, each specialized in the rapid and automatic processing of one type of data (e.g., language). Each module delivers information to a central processing unit which compares the different entries as well as all the other knowledge available to the organism, making it possible to elaborate the long-term planing of actions.

It is quite obvious that we have not yet been able to explore this extremely complex modular architecture in detail. We are still taking the first baby steps in a discipline which is centuries behind the natural or exact sciences. This functionalist representation of the psychological mechanism is above all a guideline: it enables us to formulate hypotheses and submit them to experimental verification. The actual existence of a particular system or a particular exchange of data is not a metaphysical postulate. The beauty and perfection of the theory matter less than its ability to raise questions that experiments can then proceed to answer.

If language, then, is a specific module that is rooted in cerebral structures intrinsic to humans, learning a language must depend on mechanisms specifically determined by our genetic heritage. We should, therefore, be able to find the elementary aptitudes that attest to this in the newborn. After having shown that, unlike the animals closest to them, only humans can access language by virtue of their cerebral capacities, it now behooves us to explore these linguistic manifestations themselves.

How Babies Access Language

These tiny creatures, newly born and sleeping in such peaceful ignorance of what awaits them in the world, how will they ever attain mastery of language? It actually takes them just three or four years to learn to talk. A foreign diplomat will have trouble mastering Japanese after spending two or three years in that country, and generally needs to take lessons. But children manage all by themselves. Even the most limited in other respects quickly become quite adept, more so, in any case, than the average adult learning a foreign language. This is because their cerebral mechanism predisposes them to acquire the necessary knowledge with ease and rapidity.

As we have seen, this machinery knows how to process data from the environment, not only visual data but also sounds which help in identifying and localizing objects, and in evaluating their movements. The auditory system thus participates in the elaboration of a coherent and orderly perceptual world, and does so for all the higher animals. But in the case of humans, it also plays another major role. Sound is, in fact, the privileged vehicle of spoken language, with which humans encode and exchange information, and develop and transmit a culture, knowledge, or a passing thought.

Recognizing Words, Identifying One's Own Language

Babies do not live under ideal laboratory conditions hearing nothing but perfect linguistic signals. Their environment, on the contrary, is fraught with all kinds of noises. How can they extract the stimuli pertinent to speech from this confused clamor in which words are randomly mixed with the general brouhaha, with the rustling, whistling, and grinding of miscellaneous objects? How do they tell the difference between a word and a tune, a shout, the roar of a motorcycle, or the gush of water running from a faucet? In order to learn language, wouldn't they need a mechanism that allows them to sort out sounds produced by human vocal cords?

We have seen earlier that babies have a very highly developed sense of hearing at birth.[31] Not only do they turn toward sounds, but they also discriminate between tones of different volume and organize sounds into melodies and voices. We also remarked that four-month-old babies prefer listening to words than to other noises or to silence.[32] These results indicate a propensity to be attentive to linguistic signals. But are all speakers equally attractive to the baby? To find out, we focused our inquiry on the baby's capacity to recognize different speakers, his or her mother in particular.[33] At three and a half months, babies are more attentive to their mother's voice than to a stranger's, and we were able to produce these results at an even younger age in our laboratory.[34] They are especially attentive to their mother's voice when she speaks in a natural manner. On the contrary, if she reads a text backwards – a condition which makes a natural intonation impossible – they no longer show any preference. It would seem, therefore, that they are sensitive principally to intonation. At four months babies generally prefer listening to someone talk in a style the English-speaking countries call *baby talk*, (or "motherese"), rather than to normal speech.[35] Baby talk is the speech used by mothers the world over for talking to their babies: the voice is high-pitched and the intonation exaggerated.

The first studies on recognizing mother's voice were conducted on babies two to three months old. But a few years later American researchers detected a similar preference at the age of only a few days.[36] The results, however, are less marked at twelve hours after birth.[37] Regardless of the exact age at which babies show this kind of preference, it must be noted that their performances were far superior to those of many systems of automatic word recognition.

It is undoubtedly this attraction to human speech that allows babies to disregard noises that do not correspond to a voice and, more precisely, to recognize the intonation and rhythms of their native tongue. Mother's voice would therefore serve as the model from which to determine the rules of a language.

But this explanation does nor solve all problems. What would happen, from this perspective, if babies attached the same importance to their French-speaking mothers and their grandmothers who speak Vietnamese? Cases of this sort are common enough, and many newborns are plunged into a multilingual environment. How do they manage to discern coherent principles? Don't they get everything confused and, as some people think, take longer to master any one language? It is therefore appropriate to determine if a baby can distinguish between two languages and at what age.

In their first months, as we have already said, babies can tell the difference between words and the noises produced by natural or artificial objects. But at what age can they distinguish between their native tongue and a foreign language? To learn this, we taped a perfectly bilingual speaker telling the same story in French and in Russian, and another, English-Italian bilingual made similar recordings.[38] These narrations were divided into fifteen-second sequences and presented to babies alternately in one language and the other. They were tested at the ages of four days and two months. (Four-day-olds were tested in France whereas two-month-olds were tested in the United States.) At first, it seemed likely that the younger infants might not be capable of differentiating between the two languages (Russian and French), while the older infants, after two months of exposure to their native language, might be able to tell the difference between Italian and English.

In fact, it turned out that both groups can detect a change in stimulation between the mother tongue and the new language. Furthermore, while two-month-old babies know the difference between their language and another, they show no preference for one or the other. At four days, however, a clear preference can be observed. The difference between the two groups will be clarified by further experiments. One hypothesis might be that at two months babies have extracted all the relevant parameters from their mother tongue and can turn to a new one.

If babies can tell the difference between several languages, the question arises of how. What enables them to make this differentiation and classification? It is hard to believe that four-day-old infants can master the phonology of French. But perhaps they use a simple acoustic datum that helps them identify what is French and what is not: the overall pitch or average energy of the statements, for example. In order to test this hypothesis, we ran the tapes used for the experiments backwards. The intonation, melody, and other acoustic details were thus modified, while absolute parameters like voice pitch and the energy of the signal remained the same. If babies rely on an absolute parameter to distinguish French from Russian, or English from Italian, they should exhib-

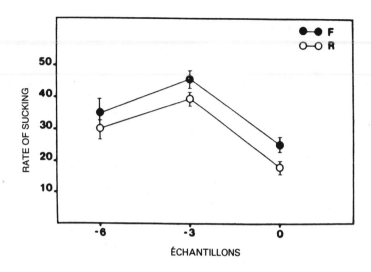

Figure 5.7   Rate of sucking of four-day-olds when they are exposed to French or Russian phrases uttered by the same person, a bilingual speaker (Mehler et al., 1987 and 1988).

it the same behavior listening to the tape run backwards or forwards. This was not the case, which suggests that they rely, then, on complex and dynamic elements of the acoustic signal.

What is involved is intonation. A language like French has melodic contours, but also a rhythm and an accentuation uniquely its own. A phrase like "L'arvonette ratoupi lu pluc notuir tincaudiment," pronounced by a French speaker, sounds like French, even though not one of its words exist in reality. Why? Because it can be pronounced with a uniquely French intonation. The same is true for English or any other natural language.

We next presented four-day-olds with the same sequences as in the preceding experiment, but filtered, so as to eliminate frequencies above 400 Hz. This operation has the effect of keeping the intonation intact while eliminating everything concerning the identity of the sounds of the language, as little as if we were listening to a conversation with our heads submerged in a bathtub. We can recognize French, but cannot identify a single word.[39] Under these conditions, newborns can tell the difference between Russian and French. A corresponding experiment was carried out in the United States with two-month-olds and they also were still able to distinguish English from Italian.

Further experiments should be conducted to supply more precise details about the acoustic factors babies use, although these results have been reproduced by comparing English and Spanish.[40] It was also noted that babies can only tell the difference between two languages if one of them is already familiar. Thus French children cannot distinguish between English and Italian, any more than American babies can differentiate French from Russian.

Long before they can talk, babies are sensitive to the intonational contours that characterize a clause or sentence. A study of their sensitivity to pauses shows this in babies aged six to ten months. They react to where pauses are placed in statements and show a preference for a pattern that conforms to syntactic boundaries.[41] It would of course be false to say they have already acquired the syntax of their language. It is more likely that syntactic boundaries have as correlates certain acoustic factors linked to intonation, rhythm, and melody. Between six and ten months, these prototypical factors are already extracted and serve to identify statements that violate the regularities of the language and those that respect them.

Very early on, then, babies can compare groups of relatively similar stimuli and focus more on the linguistic coherence of the sounds they hear than on superficial variations linked to the speaker. This mechanism, which is used in accessing language and in learning a native tongue, begins to function at a very early age. But does this mean at birth?

According to many researchers, the fetus has already started to learn, particularly in regard to its mother's voice, whose vibrations are transmitted to the amniotic fluid. We know, from other sources, that it can receive sounds, especially of low frequencies.[42] This would explain the later preference for sounds heard during intrauterine life.[43] But how can principles that will help after birth with orientation in the sensory world be discerned by the embryo itself? This is an enigma which psycholinguistics must devote itself to exploring.

By whatever means, it is clear that, at least at birth, the human brain possesses structures specialized for acquiring a native tongue. They are what permit the discrimination of words and the preference for human speech over other sounds. This selection rests on spectral parameters unique to speech, but does not only involve basic acoustic properties. If this were the case, animals like cats which have the same type of auditory mechanism as humans would show a more marked preference for human speech than for the sounds proper to their own species. On the contrary, each species develops a particular sensitivity to sounds emitted only by its members, which are processed by specialized cortical areas. Signals proper to each species are no doubt identified in a special manner because they correspond to sounds the animal itself can produce. Hearing a certain stimulus, it might mentally represent it as the articulatory gesture that is specifically used to produce it, while representing other sounds in a merely acoustic fashion. This hypothesis might also apply to the perception of speech in humans.[44]

This capacity to select sounds according to a specific model no doubt has its source in the brain and in particular in what we have termed the organ of language. We might wonder, however, if this cerebral asymmetry is in place at birth or of it is a result of interaction with the environment. Broca, updating the teachings of the embryologist Gratiolet, maintained that "the more advanced development of the left hemisphere predisposes us, in our first groping attempts, to execute the most complicated material and intellectual acts with this half of the brain, among which certainly must be numbered the expression of ideas by means of language, and, more particularly, of spoken language.[45] More recently, Lenneberg became the spokesman for the concept of the progressive migration of the linguistic function toward the left hemisphere. He asserts that "at the beginning of language development, both hemispheres seem to be equally involved; the dominance phenomenon seems to come about through a progressive decrease in involvement of the right hemisphere."[46]

For some time now, we've known that the hemispheres are already very asymmetrical by the sixth month of gestation. But it took a lot of work to learn more about the emergence of asymmetrical functions per se and to be able to conclude that they are detectable at birth. In our laboratory we used dichotic listening, a technique that consists of presenting two different sounds simultaneously, one in each ear. With the adult, we observe that the syllable heard in the right ear is generally better perceived and retained than the one in the left. According to neuropsychologists, the right ear's superiority for language is due to the fact that speech is processed in the left hemisphere and that each ear is better connected with the contralateral hemisphere, that is, located on its opposite side. This is no doubt why asymmetries of this kind, favoring the left ear in this case, have been observed during dichotic listening to musical notes or chords, music being dependent on mechanisms linked to the right hemisphere.

This method allowed us to evaluate functional asymmetries in newborns.[47] At under four days, infants are more sensitive to minimal linguistic contrasts when they are presented to the right ear. It is the opposite for notes of music which are better discerned by the left ear. Figure 5.8 shows the contrasts obtained with music and language. Special structures of the cortex are already disposed to process acoustic stimuli in a specific manner according to whether they are linguistic or musical. Analogous results have been obtained with other methods.[48] A cerebral mechanism, anchored in structures located preferably on the left, thus directs attention to acoustic signals capable of carrying speech. Then, through a mechanism still not completely understood, newborns quickly identify productions relating to their mother tongues. And it is then and only then, thanks to these innate predispositions, that they can learn to talk.[49]

We can therefore no longer think, as we did in the 1960s, that human children learn language as they later learn chess, geography, or the multiplication tables. We don't need the tricks or threats of the teacher, the carrot or the stick, to teach them how to talk. The fact is that the mind is in and of itself organized according to structures that predispose it to certain fundamental acquisitions.

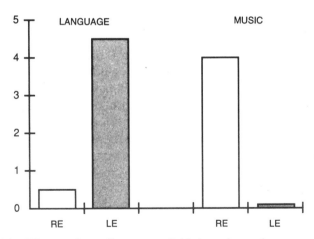

Figure 5.8   When newborns listen to a syllable in each ear, they react more when we change the one in the right ear (RE) than in the left (LE). On the other hand, if we present two musical notes, they react more if we change the one in the left ear (LE) than in the right (RE). This behavior corresponds to the superiority of the right ear for language and of the left ear for notes of music (Bertoncini et al., 1989).

In any case, the baby's predispositions do not stop at mechanisms that facilitate the identification of sensory data of a linguistic nature. Laboratory experiments have revealed other, far more subtle aptitudes.

The Unity of the Perception of Speech

To perceive speech from general data like intonation or voice identity is not enough. In order to learn a language, one must recognize words. Now the word *borrow* means the same thing whether it is whispered or yelled, spoken by a child or a grown-up man or woman. It is composed of different segments which determine its meaning. An error on a single segment (here a phoneme) produces another word, for example, *barrow*.

Among the segments that are necessary for identifying words, we find the syllable and the phoneme. The latter constitutes the smallest unit allowing us to distinguish between two words. Thus *p* and *b* or *r* and *l* are different phonemes in English, for this language distinguished between *pan* and *ban* or *rock* and *lock*, while other languages do not necessarily have this distinction. In fact, it seems intuitively obvious to us that the flow of speech consists of a sequence of certain basic sounds, just as a written text is made up of a sequence of letters. How are phonemes perceived? Since World War II, the Haskins Laboratory, the Karolinska Institute, MIT, and many other research centers have expended considerable effort to discover how phonemes are encoded in the acoustic signal. Scientists at first thought that a simple correspondence between acoustic signals and phonemes existed which allowed the automatic transcription from speech to writing and vice versa. But this blithe optimism gradually faded over decades of research conducted by the most brilliant scientists, and though much has been learned we are still seeking the acoustic invariants of consonants.

The problem is, in fact, highly complex. How do humans recognize speech, detect phonemes, and identify words no matter who is speaking, even if they have a foreign accent or a speech defect? This operation involves extremely complex processes, which are accomplished in a largely unconscious manner. And this is one of the great lessons of the cognitive sciences: humans spontaneously perform a great many very complex tasks without knowing how they manage them and even the most gifted scientists have a hard time understanding how these tasks are performed.

How are the basic sounds of language identified in the acoustic signal? The phoneme *p*, present in the syllable *pa*, has different acoustic
properties when spoken by a woman, a man, or a child. They in fact also
vary greatly according to the context, although we think we always hear
the same *p*. And the more complex the structures in which a phoneme
appears, the more blurred and imprecise its pronunciation.[50] After decades of research, we still don't know how to characterize the acoustic
properties of consonants like *p*, *t*, *k*, *b*, *d*, or *g*. The question therefore
arises of how babies arrive at a representation of speech stable enough
for them to be able to ignore attendant variations in the signal (voice
and delivery of the speaker) and yet conserve the phonological data that
allows them to build a vocabulary of words in their language. Some
writers have suggested that this representation is the syllable.[51]

Even for adults, the syllable seems to have a special perceptual role.
In a word like *concrete*, a speaker identifies the syllable *con* faster than
the phoneme *c*.[52] If phonemes are perceived in a sequential manner,
one by one, and one after the other, how do we explain this result? Research on illiterates attests to a similar phenomenon: they respond to
the syllable *con*, but not to the phoneme *c* in *concrete*.[53] Why then, contrary to what we might imagine, are longer and more complex segments
recognized with greater rapidity and ease?

In fact, it seems that for both children and illiterates, phonemes have
a subsidiary status in relation to syllables. For them, words are composed of syllables. Similarly, the Chinese, who read only ideograms,
have no concept of phonemes. The idea that vocabulary is built from
phonetic units emerges from the system of writing taught in school and
not from the perceptual processing of speech: it is "evolved" and contingent, not spontaneous and natural.

Nevertheless, all languages use a finite and relatively limited number
of segments which recur and structure the flow of speech. Thus, when
we hear a French person talk, a temporal regularity emerges: the duration of vowels is more or less constant. But this is not the case in English. Here, vowels vary in duration according to whether or not they
are accented. In Japanese, periodicity is marked by *morae*, units shorter
than the syllable but longer than the phoneme. Despite these differences, several writers have proposed thinking of the syllable as the universal building block on which speech perception depends. This is the case
with Jakobson,[54] for whom the alternation of consonants and vowels

plays a fundamental role in the acoustic structure of all languages. For him, long sequences of consonants like *vtvt* or *qvqv* are impossible and instances where they have been reported in languages like Koriak or Bellacoola are due to the omission of vowels in transcriptions made by specialists. The alternation of vowels and consonants is the basis of syllables. To say that it is universal is therefore to affirm that syllabic differentiation is universal as well.

When, as we have done in our laboratory, we present a syllable alternating consonant/vowel/consonant, we notice that babies distinguish, for example, *pat* from *tap*.[55] Only the order of the phonemes changes. However, babies have trouble distinguishing the sequential order of events in general: they must rely on a global property that is modified by a change in the order of its elements, melody, for example, which differs according to the order in which the notes are played.[56] It therefore seems probable that babies do not have separate representations for each of the phonemes, although they can distinguish "pat" from "tap." They instead represent an comprehensive entity, the syllable, which they distinguish from another syllable. This hypothesis is analogous to that of the Gestaltists, for whom it is unthinkable that a human could distinguish one triangle from another by proceeding part by part, comparing the value of each angle and the length of each arm. It is the shape in its entirety that is grasped directly and differentiated from another shape. But how can we demonstrate this with syllables?

In a second experiment, we replaced the *a* in *pat* and *tap* with a synthetic sound close to *s*, producing the two stimuli *pst* and *tsp*. They are not syllables, for they involve no alternation between consonants and vowels. In natural languages, in fact, there are no examples of words made up only of three consonants of this kind. However, we can synthesize such sounds and even find them in interjections. That they are not found in any language is therefore not the result of any physical or articulatory impossibility, but is rather linked to the structure of our linguistic mechanism itself, and not to our senses. The babies proved to be incapable of distinguishing between the two synthetic stimuli *pst* and *tsp*. During the course of these two experiments, the serial order of the phonemes was modified in the same way. But it was only in the earlier instance that the babies had a syllable to work with.

While natural languages do not contain words made up of only three consonants, many words do have clusters of three or more consonants, such as *abstract*. Can babies distinguish words that are only differentiated in this way? Through synthesis, we added a vowel sound onto the beginning and end of each "pseudo-syllable" *pst* and *tsp*, creating, for example, *upstu* and *utspu*, now perfectly acceptable linguistic sequences. If newborns perceive speech the same way as adults, they should differentiate them and hear the first of these stimuli as a sequence formed of the syllables *up* and *tsu* and the second as the succession *ut* and *spu*. The babies then would only have to retain one of the two syllables in order to distinguish the first stimulus from the second.[57] The tests proceeded precisely according to this hypothesis, proving that the syllable plays a role of primary importance in the organization of sounds linked to words in the young baby.

But do babies actually divide the acoustic sequence into syllables? Are they capable of segmenting a polysyllabic entity into its component parts? We know that very young infants can discriminate between groups of objects that differ only in number.[58] Can we exploit this ability to test their perception of items differentiated by their number of syllables? If this were the case, they could distinguish a list like *mati/ copu/deta* from another like *napigo/dusaki/fumashu*. In the laboratory,[59] we presented newborns with a group of sounds quite varied in their phonetic composition, but which all were actual bisyllables. Another group was made up only of trisyllabic items. If newborns discriminated these two groups, it meant they could organize polysyllabic sequences by breaking them down into their basic components.

In a first experiment, newborns received natural polysyllabic sequences produced by a female voice. They distinguished the two series. However, the lists differed not only in the number of syllables in their parts, but also in their duration. It was therefore necessary to circumvent this bias by using synthesized sounds that equalized the duration of the stimuli while conserving their quality and perceptibility for adults. The babies again distinguished between the series. They therefore actually were processing polysyllabic groups by dividing them into basic syllables.

If syllables really are the "building blocks" of language perception, gestalts, newborns should show a perceptual constancy similar to that observed in the visual world. We know that adults can identify consonants and vowels when we present the first twenty milliseconds of a syllable to them.[60] This extremely short duration represents less than a tenth of the total duration of a natural syllable. However, subjects are capable of accessing data on the syllable and its components from its first milliseconds, even if the speaker has the impression that the segments are organized in a temporal sequence.

This faculty could be the product of a learning process. It could be that, through habit and anticipation, we would eventually succeed in extracting very subtle factors from listening to syllables. To determine this, four-day-old infants were tested with shortened sounds derived from syllables like *ba*, *da*, and *ga*, and *bi*, *di*, and *gi*. We noted that they could tell the difference between the shortened *ba* and *da*, and also between *ba* and *bi*, with stimuli an average of thirty milliseconds long.[61] The processing of syllables therefore requires only minimal learning experience: classes of the equivalence between syllables seem to be spontaneously constructed, depending on the phonemes that comprise them.

Thus we find a form of perceptual constancy for hearing similar to the one we observe for vision. Recent experiments have in effect shown that babies habituated to the prototype of a vowel or a very similar sound recognize many other sounds even quite different from that vowel.[62] Others, habituated to an imperfect model of a vowel, have more difficulty generalizing. This remarkable ability to handle prototypes was not found in the apes studied, which seems to show that the perception and representation of speech in humans is very different from what it is in animals.[63]

But what happens when the perceived delivery of speech varies? Most adults, under normal conditions, utter between two hundred and ten and two hundred and twenty syllables per minute, although we can easily increase that to five hundred without affecting the clarity of the statement. Digital and computer techniques permit us to vary the delivery without changing other properties of speech such as the timbre of the voice or its relative pitch. Words whose duration have been shortened by half can still be identified correctly.[64] Just as for differences linked to the speaker, a perceptual constancy therefore exists in audition which withstands considerable changes in delivery. It remains to be seen whether this constancy is spontaneous or whether it results from learning. Unfortunately, the majority of experiments conducted on this question have used only adult subjects. It is therefore hard to know with certainty if, before they even know how to talk, children can recognize identical syllables despite the differences in their duration. However, we haven't heard parents complain of having to repeat the same word at different speeds before their child can understand and retain it.

With adults, we have a fairly good idea about the perceptual effects that changes in the duration of the acoustic signal can produce. For example, the classification of a consonant can depend on the duration of the vowel that follows it. For the same physical signal, we can hear *ba* or, if the vowel is longer, *wa*. The delivery speed of the context preceding it can further influence our categorization, as if our perceptual system were able to adapt to a particular word flow.[65] Experiments done with babies produce very similar results.[66] Much research is still necessary to determine the mechanism that allows us to disregard acoustic variations due to changes in delivery or speakers. But no matter what this mechanism is, we have every reason to believe that it is already operating in the very young child.

Whether they are processing syllables or phonemes, it therefore seems clear that newborns have an aptitude that does not depend on postnatal learning experience. Of course, if his back were to the wall, an inveterate empiricist might say that the newborn perhaps learns *in utero*. This is possible, but not very probable. Actually, the fetus's auditory system is hardly developed before the thirtieth week of gestation.[67] And even if its hearing were able to transmit pertinent data to the brain after reaching that stage, we must point out that amniotic fluid greatly distorts the acoustic signal. How then could warped stimuli and a still-deficient auditory mechanism assure a valid learning experience? As recordings made *in utero* demonstrate, the fetus hears mostly stomach rumblings and various other noises. If it had to rely on intrauterine experience alone for its acquisitions, it would have a curious notion indeed of spoken language. But intrauterine exposure cannot be ruled out. The issue is to understand how it might be exploited by the gestating brain.

The fetus is unquestionably already in contact with an acoustic world, but in order to orient itself in this milieu it would have to have a system of prior references in place that would induce it to focus attention on certain sounds and not on others. Once again we run into the circularity peculiar to learning theories which seek a universal principle of explanation in this mechanism but cannot account for its emergence. We must, therefore, conclude that babies already know a great deal, even though they still have a lot to learn.

Sounds and Categories of Language

We have just seen that babies are capable of sorting very different acoustic sounds into stable representations. In fact, they have no problem ignoring the differences introduced by speakers and their varying deliveries. This special ability is one of the conditions necessary for learning the words of one's own language. Conversely, we can wonder if they really make all the subtler distinctions which the adult is capable of, or if they settle for sorting sounds into rough categories in order to refine them later.

One of the first studies of the perception of language in infants was published in the early 1970s, and unquestionably remains the most frequently cited experiment today.[68] We now know that infants possess very developed abilities at birth. But at that time, Eimas' research opened up a new field, and became the model for future experiments on the subject. Eimas and his associates examined the perception of phonetic categories in infants one to four months old.

The concept of perceptual category applied to sounds evolved with the development of the first synthesizers. Without these machines, we could not obtain sounds located between *p* and *b*, for example. With them, on the other hand, we can produce a whole gamut of sounds whose acoustic characteristics vary continuously between *b* and *p*. We do not, however, actually hear these changes for we identify them as belonging to either one or the other of these categories. It therefore seems that we classify sounds, at least consonants, in broad categories with well-defined boundaries. Within a category, subjects are fairly sure they are hearing a prototypical sound. At the boundary, they are less sure and their responses are divided between the adjacent categories. But the boundary is stable from one experiment to the next and one speaker to the next. Sounds are therefore perceived in a discontinuous fashion, though, from a physical point of view, they constitute a continuous series: our perception divides them into categories and makes abrupt jumps from one to the other.

Eimas and his colleagues specifically wondered if infants perceive the sounds of language in a categorical fashion, like adults. They habituated babies to hearing, for example, a model of the syllable *pa* for several minutes. Then they presented them either with a physically different sound that was perceived by adults as a *pa*, or with a sound that differed from the first by the same physical dimensions but which, on the con-

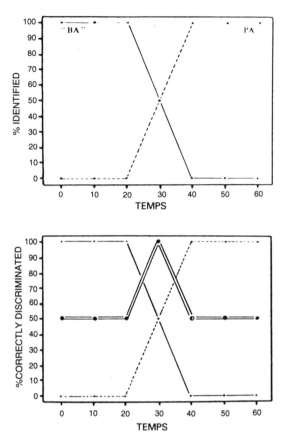

Figure 5.9   In the upper box, the denomination of synthesized sounds which vary with the voice-onset time begins once the articulators have taken on their configuration. While sounds can vary physically in a continuous manner, what we hear varies in an abrupt fashion. As indicated in the lower box, when we categorize a physical continuum, the aptitude for discriminating two sounds is maximal near the category boundaries.

trary, was perceived as a *ba*. It turned out that babies behave exactly as if they possessed the same categories as adults. They distinguish the phonemes of natural languages and sort them, as their parents do, into categories.

   The method employed by Eimas was later extensively used to show that newborns are capable of making the most subtle distinctions that serve to locate contrasts in natural languages. But, in reality, such a result is not all that astonishing. We know that toads have special detectors for flies, that cats have cells sensitive to meowing, and that canaries possess neurons that react to certain specific songs. It might seem to follow naturally that humans are similarly equipped with detectors specialized in the perception of speech. This theory is unfortunately very difficult to prove because it seems probable that we have built our categories around areas where the ear of the vertebrates that we are has maximal sensitivity. In fact, animals also make very subtle acoustic distinctions, but do not have a natural tendency to classify the sounds of language in the same manner as newborns.[69] Thus, it takes from four to twelve thousand training sessions before Japanese quail are able to learn

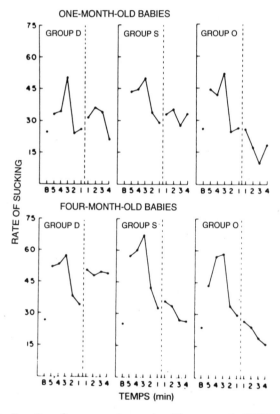

Figure 5.10   Results of an experiment by Eimas et al. (1971). During the habituation phases of the test, group D receives stimuli that differ by 20 msecs, but are heard as *ba* and *pa* by adults. Group S receives stimuli that differ by 20 msecs, but both of which are heard as *ba* or as *pa*. Group O, the control group, receives the same sound during the test and the habituation.

to peck at a certain key each time a syllable starts with the phoneme d.[70] Happily for us, babies manifest their categorizations the first time they are confronted with an experiment like the one that was conducted.

The thesis that sensitivity to units of speech is specifically rooted in humans is, in fact, simpler and above all more consistent with what much research has shown. Patricia Kuhl demonstrated that humans perceive different manifestations of a vowel like i and reduce their perception to a prototype of the category. In this they differ from apes, who do not have prototypes of vowels.[71] Language appeared late in the course of the evolution of the species. It is therefore plausible that it established phonetic categories in very sensitive areas of the auditory system. There would thus be nothing astonishing about the fact that animals, despite their lack of phonetic categories, can be trained to make the same distinctions as humans.

This is why the regnant idea today is that the system for speech perception is grafted onto a more primitive system for perceiving acoustic qualities. A certain number of properties which characterize it derive, then, from more general acoustic principles. Categorical perception is found also in nonlinguistic or even musical sounds.[72] This does not mean, however, that it is not specific to language and, consequently, to humans. The localization of sounds is based on the subtle properties of the temporal and spectral resolution of hearing. But it requires processes specific to the localization of sounds, and uses data that cannot serve other purposes. The same applies for the classification of the sounds of language: certain factors are unique to it. We could therefore conclude that the criteria which serve to identify linguistic categories are part of our genetic heritage.

Armed with the investigative methods described above, we can then ask what the repertory of phonetic distinctions that newborns are capable of is like. Do they possess a subgroup of the contrasts used throughout the world, or do they possess them all?

In fact, the capacity of month-old infants to distinguish minimal contrasts is remarkable. They distinguish contrasts between place of articulation (p, t, k),[73] manner of articulation (occlusive and nasal [d and n], occlusive and liquid [d and l],[74] [l and r]),[75] between vowels (a or i, i or u), and between nasal and non-nasal vowels (a and an).[76] Even if they all have not been tested, we infer, as a working hypothesis, that newborns are sensitive to *all* contrasts that can appear in *all* natural languages, and in exactly the same way as adults.

Learning by Forgetting

The astonishing array of the newborn's capacities for processing sounds unique to natural languages are not limited to those of its mother tongue. A French baby can categorize the sounds of all languages.

The *p* in *poem* can be aspirated or not. We still hear the same word even when it is pronounced with an English accent, giving it a rather snobbish ring. In Hindi, on the other hand, this contrast between the aspirated and unaspirated *p* denotes differences between words. How do we learn the contrasts pertinent to a language when we don't even know its words yet? This is one of the problems babies must resolve.

We have seen that at two months babies easily distinguish *r* and *l*, whereas Japanese adults, for example, have great difficulty doing this. Babies are not *just as* gifted as adults, they are much *more* so. Learning a language in fact involves a partial loss, through the selection of certain contrasts and the forgetting of others which are not relevant. Upon contact with their own language, the Japanese thus lose their sensitivity to the contrast between *r* and *l*. Babies born in Toronto and English-speaking adults were tested on English and Czech phonetic contrasts. The babies could distinguish both, but the adults only those characteristic of English. Young Kikuyu babies tested in Africa on Kikuyu and English contrasts proved that they were capable of distinguishing both.[77]

At what age do babies start disregarding certain contrasts and begin to exhibit adult behavior? Most likely at around ten to twelve months, as shown by a Canadian study whose results are reproduced in figure 5.11.[78]

Several studies have been conducted either by testing groups of subjects at different ages or the same subjects over a period of time. The results always lead to the same conclusion: the very youngest babies discriminate all the contrasts they are confronted with, while at about eight or ten months they exhibit the same aptitude, but only for the contrasts of their own language. At twelve months, they behave like adults and are no longer sensitive to foreign contrasts.

What is the nature of this loss? Does it involve a loss of acoustic sensitivity to contrasts that are not heard frequently during infancy? Is the loss neurosensory or attentional and cognitive? It seems we must opt for the second answer. A recent study explored our capacity to discriminate contrasts that are not used in our own language such as Zulu "clicks," very different from anything we find in Western language.[79] A

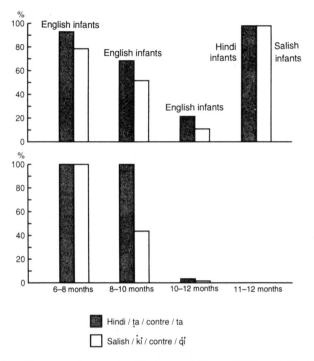

Figure 5.11   Two experiments by Werker and Tees (1984) and Werker et al. (1981). Groups of children at three age levels who distinguish Hindi or Insle-kampx (Salish) contrasts according to their linguistic milieu. In the upper pannel, the age groups correspond to different children. Below, the study is longitudinal. We see in the two studies that babies gradually lose the ability to distinguish contrasts foreign to their own language.

person who has never been exposed to these kinds of linguistic sounds should be even less adept at them than at aspirated consonants, for example, which exist in French and English but are not used to differentiate words. This is not the case at all, however. English-speaking adults notice these "clicks," even in conditions of very poor emission and reception. Furthermore, at around twelve months, babies do not show a loss of sensitivity to these sounds the way they do with other contrasts not relevant to their native language. Only contrasts that are in "competition" with, or share the same dimension with, those of the mother tongue are lost at around a year. The others, which have no equivalent in their own language and therefore do not interfere with its processing, remain perceptible to the child as well as to the adult.

The loss of capacity is, therefore, not sensory.[80] Under special experimental conditions, English-speaking adults can distinguish Hindi contrasts (a nonaspirated and nonvoiced consonant whose place of
articulation is either retroflexive or dental) or Inslekampx contrast
(place of articulation velar glottal as against uvular glottal). So we do
not observe irreparable perceptual loss through a degeneration of the
nerve connections. If foreign contrasts are disregarded, it is instead because at a certain stage in cognitive development a new system of representation emerges which permits the coding of heard sounds in
memory. Very subtle distinctions can still be made, but the phonetic
code of the mother tongue takes precedence. It is, then, not because the
Japanese have problems consciously distinguishing an *r* from an *l* that
they do not perceive them separately and do not use them for recognizing adjacent segments.[81]

Be that as it may, sensitivity to phonetic contrasts declines in favor of
the phonemes actually used in the mother tongue. Only very rigorous
experimental conditions can affirm that this loss is not irreparable and
therefore does not affect the neuro-sensitive mechanism. So it is not
surprising that after puberty we usually have a very difficult time learning a new language and mastering its pronunciation. Our cultural and
intellectual level has nothing to do with this; it is our age that counts, so
that it is much harder to learn a foreign language after the age of twenty-
five and impossible to ever speak it as if it were one's native tongue. We
can, however, learn to speak a few phrases flawlessly. This is no doubt
why French-speaking opera singers who normally have an accent you
could cut with a knife can sing their parts in German or Italian to such
perfection. The method of perceiving and producing speech crystalizes
at a given age in relation to the language spoken in the environment.
From then on, everything happens in a more or less automatic manner.

But how do babies manage to sort out all these acoustic contrasts,
these phonemes and syllables? How can they relate them to the appropriate language? An English-speaking person can accidentally produce
a sound that corresponds to a Kikuyu or Thai phoneme. Adults who
hear the sound pay no attention to it, since it is not relevant to English.
But babies do. Why aren't they thrown into the most utter confusion,
fabricating arbitrary pseudo-languages from all the sounds they hear?
Why do bilingual children bring order to the linguistic blend they listen
to, even when they have not yet learned the vocabularies used around
them? If children mixed up sounds like this, only those living in very

uniform, isolated monolingual communities would ever learn to talk. The rest would get lost in the shuffle.

In fact, it is probable that at a very early age babies notice native statistical regularities in speech. Certain sounds are repeated more often with certain other sounds. Actually, the frequency of emission of sounds increases as we approach the centers of the linguistic categories used by a language. On the other hand, the frequency of emission diminishes greatly near the boundaries between two categories. The less a language is used, the lower the frequency of the sounds close to its basic categories. This "natural statistic" would explain the baby's progressive tendency to ignore certain sounds that are not distinctive in her or his mother tongue.

Babies born into a bilingual or even trilingual environment can learn all the languages spoken around them at the same time, without mixing them up. No Franco-English baby uses French vocabulary with English syntax. Similarly, for bilingual individuals, the passage from one language to another in the course of conversation is governed by precise linguistic rules.[82] Consequently, in one way or another, the mechanism for acquiring languages must be guided by purely phonetic and prosodic properties, so that languages can be isolated very early on and new statements automatically stored in the language to which they belong. We have seen that traces of these mechanisms can be found in four-day-old babies.

This does not mean, however, that learning a second or third language before puberty is easy. A recent study exploiting a curious fact discovered in our laboratory shows this clearly.[83] A French speaker takes less time discerning the segment *ba* in the word *balance* than in the word *balcon*, but perceives the segment *bal* faster in the word *balcon* than in the word *balance*. For a French-speaking subject, the first syllable of a word is easier to recognize than a shorter or longer segment. This is not true for subjects who speak English.[84] It therefore appears that French-speaking persons access words by dividing the spoken sequence into syllables, but not English-speaking people. These mechanisms are carried over to other languages: thus the English, when speaking French, often fail to divide French words into syllables, while the French have this tendency when they are speaking in English.

What happens with bilingual subjects? By bilingual, we mean only subjects who speak two languages equally well. These are usually children born into mixed marriages, no matter what the birthplace, and raised in a very balanced bilingual atmosphere. Do they divide the French acoustic sequence into syllables and process English by separating its sounds differently? A study revealed that their behavior varies enormously.[85] So we asked them a number of questions whose aim was to determine which language they would choose if they had to speak only one from then on. This inquiry, which threw more than one of them into a state of confusion, allowed us to separate the subjects into dominant French-speaking or English-speaking groups. It then emerged that the dominant French-speaking subjects utilized syllabization, but the dominant English-speaking subjects did not.

Bilingual individuals, even under very equal linguistic conditions, therefore never behave as if they were juxtaposing two equal monolingual behaviors. A dominant language always emerges, so that one of the two languages is in certain respects processed like the other. Even at a very early age, we never learn a second language the way we do the first, the one that by virtue of even the slimmest of margins enjoys the status of mother tongue. The acquisition of a language through the bias of the mother tongue therefore relies on specialized mechanisms that differ from the general procedures of the learning process.

Human infants, then, know how to discriminate all the minimal potential differences used in natural languages. They can discern changes in the speaker, intonation, or delivery and, at the same time, link them to syllables they have memorized in a rather crude form.[86] Usually sensitive to the more general features of speech, they can also, under the proper conditions, focus their attention on the finer aspects of acoustic signals conveying statements. Their native disposition for speech can, then, no longer be in any doubt. But very quickly, on contact with their environment, they incorporate statistical regularities that limit their attention to categories pertinent to what becomes their native language. Possibly the more global properties of speech are attained earlier than the more specific ones. Intonation and other phonetic qualities are coded within the first few weeks, vowels within the first six months, and consonants within the first year of life. At this point the phase of original flexibility is succeeded by a period in which the structures solidify and become more effective. The brain then ceases to function only according to a universal model for entering the world of cultural diversities and particularities. Similarly, cortical lesions which occur very early may not seriously affect the mastery of language. Yet once the period of acquisition of the first language is over, the consequences can be irreparable.[87] The brain, therefore, seems to be structured to allow us to learn a language, and to do so through mechanisms that bear a strong resemblance to what biologists call instinctive learning.[88] This is one of the fundamental elements, perhaps the most essential one, of human nature.

Language, the instrument essential to the species for communicating, building societies, and transmitting culture, is therefore based on genetically transmitted predispositions and aptitudes inherent to the human brain. We cannot suppose, therefore, that its emergence is due merely to the brain's ability to learn anything and everything.

Conclusion: Human Nature and the Cognitive Sciences

What are the specific psychological aptitudes of the human being? In the past, this question could only generate speculation or dinner table conversation, but for about thirty years we have been able to approach it in a truly scientific manner. In this sense, the study of human behavior and psychological aptitudes has entered a new era. Empirical investigative methods born of many disciplines such as linguistics, psychology, neurobiology, and even computer science, have finally allowed us to elaborate theories susceptible to refutation by the facts, and to break with approaches solely inspired by commonsense or superficial observations.

The End of Vitalism

Naive psychology, we have seen, is based on common sense. No one could or would want to do without its concepts in everyday life. But the crude and often erroneous insights to which they lead are useless once we seek to explain behavior scientifically. No scientist would claim to limit him or herself to naive physics or chemistry any more. Naive psychology, on the other hand, still has a considerable influence on the human sciences: they operate as if they were unable to transcend the thinking the natural sciences were stuck in when they claimed that bodies fall because of a "yearning for the abyss."

Naive psychology attributes to living beings a unique and indissociable quality or substance – intelligence – constructed in principle from a base incorporating all behaviors. As we have seen, this concept is circular and explains nothing. However, the tendency to see a substantial principle in intelligence is still alive and well. Attesting in particular to this is the notion that it can be quantified and measured. The impact of "intelligence tests" clearly shows how much weight this somewhat pre-scientific notion still carries. But it is a dangerous idea. It suggests, in effect, that a single objective scale exists that permits a natural classification of individuals or groups of individuals – one can only guess at the travesties that might ensue.

This way of thinking has no more basis in reality, however, than the idea that the Earth is flat and located at the center of the universe, or the notion of spontaneous generation. Intelligence is not, in fact, a substantial principle, but a collection of distinct faculties like memory, language, mental imagery, perception, and attention, which themselves rest on a great number of specialized processes. It is, therefore, not a measurable quantity any more than "life" is: neither one is homogeneous, and both encompass a host of disparate and independent phenomena. To establish an "intelligence quotient" or "life quotient" scale is therefore as absurd as linking social rank to the size of the femur or to cardiac capacity, or adjusting salaries on the basis of the rotation speed of mental images or the quality of short-term memory.[1]

Biology has rejected the concept of the vital principle. It is interested only in the different mechanisms that allow living beings to perform such and such a task or to transmit the characteristic properties of their species to their descendants. As for psychology, it must likewise avoid all recourse to intelligence considered as an explicative fundamental principle, and interest itself only in the components of intelligent behavior. It is, moreover, the nature of the scientific process to divide up the problem and not to attack it head-on, in its totality. We must separate our investigation into a series of more modest, more clearly defined subproblems, and then proceed one step at a time. Under these conditions, the complexity of phenomena as a whole might, upon closer scrutiny, be better understood.

What should the sources of inspiration for psychology and the cognitive sciences be? At first glance, it seems that they should draw inspiration from biology rather than from physics. In psychology, we observe behaviors which have similar causes and ways of operating without being able to assign them an invariant physical basis. E. Sober demonstrated that central concepts in biology also have this property.[2] The Darwinian concept of the survival of the fittest differs depending on whether it involves a zebra trying to escape from lions or an insect developing an immunity to DDT. Each of these organisms was selected in relation to an aptitude, but it would be foolish to try to find a physical basis common to the properties of the zebra's hooves and the insect's digestive tract. However, it does seem that functional notions play a central role in cognitive psychology, as in biology, while this is rarely the case in physics. There is nothing vitalist in these notions, however, for although two physically different systems can have the same function, two physically identical systems must both have an identical function.

Furthermore, the cognitive sciences have much to learn from disciplines like theoretical computer science and generative linguistics. These disciplines in effect furnish the tools that allow us to analyze complex behaviors in relation to purely mechanical operations. They teach us that material systems – what is more physical than a computer? – can nevertheless exhibit very complex and even unpredictable behaviors.

The same computer in two very similar physical states (in terms of electric activity) can exhibit extremely different behaviors. Conversely, one machine can display very similar behaviors even though the distribution of electrical activity in its memories varies considerably. However, these machines become completely regular when we consider them at the level of the data structures they can develop and their way of processing them. Computer science, therefore, gives us hope of clarifying mental processes by comparing them to one or several abstract machines that operate mechanically on internal representations. Generative linguistics is an example where the fruitfulness of this computer model has been explored with success.

It is clear that this book has not been able to do justice to all the work that has been done on mental imagery, memory, spatial perception, language processing, reasoning, or the planning of actions. Our aim was not an exhaustive review of these fields. We were concerned, rather, to use a few examples to illustrate a new way of approaching the study of psychological phenomena, and to point out its relevance. Contrary to our naive representations, the mind must be studied without reference to a comprehensive principle – by examining the mechanisms themselves. The behaviorists had already anticipated this approach, indispensable to a truly scientific psychology. But, by rejecting all references to subjective mental states and internal representations, in their hygienic zeal they . . . threw the baby out with the bath water. The idea of modularity specifically allows us, as we have seen, to circumvent this obstacle: the diverse systems that constitute the "mind" appear as autonomous mechanisms whose function is rigorously regulated by procedures in themselves "intelligent." A "naturalistic" and "mechanistic" approach can then demonstrate its complete relevance.

The Return of Rationalism and the Permanence of Humanity

A hundred and fifty years ago, only an iconoclast would have claimed that what little soul we have is contained in our brain. Fifty years later, we had acquired the right to think that certain functions are properties of the encephalon. The essence of humans, their emotions, their originality remained, however, the realm of the "mind" or the "soul." Today, despite the mysteries still surrounding who we are, when we study human psychology, it is biological phenomena that we explore, even though our methods may seem quite removed from those of biology.

Once the idea that our cognitive mechanism consists of distinct, autonomous elements is accepted, the question of their origin arises. One tradition that dominated the human sciences for a long time has it that our capacities are derived from the cultural and social milieu, so that no human prototype could legitimately be retained. But the scientific study of human aptitudes profits greatly, as we have seen, from considering the cognitive mechanisms of all members of the species to be identical. The idea of *human nature*, as this book seeks to show, thus must become the key to research in the cognitive sciences.

Cognitive aptitudes, stable from puberty until the age when senility or illness begin to take their toll, can be explored and described as if they were alike in every human. This is why we must functionally, formally, and biologically study the properties of memory, attention, and language; build bridges to other disciplines like linguistics and logic; and also examine the manner in which cognitive functions are embedded in the human nervous system.

Mental aptitudes seem to define a prototype or an *idealized human being*.[3] Is it not evident that all human beings possess a grammar that allows them to master and use a natural language, and that they all have a natural logic, axioms and principles that enable them to plan their actions in terms of their desires and beliefs? Is it not obvious that everyone is capable of representing for him or herself the situations they encounter and even of representing their own ability to represent these things?[4] As a result, linguistics, logic, and mathematics are, in part, theories bearing on the aptitudes of the human brain. These aptitudes come into being by virtue of the process of selective stabilization that the environment performs on our genetic heritage. The environment, therefore, does not explain everything we do and think, but it does play a role in the development of dispositions into effective intellectual aptitudes. This is why, for example, generative linguistics can make an essential contribution to cognitive science: it explains how a particular individual can move from the universal grammar to a specific grammar, be it that of Chinese, French, or Hebrew.

This book has specifically shown the importance for the cognitive sciences of the study of the *initial state* of psychological functions. Babies, because they are human, carry within them a determined genetic heritage. The initial state, in as much as it can be studied precisely in newborns, thus defines (though it may underestimate) the realm of the possible. The study of the *stable state*, on the other hand – the constant cognitive faculties of the prototypical individual – reveals the realm of the realizable in the selective environment to which human beings are subjected.

We are born with a predetermined heritage and therefore have the capacity to express it. *To be born human* means to be born to achieve a certain stable state. This thesis, however, presents a number of problems which we must address. Does the fact that some individuals are deprived, at birth or by accident, of certain aptitudes, allow us to consider them no longer human? Do the mute, the blind, the insane, and even the handicapped elderly still belong to our species?[5] This question is not as easy to answer as it might seem. Some concepts are defined by one and only one property: it is easy, for instance, to determine if a number is even or odd, or, in other words, if a specific example does or does not correspond to the general concept. Conversely, many concepts involving a combination of several properties are not so easy to define: it is difficult, for example, to say exactly what a table is, although the way we use it helps. This is why you call the thing you work on or eat your meals at a table. But if one of your children amused himself scratching it up, what would you say? That it is a scratched-up table? And what if he sawed off one or two of its legs? Would it still be a table? Eventually you would throw the thing away since you would no longer have a table, but a useless hunk of wood, a piece of junk.

Does the same reasoning apply to humans? A table is a simple, replaceable object. A human being, on the other hand, is both complex and unique. Our attitude must therefore be different. A blind person does not stop being human because one of the faculties proper to humans is lacking. Our propensity for sympathy, particularly for those who are injured or fragile, does, however, present us with painful choices. What do we do when elderly persons we love are dying? We cannot think of them as utilitarian objects that have ceased to function normally, but for all that, should we let them suffer? The same goes for the newborn baby who, we know, is genetically handicapped. Confronted with this kind of problem, we all have more or less set convictions, and this book cannot claim to put forth another one. It can only provide a framework for reflection and discussions which might otherwise veer off into fruitless clashes of opinion.

The concept of human nature must also respond to another objection. Each individual is unique and cannot be reduced to an *ideal human being* or a universal stable state. However, throughout the diversity of cultures and individuals, the general mechanisms that make these behaviors possible must be more or less identical. It is best, then, to describe this stable state not according to what someone says or does, what Einstein calculates or Balthus paints, but at a level where the aptitudes under consideration are identical whether we are studying an illiterate or a college graduate, a politician or a Bushman from the Australian outback.

Obviously, a person may seem handicapped if he cannot see without corrective lenses, and another appear superior if he is endowed with an exceptional musical memory. Obviously, individuals differ – this cannot be denied. Yet to describe all these differences would take a book longer than all the encyclopedias ever written, an endless book, actually, as vast and complex as the world itself. Each individual would read in it the exhaustive list of his or her unique properties and qualities. But, at each new birth, work would have to start up again, with no hope of ever ending.

This is why no science can begin or advance unless it analyzes phenomena into simple and therefore general elements, rather than losing itself in the complexity and diversity of reality. The concept of the human prototype should specifically permit a simplification and foster progress in the establishment of a truly illuminating psychological theory. But is it legitimate to maintain that all humans are identical? Is not the concept of a universal human nature in conflict with what everyone and his uncle can observe?

Simplifications can indeed be misleading, and even dangerous. Imagine a doctor obsessed with similarities who asked his associates to ignore the varieties of antigens present in blood. The transfusion-related death rate in his practice would soar. His colleagues, the authorities, and even the press, would no doubt call for an investigation. "I made a mistake," he would admit, "but above all, I had bad luck. Most differences are random and involve unimportant elements, but some can contain crucial regularities. I guessed wrong. . . ." How can we classify the different types of variations, how to distinguish those that are essential from those that are superficial? How can we be sure that we are not making the same mistake as that doctor?

Science advances gradually, largely through correcting its errors and proposing simplifications. When Lamarck conceived the notion of the hereditary transmission of acquired characteristics, he seemed to be making a valid, illuminating simplification of the data. But modern biology has shown that he was in error. When Newton concluded that all bodies fall at the same rate of speed in a void, he conceptualized a powerful simplification of mechanics which, itself, later led to considerable scientific progress. Lamarck's so-called simplification seems intuitively correct, while Newton's seems false. Yet in fact, just the reverse is true. It is therefore hard to tell a priori which hypotheses are correct.

To plead in favor of the concept of a human nature and to place into evidence the characteristics of the human prototype does not necessarily mean to condemn all psychology concerned with the differences. It simply involves proposing an alternative, a path that would lead to productive research. Since the beginning of humankind, one individual has never been the exact copy of another. Nor have two humans ever had the same fingerprints. This does not prevent us from describing properties common to all fingerprints, each different, of course, but within a limited range of possibilities. Similarly, all hands are different, but all have five fingers, and every human finger has three phalanxes, with the exception of the thumb. Reality therefore not only contains infinite differences: it also presents constants which must be the subject of the sciences and which underlie the legitimacy of their projects.

Thus, anatomy became a science when scientists stopped being obsessed with the individual organs they observed and created from them general and invariant models. Blood types, moreover, which permitted the classification and differentiation of individuals, were not conceived by researchers attentive only to differences, but by those striving to describe the general properties of the antigens carried by red blood cells. Once the basic composition of blood was determined, it seemed that certain incompatibilities could be due to antigens linked to genetic inheritance. But the anatomist must avoid the same trap our unwary doctor fell into. He runs the same risks. This is why, even in anatomy, one must seek to curtail errors caused by theoretical simplifications.

Psychology is therefore faced with two fairly obvious alternatives. Either it renounces becoming a science and contents itself, as it were, with spelling out individual differences ad infinitum, or else it ignores them and seeks to simplify the representation it gives of reality. In any event, what separates the jovial jazz musician from the distraught, antisocial mathematician is paltry indeed compared to what they have in common. Both can recognize visual and auditory stimulations, construct a three-dimensional world full of stable objects, localize sounds, and compare physical sizes. Both can memorize, count, and produce and understand sentences. The list is long indeed of the aptitudes they share with every member of the human species. This is precisely why psychology, if it wishes to succeed in giving an idea of what is truly human, must dedicate itself to common characteristics.

The cognitive sciences, then, do not risk running into a dead end if they disregard individual differences. Quite the contrary. They need only navigate clear-sightedly to discern the simplifications necessary for their progress, for increasing the explanatory power of their hypotheses, for including ever-greater complexities in their schematisms, and for eliminating fallacious simplifications. This road full of pitfalls is the path all the sciences must take. And it is wrong to say that science desiccates reality by draining it of all its richness, its spontaneity. It is the role of scientific description to subject the observation of variety to the laws that serve to explain, organize, and predict phenomena. Theoretical simplifications do not give us an impoverished representation of the world. On the contrary, they reveal aspects which, without them, would have remained hidden and which, in turn, lead to further hypotheses and other more powerful explanatory models. Psychology, in this respect, is no exception. This is why affirming the existence of a universal human nature does not impoverish humanity or reduce people to abstract, lifeless diagrams. Instead, it gives us a chance to discover, at last, who we are.

Notes

Chapter 1 Explaining Our Behavior

1. Galaburda, Rosen, and Sherman (1989).
2. Norman (1988).
3. Reason (1989).
4. Bruce (1988).
5. In addition, Loftus (1979) demonstrated that nonexistent objects like a streetlight or a fence can be inserted into the minds of witnesses at the time of questioning ("Did you see a/the broken streetlight?"). Tested a week later, the witnesses showed a tendency to reconstruct the scene, not as they saw it, but by inserting foreign elements which were suggested during questioning.
6. We are indebted to S. Moscovici (1981) for important research on social pressure.
7. Loftus (1979).
8. Hadamard (1945).
9. Freud (1971).
10. An excellent description of this work is given by Humphrey (1951).
11. Ericsson and Simon (1984).
12. One of the fathers of research in artificial intelligence assigned the problem of vision to one of his students as vacation homework.
13. The organization of information and the computerization of expertise have now become a technology. Those who practice it call themselves "cogniticians." Despite its name, this activity has little in common with the cognitive sciences.
14. Certain behaviorists are very clear on this issue. For example, Lieberman (1984) wrote: "The formal rules at the fixed core of Chomsky's thought are linked in the final analysis to the way lizards move their tails."
15. See Ewert (1987) for a survey.
16. Pavlov (1927).
17. Skinner (1959).

18. This term is misleading, for it suggests that the pigeon believes occult forces are driving it to perform an always identical ritual. On the contrary, it only demonstrates the profoundly unintelligent character of operant conditioning.
19. Lawrence and DeRivera (1954).
20. In other words, to get to its food, our monkey solved the difficult problem of the "traveling salesman" (Menzel 1973).
21. Piaget (1973), p. 23.
22. Lorenz (1958).
23. Changeux (1983).
24. Marler (1970); Marler and Peters (1982); Notebohm (1984); Changeux and Dehaene (1989).
25. Gregory (1987), p. 808.
26. Chomsky (1975).
27. Lenneberg (1967).
28. Walk and Gibson (1961).
29. Changeux and Dehaene (1989).
30. Amiel-Tison and Grenier (1986); Peiper (1963).
31. Zelazo, Zelazo, and Kolb (1972).
32. Siqueland and DeLucia (1969) were the first to demonstrate the validity of the differences in habituation with regard to the different types of stimulations.
33. Held and his associates (1980) utilized the preferential fixation method, another of the methods developed by Fantz (1963).

Chapter 2 Seeing and Hearing

1. Gwiazda, Brill, Mohindra, and Held (1978); Gwiazda, Wolfe, Brill, Mohindra, and Held (1980).
2. Adams (1987).
3. Shepherd, Fagan, and Kleiner (1985).
4. Annis and Frost (1973).
5. Adams and Maurer (1984).
6. Thomas & Autgarden (1966).
7. Schneider, Trehub, and Bull (1980).
8. Aslin (1987); Sinott, Pisoni, and Aslin (1983); Trehub, Schneider, and Endman (1980). There is a very good survey of sensitivity and the functions of discrimination in very young children in Eisenberg (1976) and Aslin (1987).
9. Eisenberg (1976).
10. This difference is particularly striking if we compare the state of myelination in the nerve fibers corresponding to each of these modalities.
11. Lewkowicz (1985, 1988).
12. Whorf (1956).
13. Berlin and Kay (1969).
14. Lenneberg (1967) as well as Lantz and Stefflre (1964).
15. Bornstein, Kessen, and Weiskopf (1976).
16. Bornstein (1985).

17. Oxbury, Oxbury, and Humphrey (1969).
18. Bomba and Siqueland (1983).
19. Bomba (1984).
20. Fisher, Ferdinandsen, and Bornstein (1981); Bornstein, Ferdinandsen, and Gross (1981).
21. Bornstein and Krinsky (1985).
22. Certain experimenters actually put forward such a theory.
23. Ehrenfels (1890).
24. Herlse and Page (1988).
25. Köhler (1959); Koffka (1935).
26. Bertenthal, Campos, and Haith (1980).
27. Antell and Caron (1985).
28. Van Giffen and Haith (1984).
29. Milewski (1979).
30. Slater, Morison, and Rose (1983).
31. Bower (1967, 1972).
32. Kellman and Spelke (1983).
33. Milewski (1976).
34. Bushnell (1979).
35. Ghim Hei-Rhee and Eimas (1988).
36. The process by which nerve fibers (axons) are wrapped in an isolating and protective sheath (the myelin).
37. Chang and Trehub (1977); Demany, McKenzie, and Vurpillot (1977); Mehler and Bertoncini (1979).

Chapter 3 The World and Its Objects

1. Piaget (1966).
2. Held, Birch, and Gwiazda (1980).
3. Fox, Aslin, Shea, and Dumais (1980).
4. Gibson (1966).
5. Yonas and Granrud (1985).
6. Held, Birch, and Gwiazda (1980).
7. Abramov, Gordon, Hendrickson, Hainline, Dobson, and Laboussier (1982).
8. Held (1985).
9. Bower, Broughton, and Moore (1971)
10. Yonas, Bechtold, Frankel, Gordon, McRoberts, Norcia, and Sternfels (1977).
11. Alégria and Noirot (1978, 1982).
12. Aronson and Rosenbloom (1971).
13. Wertheimer (1971).
14. McGurk and Lewis (1974); McGurk, Turnure, and Creighton; (1977), Butterworth and Castillo (1976).
15. Muir and Field (1979).
16. Clarkson, Clifton, and Morrongiello (1985).

17. Clifton, Morrongiello, Kulig, and Dowd (1981).
18. Quoted in Boring (1942), p. 263.
19. McKensie, Tootell, and Day (1980)
20. Granrud (1987); Slater, Mattock, and Brown (1990).
21. Day and McKenzie (1973).
22. Caron, Caron, and Carlson (1979).
23. Slater and Morison (1985).
24. Kellman and Spelke (1983).
25. Spelke (1985).
26. Quoted in Mehler and Fox (1985).
27. Schwartz (1982).
28. Bower and Patterson (1972).
29. Bower and Wishart (1972).
30. Baillargeon, Spelke, and Wassermann (1985).
31. Baillargeon and Graber (1987).
32. As Diamond and Goldman-Rakic think (1989).
33. Bower (1977).
34. Aronson and Rosenbloom (1971).
35. Spelke (1981).
36. Spelke (1976).
37. Spelke and Owsley (1979).
38. Do children have a conception of the connections between articulatory facial movements and speech? MacKain, Studdert-Kennedy, Spieker, and Stern (1983) showed that at five months, they can already correlate filmed faces and syllables like "mama" and "zouzou." Kuhl and Meltzoff (1984) observed the same phenomenon with isolated vowels.
39. Lewkowicz (1985).
40. Meltzoff and Borton (1979).
41. Bahrick (1988).
42. Starkey and Cooper (1980).
43. Treiber and Wilcox (1984); Strauss and Curtis (1981).
44. Antell and Keating (1983).
45. Starkey, Spelke, and Gelman (1983).
46. Wynn, K. (1992).

Chapter 4 Self and Others

1. Peiper (1963) cites studies like those of Buhler and Hetzer, and Guernsey and Kaila, which all report having noted imitations in the newborn.
2. Maratos (1973, 1982).
3. Hayes and Watson (1981); Koepke, Hamm, Legerstree, and Russell (1983); McKenzie and Over (1983).
4. Abravanel and Sigafoos (1984); Fontaine (1984); Field, Cohen, Garcia, and Greenberg (1986).

5. Meltzoff and Moore (1977, 1983).
6. Tinbergen (1953).
7. Bower (1979), p. 304.
8. Jacobson and Kagan (1979).
9. Meltzoff (1988).
10. Goren, Sarty, and Wu (1975).
11. Maurer and Young (1983).
12. Maurer and Barrera (1981).
13. Morton and Johnson (1991); Dannemiller and Stephens (1988).
14. Johnson and Morton (in press); Morton & Johnson (1991).
15. Barrera and Maurer (1981).
16. Field, Cohen, Garcia, and Greenberg (1984); Bushnell and Sai (1987).
17. Bertenthal, Proffitt, and Cutting (1984).
18. Sometimes our thoughts are not purely operative, however. One of the authors of this book does not have much confidence in airplane pilots, and yet this very fear seems to him to ward off danger. We are not, after all, so different from lizards.
19. Woodruff and Premack (1979).
20. Wimmer and Perner (1983).
21. A good recapitulation of the works of Piaget as well as of the main criticisms directed against his system can be found in the proceedings of the Royaumont symposium, during which Chomsky and Piaget set forth their points of view. See Piatelli-Palmarini (1980).
22. Mehler and Bever (1967).
23. Wellman and Bartsch (1988).
24. Mehler and Bever (1967); Mehler (1971, 1974, 1982).
25. McGarrigle and Donaldson (1974–75).
26. Fodor has recently argued that the literature which suggests that children have to develop an adult belief-desire psychology may benefit from a less radical interpretation. He suggests that young children have the same belief-desire psychology as adults but avoid engaging in difficult computations whenever possible.
27. Leslie (1987).
28. Dasser, Ulbaek, and Premack (1989).
29. Fodor (1975).
30. We would never mistake a snake or a tree for one of our kind. It is this predisposition that inclines us to protect little humans until they can survive on their own. But humans are not, for all that, "noble savages." In the social realm, they exacerbate crime and war. And even though language and perception depend on innate predispositions, it would be absurd to say that the entire *Romance of the Rose* or the *Odyssey* are part of the human heritage. Humans rely on their heritage to elaborate constructions containing both the arbitrary and the creative. The same goes for social relationships. The human being is predetermined to live in society, but social life is not, for all that, limited to these predeterminations.

Chapter 5 The Biological Foundations of Language

1. Kellog and Kellog (1933).
2. Hayes (1951).
3. Premack and Schwartz, (1966).
4. Gardner and Gardner (1969).
5. Seidenberg and Pettito (1979).
6. Premack (1971, 1976).
7. For an excellent history of the sources of the language of deaf-mutes, see Lane (1979).
8. Lane (1979), pp. 83–84.
9. Klima and Bellugi (1979).
10. Peritto and Marentette (1991).
11. Brown and Bellugi (1964).
12. See the fascinating book by Landau and Gleitman (1985).
13. Broca (1865).
14. James (1893).
15. Segalowitz and Bryden (1983).
16. Sperry (1974).
17. Wada (1949).
18. Goldman-Rakic (1985).
19. Fodor (1983).
20. Gall (1835).
21. Flourens (1842).
22. Lashley (1950).
23. Benson, Segarra, and Albert (1974).
24. Sacks and Wasserman (1987).
25. Signoret, van Eeckhout, Poncet, and Castaigne (1987).
26. Basso and Capitani (1985).
27. To present data to one hemisphere only, experimenters used the following device: since the right side of each retina is anatomically connected to the left hemisphere (and vice versa for the left side), one can, by briefly flashing a word to the left or right of a fixation point, ensure that only one hemisphere has been stimulated.
28. See Sperry (1974) for a discussion of these phenomena.
29. Warrington and Shallice (1980, 1984).
30. Fodor (1983).
31. Eisenberg (1976); Aslin (1987); Aslin, Pisoni, and Jusczyk (1983).
32. Colombo and Bundy (1983).
33. Mills and Meluish (1974).
34. Mehler, Bertoncini, Barrière, and Jassik-Gerschenfeld (1978).
35. Fernald (1985).
36. DeCasper and Fifer (1980).
37. Spence and DeCasper (1987).
38. Mehler, Lambertz, Jusczyk, and Amiel-Tison (1987); Mehler, Jusczyk, Lambertz, Halsted, Bertoncini, and Amiel-Tison (1988).

39. The signal resembles what the fetus hears when it perceives its mother's voice.
40. Bahrick and Pickens (1988).
41. Hirsh-Pasek, Kemler Nelson, Jusczyk, Druss, and Kennedy (1987).
42. Querleau and Renard (1981).
43. Spence and DeCasper (1987); Lecanuet, Granier-Deferre, DeCasper, Maugeais, Andrieu, and Busnel (1987).
44. Liberman (1970); Liberman and Mattingly (1985).
45. Lecours and Lhermitte (1979), p. 29.
46. Lenneberg (1967).
47. Entus (1977); Vargha-Khadem and Corballis (1979); Bertoncini, Bijeljac-Babic, McAdams, Peretz, and Mehler (1989).
48. Best (1988).
49. The research done by Entus (1977), never published in full, yielded similar results. On the other hand, Vargha-Khadem and Corballis (1979) reported results that suggested an absence of functional asymmetry at about two weeks. Bertoncini et al. (1989) used a more refined experimental technique, which allowed them to observe the conduct described.
50. Ohman (1966).
51. Mehler (1981); Mehler, Dupoux, and Segui (1990).
52. Savin and Bever (1970); Segui, Frauenfelder, and Mehler (1981).
53. Morais, Cary, Alégria, and Bertelson (1979); Morais, Bertelson, Cary, and Alégria (1986).
54. Jakobson and Waugh (1980).
55. Bertoncini and Mehler (1981).
56. Trehub and Chang (1977).
57. Thanks to experiments conducted by Jusczyk and Thompson (1978), and also by Gottlieb and Karzon (1985), we know that they are capable of distinguishing a change in one of the syllables in a bisyllabic item.
58. Starkey and Cooper (1980); Starkey, Spelke, and Gelman (1983); Strauss and Curtis (1981); Moore, Benenson, Resnick, Peterson, and Kagan (1987).
59. Bijeljac-Babic, Bertoncini, and Mehler (in preparation).
60. Blumstein and Stevens (1980).
61. Bertoncini, Bijeljac-Babic, Blumstein, and Mehler (1987).
62. Grieser and Kuhl (1989).
63. Kuhl (1991).
64. Dupoux and Mehler (1990)
65. Miller and Liberman (1979).
66. Miller amd Eimas (1983).
67. Northern and Downs (1974).
68. Eimas, Siqueland, Jusczyk, and Vigorito (1971).
69. Kuhl and Miller (1975).
70. Kluender, Diehl, and Killeen (1987).
71. Kuhl (1990).
72. Miller, Weir, Pastore, Kelly, and Dooling (1976).
73. Eimas (1974).
74. Miller and Eimas (1983); Eimas and Miller (1980b).

75. Eimas (1975).
76. Trehub (1976).
77. Trehub (1976); Streeter (1976); Werker, Gilbert, Humphrey, and Tees (1981).
78. Werker and Tees (1983). Since the appearance of the French edition of the present book, this age may have to be revised downward, at least for vowels. P. Kuhl and her colleagues (1992) have shown that six-month-old infants react to the vowels of the language of their milieu. The quality of the vowels is not identical in Swedish and English. Kuhl and collaborators demonstrated that by the age of size months the behavior of Swedish and American babies is different retarding these vowels. The only way these differences can be explained is by postulating that by six months of age babies have already extracted the relevant properties of the vowels of their native language.
79. Best, McRoberts, and Sithole (1988).
80. Werker and Tees (1984).
81. Mann and Liberman (1983).
82. Joshi (1985).
83. Mehler, Dommegues, Frauenfelder, and Segui (1981).
84. Cutler, Mehler, Norris, and Segui (1983).
85. Cutler, Mehler, Norris, and Segui (1989).
86. Bertoncini, Bijeljac-Babic, Jusczyk, Kennedy, and Mehler (1988).
87. Lenneberg (1967).
88. Gould and Marler (1987).

Conclusion Human Nature and the Cognitive Sciences

1. This is not to say that the IQ tests that are regularly administered in many studies are useless or an indication of bad science. The fact is, IQ tests reflect quite accurately something like "the subject's cooperativeness and ability to concentrate on a set of unrelated, time-limited artificial tasks." Although this may have nothing to do with "intelligence," it is certainly a variable that one wants to control for, say, when comparing the performance of different populations on an experimental task.
2. Sober (1984).
3. This proposition is familiar to those who have been following the development of the rationalist turn of the cognitive sciences since the 1950s, subsequent to Chomsky.
4. This astonishing faculty for recursive representation was noticed by many theoreticians, but it was Dan Sperber who stressed the importance of this concept for all cognitive theory.
5. Müller-Hill (1989).

References

Abramov, I., Gordon, J., Hendrickson, A., Hainline, L., Dobson, K. & Laboussier, E. (1982). The retina of the newborn human infant. *Science, 217,* 265–67.

Abravanel, E. & Sigafoos, A. D. (1984). Exploring the presence of imitation during early infancy. *Child Development, 55,* 381–92.

Adams, R. J. (1987). Visual acuity from birth to 5 months as measured by habituation: A comparison to forced-choice preferential looking. *Infant Behavior & Development, 10,* 239–44.

Adams, R. J., & Maurer, D. (1984). Detection of contrast by the newborn and 2-month-old infant. *Infant Behavior & Development, 7,* 415–22.

Alégria, J. & Noirot, E. (1978). Neonate orientation behavior towards human voice. International Journal of Behavior Development, 1, 291–312.

Alégria, J. & Noirot, E. (1982). Oriented mouthing in neonates: Early development of differences related to feeding experiences. In J. Mehler, E. Walker & M. Garrett (Eds), *Perspectives on Mental Representation,* Hillsdale, N.J.: Lawrence Erlbaum.

Amiel-Tinson, C. & Grenier, A. (1986). *Neurological Assessment During the First Year of Life.* New York: Oxford University Press.

Annis, R. C. & Frost, B. (1973). Human visual ecology and orientation anisotropies in acuity. *Science, 182,* 729–31.

Antell, S. E. G. & Keating, D. P. (1983). Perception of numerical invariance in neonates. *Child Development, 54,* 695–701.

Antell, S. E. G., Caron, A. J. (1985). Neonatal perception of spatial relationships. *Infant Behavior & Development, 8,* 15–23.

Aronson, E. & Rosenbloom, S. (1971). Space perception in early infancy: Perception with a common auditory-visual space. *Science, 172,* 1161–63.

Aslin, R. N. (1987). Visual and auditory development in infancy. In J. Osofsky (Ed.), *Handbook of Infant Development*. New York: Wiley.

Aslin, R. N., Pisoni, D. B. & Jusczyk, P. W. (1983). Auditory development and speech perception in infancy. In M. Haith and J. Campos (Eds). *Carmichael's Handbook of Child Psychology: Infancy and Development Psychobiology*. New York: Wiley.

Bahrick, L. E. (1988). Intermodal learning in infancy: Learning on the basis of two kinds of invariant relations in audible and visible events. *Child Development, 59*, 197–209.

Bahrick, L. E. & Pickens, J. N. (1988). Classification of bimodal English and Spanish language passages by infants. *Infant Behavior and Development, 11*, 277–96.

Baillargeon, R., Spelke, E. S. & Wasserman, S. (1985). Object permanence in five-month-old infants. *Cognition, 20*, 191–208.

Baillargeon, R. & Graber, M. (1987). Where's the rabbit? 5.5-month-old infants' representation of the height of a hidden object. *Cognitive Development, 2*, 375–92.

Barrera, M. E. & Maurer, D. (1981). Recognition of mother's photographed face by the three-month-old infant. *Child Development, 52*, 714–16.

Basso, A. & Capitani, E. (1985). Spared musical abilities in a conductor with global aphasia and ideomotor apraxia. *Journal of Neurology, Neurosurgery and Psychiatry, 48*, 407–12.

Benson, J. F., Segarra, J. & Albert, M. L. (1974). Visual agnosia-prosopagnosia, a clinicopathological correlation. *Archives of Neurology, 20*, 307–310.

Berlin, B. & Kay, P. (1969). *Basic Color Terms: Their Universality and Evolution*. Berkeley, Calif.: University of California Press.

Bertenthal, B. I., Campos, J. J. & Haith, M. M. (1980). Development of visual organization: The perception of subjective contours. *Child Development, 51*, 1072–80.

Bertenthal, B. I., Proffitt, D. R. & Cutting, J. E. (1984). Infant sensitivity to figural coherence in biomechanical notions. *Journal of Experimental Child Psychology, 37*, 214–30.

Bertoncini, J. & Mehler, J. (1981). Syllables as units in infants' speech behavior. *Infant Behavior and Development, 4*, 247–60.

Bertoncini, J., Bijeljac-Babic, R., Blumstein, S. & Mehler, J. (1987). Discrimination of Very Short CVs in Neonates. *Journal of the Acoustical Society of America, 82*, 1–37.

Bertoncini, J., Bijeljac-Babic, R., Jusczyk, P., Kennedy, L., Mehler, J. (1988). An investigation of young infants' perceptual representations of speech sounds. *Journal of Experimental Psychology: General, 117*, 21–33.

Bertoncini, J., Bijeljac-Babic, R., McAdams, S., Peretz, I. & Mehler, J.

(1989). Dichotic perception of laterality in neonates. *Brain and Language, 37,* 591–605.

Best, C. T. (1988). The emergence of cerebral asymmetries in early human development: A literature review and a neuroembryological model. In D. L. Molfese and S. J. Segalowitz (Eds), *Brain Lateralization in Children.* New York: Guilford Press.

Best, C. T., McRoberts, G. W. & Sithole N. M. (1988). Examination of perceptual reorganization for nonnative speech contrasts: Zulu click discrimination by english-speaking adults and infants. *Journal of Experimental Psychology: Human Perception and Performance, 14,* 345–60.

Bever, T. G., Mehler, J. & Epstein J. (1968). What children do in spite of what they know. *Science, 162,* 921–24.

Bijeljac-Babic, R., Bertoncini, J. & Mehler, J. (in preparation). Les unités de traitement de la parole chez le nouveau-né.

Blumstein, S. & Stevens, K. N. (1980). Perceptual invariance and onset spectra for stop consonants in different vowel environments. *Journal of the Acoustical Society of America, 67,* 648–62.

Bomba, P. C. (1984). The development of orientation categories between 2 and 4 months of age. *Journal of Experimental Child Psychology, 37,* 609–36.

Bomba, P. C. & Siqueland, E. R. (1983). The nature and structure of infant form categories. *Journal of Experimental Child Psycholgy, 35,* 294–328.

Boring, E. G. (1942). *Sensation and Perception the History of Psychology.* New York: Appleton Century-Crofts.

Bornstein, M. H. (1985a). Infant into adult: Unity to diversity in the development of visual categorization. In Jacques Mehler and Robin Fox (Eds). *Neonate Cognition: Beyond the Blooming Buzzing Confusion.* Hillsdale, N.J.: Lawrence Erlbaum.

Bornstein, M. H. (1985b). Human infant color vision and color perception. *Infant Behavior and Development, 8,* 109–113.

Bornstein, M. H., Kessen, W. & Weiskopf, S. (1965). Color vision and hue categorization in young human infants. *Journal of Experimental Psychology: Human Perception and Performance, 2,* 115–29.

Bornstein, M. H., Gross, C. G. & Wolf, J. Z. (1978). Perceptual similarity of mirror images in infancy. *Cognition, 6,* 89–116.

Bornstein, M. H., Ferdinandsen, K. & Gross, C. G. (1981). Perception of symmetry in infancy. *Developmental Psychology, 17,* 82–86.

Bornstein, M. H. & Krinsky, S. J. (1985). Perception of symmetry in infancy: The salience of vertical symmetry and the perception of pattern wholes. *Journal of Experimental Child Psychology, 39,* 1–19.

Bower, T. G. R. (1967). Phenomenal identity and form perception in an infant. *Perception and Psychophysics, 2,* 74–76.

Bower, T. G. R. (1972). Object perception in infancy, *Perception, 9,* 15–30.

Bower, T. G. R. (1977). *A Primer of Infant Development*. San Francisco: W. H. Freeman.

Bower, T. G. R. (1979). *Human Development*. San Francisco: W. H. Freeman.

Bower, T. G. R., Broughton, J. M. & Moore, M. K. (1971). Infants' responces to approaching objects: An indicator of responce to distal variables. *Perception and Psychophysics, 9*, 193–96.

Bower, T. G. R. & Patterson, J. G. (1972). Stages in the development of object concept, *Cognition, 1*, 47–55.

Bower, T. G. R. & Wishart, J. G. (1972). The effects of motor skill on object permanance, *Cognition, 1*, 165–72.

Broca, P. (1865). Sur le siége de la faculté du langage articulé. *Bulletin de la Société d'Anthropologie, 6*, 337–93.

Brown, R. (1976). Reference – In memorial tribute to Eric Lenneberg. *Cognition, 4*, 125–53.

Brown, R. & Bellugi (1964). Three processes in the child's acquisition of syntax. In E. Lenneberg (Ed.), *New Directions in the Study of Language*. Canbridge, Mass.: MIT Press.

Bruce, V. (1988). *Recognizing Faces*. Hillsdale, N.J.: Lawrence Erlbaum.

Bryden, M. P. (1982). *Laterality: Functional Asymmetry in the Intact Brain*. New York: Academic Press.

Bushnell, I. W. R. (1979). Modification of the externality effect in young infants. *Journal of Experimental Child Psychology, 28*, 211–29.

Bushnell, I. W. R. & Sai, F. (1987). *Neonatal Recognition of Mother's Face*. University of Glasgow Report 87/1.

Bushnell, I. W. R., Sai, F. & Mullin, J. T. (1989). Neonatal recognition of mother's face. *British Journal of Developmental Psychology, 7*, 3–15.

Butterworth, G. & Castillo, M. (1976). Coordination of auditory and visual space in newborn infants. *Perception, 5*, 155–160.

Caron, A. J., Caron, R. F. & Carlson, V. R. (1979). Infant perception of the invariant shape of objects varying in slant. *Child Development, 50*, 3, 716–21.

Chang, H. W. & Trehub, S. E. (1977). Auditory processing of relational information by young infant. *Journal of Experimental Psychology, 24*, 324–31.

Changeux, J. P. (1983). *L'Homme Neuronal*. Paris: Editions Odile Jacob.

Changeux, J. P. & Dehaene, S. (1989). Neuronal models of cognitive functions. *Cognition, 33*, 63–110.

Chomsky, N. (1975). *Reflections on Language*. New York: Pantheon Books.

Chomsky, N. (1988). *Language and Problems of Knowledge*. Cambridge, Mass: MIT Press.

Clarkson, M. G., Clifton, R. K. & Morrongiello, B. A. (1985). The effects of sound duration on newborn's head orientation. *Journal of Experimental Child Psychology, 39*, 20–36.

Clifton, R. K., Morrongiello, B. A., Kulig, J. W. & Dowd, J. M. (1981). Newborn's orientation toward sound: Possible implications for cortical development. *Child Development, 53,* 833–38.

Colombo, J. & Bundy, R. (1983). Infant response to auditory familiarity and novelty. *Infant Behavior and Development, 6,* 305–11.

Cutler, A., Mehler, J., Norris, D. & Segui, J. (1983). A language-specific comprehension strategy. *Nature, 304,* 159–60.

Cutler, A., Mehler, J., Norris, D. & Segui, J. (1989). Limits on bilingualism. *Nature, 340,* 229–30.

Dannemiller, J. L. & Stephens, B. R. (1988). A critical test of infant pattern preference models. *Child Development, 59,* 210–16.

Dasser, V., Ulbaek, I., & Premack, D. (1989). Perception of intention. *Science, 243,* 365–67.

Dax, M. (1865). Lésions de la moitié gauche de l'encéphale coïncidant avec l'oubli des signes de la pensée. *Gazette Hebdomadaire Médical et Chirurgical, 33,* 259–62.

Day, R. H. & McKenzie, B. E. (1973). Perceptual shape constancy in early infancy. *Perception, 2,* 315–20.

DeCasper, A. J., & Fifer, W. P. (1980). Of human bonding: Newborns prefer their mother's voices. *Science, 208,* 1174–76.

Dehaene, S., Changeux, J.-P. & Nadal, J.-P. (1987). Neural networks that learn temporal sequences by selection. *Proceedings of the National Academy of Sciences, USA, 84,* 2727–31.

Demany, L., McKenzie, B. & Vurpillot, E. (1977). Rhythm perception in early infancy. *Nature, 226,* 5604, 718–19.

DeRenzi, E. (1986). Current issues in prosopagnosia. In H. D. Ellis, F. Jeeves, F. Newcombe & A. Young (Eds), *Aspects of Face Processing.* The Hague: Martinus Nijhoff.

Diamond, A., & Goldman-Rakic, P. S. (1989). Comparison of human infants and rhesus monkeys on Piaget's object permanence task: Evidence for dependence on dorsolateral prefrontal cortex. *Experimental Brain Research, 74,* 24–40.

Dodwell, P. C., Humphrey, G. K., & Muir, D. W. (1987). Handbook of Infant perception, Vol. 2, *From perception to cognition,* Ed. P. Salapalck & L. Cohen, p. 55.

Dupoux, E. & Mehler, J. (1990). Monitoring the lexicon with normal and compressed speech: Frequency effects and the prelexical code. *Journal of Memory and Language, 29,* 316–35.

Ehrenfels, C. von (1890). Über Gestalt Qualitäten. *Vierteljahrschrift Wissenschaftliche Philosophie, 14,* 249–92.

Eimas, P. (1974). Auditory and linguistic processing cues for place of articulation by infants. *Perception and Psychophysics, 16,* 513–21.

Eimas, P. (1975). Auditory and phonetic coding of the cues for speech: Discrimination of the (r-l) distinction by young infants. *Perception and Psychophysics, 18,* 341–47.

Eimas, P., Siqueland, E. R., Jusczyk, P. W. & Vigorito, J. (1971). Speech perception in infants. *Science, 171,* 303-6.

Eimas, P. & Miller, J. (1980a). Contextual effects in infant speech perception. *Science, 209,* 1140–41.

Eimas, P. & Miller J. (1980b). Discrimination of the information for manner of articulation. *Infant Behavior and Development, 3,* 367–75.

Eisenberg, R. B. (1976). *Auditory Competence in Early Life.* Baltimore: University Park Press.

Entus, A. K. (1977). Hemispheric asymmetry in processing of dichotically presented speech and nonspeech stimuli by infants. In S. J. Segalowitz & F. A. Gruber (Eds), *Language Development and Neurological Theory.* New York: Academic Press.

Ericsson, K. A. & Simon, H. A. (1984), *Protocol Analysis: Verbal Reports as Data.* Cambridge, Mass.: MIT Press.

Ewert, J.-P. (1987). Neuroethology of releasing mechanisms: prey-catching in toads. *Brain and Behavioral Science, 10,* 338–405.

Fantz, R. L. (1963). Pattern vision in newborn infants. *Science, 140,* 296–97.

Fernald, A. (1985). Four-month-old infants prefer to listen to motherese. *Infant Behavior and Development, 8,* 181–95.

Field, T. M., Cohen, D., Garcia, R. & Greenberg, R. (1984). Mother-stranger face discrimination by the newborn. *Infant Behavior and Development, 7,* 19–25.

Field, T. M., Goldstein, S., Vega-Lahr, N. & Porter, K. (1986). Changes in imitative behavior during early infancy. *Infant Behavior and Development, 9,* 415–21.

Fisher, C. B., Ferdinandsen, K. & Bornstein, M. H. (1981). The role of symmetry in infant form discrimination. *Child Development, 52,* 457–62.

Flourens, P. J. M. (1842). Recherches expérimentales sur les propriétés et les fonctions du système nerveux dans les animaux vertébrés, Paris: Ballière.

Fodor, J. A. (1975). *The Language of Thought.* New York: Thomas Y. Crowell.

Fodor, J. A. (1981). Imagistic representation. In N. Block (Ed.), *Imagery.* Cambridge, Mass.: MIT Press.

Fodor, J. A. (1983). *The Modularity of Mind.* Cambridge, Mass.: MIT Press.

Fontaine, R. (1984). Imitative skills between birth and six months. *Infant Behavior and Development, 7,* 323–33.

Fox, R., Aslin, R. N., Shea, S. L. & Dumais, S. T. (1980). Stereopsis in human infants. *Science, 218,* 486–87.

Freud, S. (1971). *Psychopathologie de la Vie Quotidienne.* Trans. S. Yankelevitch. Paris: Payot.

Galaburda, A., Rosen, G. D. & Sherman. G. (1989). The neural origins of developmental dyslexia: Implications for medicine, neurology and cognition. In A. Galaburda (Ed.), *From Reading to Neurons*. Cambridge, Mass.: MIT Press.

Gall, F. J., (1835). Works. Vols. 1–6: *On the Function of the Brain and Each of Its Parts*. Boston: March, Capon & Lyon.

Gardner, A. A. & Gardner, B. T. (1969). Teaching sign language to a chimpanzee. *Science, 165*, 3894, 664–72.

Ghim Hei-Rhee & Eimas P. D. (1988). Global and local processing by 3- and 4-month old infants. *Perception and Psychophysics, 43*, 165–171.

Gibson, J. J. (1966). *The Senses Considered as Perceptual Systems*. Boston: Houghton Mifflin.

Gleitman, H. (1981). *Psychology*. New York: Norton.

Goldman-Rakic, P. S. (1985). Toward a neurobiology of cognitive development. In J. Mehler & R. Fox (Eds), *Neonate Cognition*. Hillsdale, N.J.: Lawrence Erlbaum.

Goren, C. C., Sarty, M., Wu, P. Y. K. (1975). Visual following and pattern discrimination of face-like stimuli by newborn infants. *Pediatrics, 56*, 544–49.

Gottlieb Karzon, R. (1985). Discrimination of polysyllabic sequences by one- to four-month-old infants. *Journal of Experimental Child Psychology, 39*, 326–42.

Gould, J. L. and Marler, P. (1987). Learning by instinct. *Scientific American, 256*, 72–73.

Granrud, C. E. (1987). Size constancy in newborn infants. *Investigative Ophthalmology and Visual Science, 23*, 5.

Gregory, R. L. (1970). *The Intelligent Eye*. London: Weidenfeld & Nicolson.

Gregory, R. L. (ed.) (1987). *The Oxford Companion to the Mind*. Oxford: Oxford University Press.

Grieser, D. & Kuhl P. K. (1989). The categorization of speech by infants: Support for speech-sound prototypes. *Developmental Psychology, 25*, 577–88.

Guernsey, M. (1928). Eine genetische studie über nachahnung. *Zeitschrift für Psychologie. 107*, 105–78.

Gwiazda, J., Brill, S., Mohindra, I. & Held, R. (1978). Infant visual response to sinusoidally modulated spatial stimulus. *Journal of the Optical Society of America, 55*, 1154–57.

Gwiazda, J., Brill, S., Mohindra, I. & Held, R. (1980). Preferential looking acuity in infants from 2 to 58 weeks of age. *American Journal of Optometry and Physiological Optics, 57*, 428–32.

Gwiazda, J., Wolfe, J. M., Brill, S., Mohindra, I. & Held, R. (1980). Quick assessment of preferential looking acuity in infants. *American Journal of Optometry and Physiological Optics, 57*, 420–27.

Hadamard, J. (1945). *The Psychology of Invention in the Mathematical Field*. Princeton: Princeton University Press.

Hayes, C. (1951). The Ape in Our House, New York: Harper & Row.

Hayes, L. A. & Watson, J. S. (1981). Neonatal imitation: Fact or artifact? *Developmental Psychology, 17*, 655–60.

Held, R. (1985). Binocular vision – Behavioral and neuronal development. In J. Mehler & R. Fox (Eds), *Neonate Cognition: Beyond the Blooming Buzzing Confusion*, Hillsdale, N.J.: Lawrence Erlbaum.

Held, R., Birch, E. & Gwiazda, J. (1980). Stereoacuity of human infants. *Proceedings of National Academy of Sciences, USA, 77*, 5572–74.

Herlse, S. H. & Page, S. C. (1988). Towards a comparative psychology of music perception. *Music Perception, 5*, 427–52.

Hirsh-Pasek, K., Kemler Nelson, D. G., Jusczyk, P. W., Cassidy, K. W., Druss, B. & Kennedy, L. (1987). Clauses are perceptual units for young infants. *Cognition, 26*, 269–86.

Hubel, P. & Wiesel, T. (1977). Functional architecture of macaque monkey and visual cortex. *Proceedings of the Royal Society, B 198*, 1–59.

Humphrey, G. (1951). *Thinking*. London: Methuen.

Jacobson, S. W. & Kagan J. (1979). Interpreting "imitative" responses in early infancy. *Science, 20*, 215–17.

Jakobson, R. & Waugh, L. (1980). *La charpente phonique du langage*. Paris: Ed. de Minuit.

James, W. (1893). *Psychology*. New York: Henry Holt.

Johnson, M. H. & Morton, J. *Biology and Cognitive Development: The Case of Face Recognition*. Oxford: Blackwell (in press).

Joshi, A. K. (1985). Processing of sentences with intrasential code switching. In D. Dowty, L. Karttunen, A. Zwicky, (Eds), *Natural Language Processing: Psychological and Theoretical Perspective*. Cambridge: Cambridge University Press.

Jusczyk, P. W. (1985). On characterizing the development of speech perception. In J. Mehler & R. Fox (Eds), *Neonate Cognition: Beyond the Blooming Buzzing Confusion*. Hillsdale, N.J.: Lawrence Erlbaum.

Jusczyck, P. W. & Thompson, E. (1978). Perception of phonetic contrast in multi-syllabic utterances by two-month-old infants. *Perception and Psychophysics, 23*, 10–109.

Kagan, J. (1971). Change and Continuity in Infancy. New York: Wiley.

Kellman, P. J. & Spelke, E. S. (1983). Perception of partly occluded objects in infancy. *Cognitive Psychology, 15*, 483–524.

Kellog, W. N. & Kellog, L. A. (1933). *The Ape and the Child*, New York: McGraw-Hill.

Klima, E. & Bellugi, U. (1979). *The Signs of Language*. Cambridge, Mass.: Harvard University Press.

Kluender, K. R., Diehl, R. L. & Killeen, P. R. (1987). Japanese quail can learn phonetic categories. *Science, 237*, 1195–97.

Koepcke, J. E., Hamm, M. Legerstree, M., & Russell, M. (1983). Neonatal imitation: Two failures to replicate. *Infant Behavior & Development, 6,* 97–102.

Koffka, K. (1935). *Principles of Gestalt Psychology.* New York: Harcourt Brace.

Köhler, W. (1959). Gestalt psychology today. *American Psychologist, 14,* 727–34.

Kuhl, P. K. (1991). Human adults and human infants exhibit a prototype effect for phoneme categories: Monkeys do not. *Perception and Psychophysics, 50,* 93–107.

Kuhl, P. K. & Miller, J. D. (1975). Speech perception by the chinchilla: Voiced-voiceless distinction in alveolar plosive consonants. *Science, 190,* 69–72.

Kuhl, P. K. & Meltzoff, A. N. (1984). The intermodal representation of speech in infants. *Infant Behavior and Development, 7,* 361–81.

Kuhl, P. K., Williams, K. A., Laard, F., Stevens, K. N., & Lindblom, B. (1992). Linguistic experience alters phonetic perception in infants by 6 months of age. *Science, 255,* 606–8.

Landau, B. & Gleitman, L. (1985). *Language and Experience – Evidence from a Blind Child.* Cambridge, Mass.: Harvard University Press.

Lane, H. (1979). *L'enfant sauvage de l'Aveyron.* Paris: Payot.

Lantz, D. L. & Steffre, V. (1964). Language and cognition revisited. *Journal of Abnormal Social Psychology, 36,* 368–82.

Lashley, K. D. (1950). In search of the engram: *Symposia of the Society for Experimental Biology, 4,* 454–82.

Lawrence, D. H. & De Rivera, J. (1954). Evidence for relational discrimination. *Journal of Comparative Physiological Psychology, 47,* 465–71.

Lecanuet. J.-P., Granier-Deferre, C., DeCasper, A. J., Maugeais, R., Andrieu, A. J. & Busnel, M. C. (1987). Perception et discrimination foetales de stimuli langagiers mises en evidence à partir de la réactivité cardiaque: Résultats preliminaires. *Comptes Rendus de l'Academie des Sciences de Paris, 305,* 161–64.

Lecours, A. R. & Lhermitte F. (1979). *L'Aphasie.* Paris: Flamarion.

Lenneberg, E. (1967). *Biological Foundations of Language.* New York: Wiley.

Leslie, A. M. (1987). Pretense representation: The origins of "Theory of Mind," *Psychological Review, 94,* 412–26.

Lewkowicz, D. J. (1985). Bisensory response to temporal frequency in 4-month-old infants. *Developmental Psychology, 21,* 306–17.

Lewkowicz, D. J. (1988). Sensory dominance in infants: 1. Six-month-old infant's response to auditory-visual compounds. *Developmental Psychology, 24,* 155–71.

Liberman, A. M. (1970).The grammars of speech and language. *Cognitive Psychology, 1,* 301–23.

Liberman, A. M. & Mattingly, I. G. (1985). The motor theory of speech perception revised. *Cognition, 21,* 1–36.

Lieberman, P. (1984). *The Biology and Evolution of Language*. Cambridge, Mass.: Harvard University Press.

Loftus, E. F. (1979). *Eyewitness Testimony*. Cambridge, Mass.: Harvard University Press.

Lorentz, K. (1958). The Evolution of Behavior. *Scientific American, 119*, 67–78.

MacKain, K., Studdert-Kennedy, M., Spieker, S. & Stern, D. (1983). Infant intermodal speech perception is a left-hemisphere function. *Science, 219*, 1347–49.

Mann, V. A. & Liberman, A. M. (1983). Some differences between phonetic and auditory modes of perception *Cognition, 14*, 211–236.

Maratos, O. (1973). The origin and development of imitation in the first six monthe of life. Ph.D. dissertation, University of Geneva.

Maratos, O. (1982). Trends in the development of imitation. In T. G. Bever (Ed.), *Regressions in Mental Development*. Hillsdale, N.J.: Lawrence Erlbaum.

Marler, P. (1970). A comparative approach to vocal learning: Song development in white-crowned sparrows. *Journal of Comparative Physiological Psychology*, Monograph 71.

Marler, P. & Peters, S. (1982). Developmental overproduction and selective attrition: New processes in epigenesis of birdsong development. *Psychobiology, 15*, 369–78.

Maurer, D. (1985). Infant's perception of facedness. In T. M. Field and N.A. Fox (Eds), *Social Perception in Infants*. Norwood: Ablex

Maurer, D. & Barrera, M. (1981). Infant's perception of natural and distorted arrangements of schematic face. *Child Development, 52*, 196–202.

Maurer, D. & Young, R. E. (1983). Newborn's following of natural and distorted arrangements of facial features. *Infant Behavior and Development, 6*, 127–31.

McGarrigle, J. & Donaldson, M. (1974–75). Conservation Accidents. *Cognition, 3*, 341–50.

McGurk, H. & Lewis, M. (1974). Space perception in early infancy: Perception within a common auditory-visual space? *Science, 186*, 649–50.

McGurk, H., Turnure, C. & Creighton, S. (1977). Auditory-visual coordination in neonates. *Child Development, 48*, 138–43.

McKenzie, B. E., Tootell, H. E. & Day, R. H. (1980). Development of visual size constancy during the 1st year of human infancy. *Developmental Psychology, 16*, 163–74.

McKenzie, B. E. & Over, R. (1983). Young infants fail to imitate facial and manual gestures. *Infant Behavior and Development, 6*, 85–95.

Mehler, J. (1971). Le développement des heuristiques perceptives chez le très jeune enfant. In H. Hécaen (Ed.), *Neuropsychologie de la Perception Visuelle*. Paris: Masson & Cie.

Mehler, J. (1974). Connaître par désapprentissage. In M. Piatelli & E. Morin (Eds), L'Unité de l'Homme. Paris: Le Seuil.

Mehler, J. (1981). The role of syllables in speech processing: Infant and adult data. Philosophical Transactions of the Royal Society, B 295, 333–52.

Mehler, J. (1982). Unlearning: Dips and drops – A theory of cognitive development. In T. G. Bever (Ed.), Regressions in Development: Basic Phenomena and Theoretical Alternatives. Hillsdale, N.J.: Lawrence Erlbaum.

Mehler, J. & Bever, T. (1967). Cognitive capacity of very young children. Science, 158, 141–42.

Mehler, J., Bertoncini, J., Barrière, M. & Jassik-Gerschenfeld, D. (1978). Infant recognition of mother's voice. Perception, 7, 491–97.

Mehler, J. & Bertoncini, J. (1979). Infant's perception of speech and other acoustic stimuli. In J. Morton & J. Marshall (Eds), Psycholinguistic Series II. London: Elek Books.

Mehler, J., Dommergues, J. Y., Frauenfelder, U. & Segui, J. (1981). The syllable's role in speech segmentation. Journal of Verbal Learning and Verbal Behavior, 20, 298–305.

Mehler, J. & Fox, R. (Eds) (1985). Neonate Cognition: Beyond the Blooming, Buzzing Confusion. Hillsdale, N.J.: Lawrence Erlbaum, p. 122.

Mehler, J. Lambertz, G., Jusczyk, P. W. & Amiel-Tinson, C. (1987). Discrimination de la langue maternelle par le nouveau-Né. Comptes Rendus de l'Académie des Sciences de Paris, 303, 637–40.

Mehler, J., Jusczyk, P. W., Lambertz, G., Halsted, N., Bertoncini, J. & Amiel-Tison, C. (1988). A precursor of language acquisition in young infants. Cognition, 29, 143–78.

Mehler, J., Dupoux, E. & Segui, J. (1990). Constraining models of lexical access: The onset of word recognition. In G. Altmann (Ed.), Cognitive Models of Speech Processing. Cambridge, Mass.: MIT Press.

Meltzoff, A. N. (1988). Infant (1988). Infant imitation after a 1-week delay: Long-term memory for novel acts and multiple stimuli. Developmental Psychology, 24, 470–76.

Meltzoff, A. N. & Moore, M. K. (1977). Imitation of facial and manual gestures by human neonates. Science, 198, 75–78.

Meltzoff, A. N. & Borton, R. W. (1979). Intermodal matching by human neonates. Nature, 282, 403–4.

Meltzoff, A. N. & Moore, M. K. (1983). Newborn infants imitate facial gestures. Child Development, 54, 702–9.

Menzel, E. W. (1973). Chimpanzee spatial memory organization. Science, 182, 943–45.

Milewski, A. E. (1976). Infant's discrimination of internal and external pattern elements. Journal of Experimental Child Psychology, 22, 229–46.

Milewski, A. E. (1979). Visual discrimination and detection of configurational invariance in 3-month-old infants. *Developmental Psychology, 15,* 357–63.

Miller, J. D., Wier, C. C., Pastore, R. E., Kelly, W. J. & Dooling, R. J. (1976). Discrimination and labelling of noise-buzz sequences with varying noise-lead times: An example of categorical perception. *Journal of the Acoustical Society of America, 60,* 410–17.

Miller, J. L. & Liberman, A. M. (1979). Some effects of later-occurring information on the perception of stop consonant and semivowel. *Perception and Psychophysics, 25,* 457–65.

Miller, J. L. & Eimas, P. D. (1983). Studies on the categorization of speech by infants. *Cognition, 13,* 135–65.

Mills, M. & Meluish, E. (1974). Recognition of mother's voice in early infancy. *Nature, 252,* 123–24

Moore, D., Benenson, J., Reznick, J. S., Peterson, M. & Kagan, J. (1987). Effect of auditory numerical information on infant's looking behavior: Contradictory evidence. *Developmental Psychology, 23,* 665–70

Morais, J., Cary, L., Alégria, J. & Bertelson, P. (1979). Does awareness of speech as a sequence of phonemes arise spontaneously? *Cognition, 7,* 323–32.

Morais, J., Bertelson, P., Cary, L., & Alégria, J. (1986). Literacy training and speech segmentation. *Cognition, 24,* 45–64.

Morton, J., Johnson, M. H. & Maurer, D. (1990). On the reasons for newborn's responses to faces. *Infant Behavior and Development, 13,* 99–103.

Morton, J. & Johnson, M. (1991). Conspec & Conlearn: A two-process theory of infant face recognition. *Psychological Review, 98,* 164–81.

Moscovici, S. (1981). *Psychologie de Minorités Actives.* Paris: Presses Universitaires de France.

Muir, D. & Field, J. (1979). Newborn infants orient to sounds. *Child Development, 50,* 431–36

Müller-Hill, B. (1989). *Science Nazie, Science de la mort.* Paris: Editions Odile Jacob.

Norman, D. A. (1988). *The Psychology of Everyday Things.* New York: Basic Books.

Northern, J. L. & Downs, M. P. (1974). *Hearing in Children.* Baltimore: Williams and Wilkins Co.

Nottebohm, F. (1981). A brain for all seasons: Cyclic anatomical changes in song Control Nuclei of the Canary Brain. *Science, 214,* 1368–70

Nottebohm, F. (1984). Vocal learning and its possible relation to replaceable synapses and neurons. In D. Caplan & R. Lecours (Eds), *Biological Perspectives on Language.* Cambridge, Mass.: MIT Press.

Ohman, S. E. G. (1966). Coarticulation in VCV utterances: Spectrographic measurements. *Journal of the Acoustical Society of America, 39,* 151–68.

Oxbury, J. M., Oxbury, S. M. & Humphrey, N. K. (1969). Varieties of colour anomia, *Brain, 92*, 847–56.

Pavlov, I. (1927). *Conditioned Reflexes*. London: Oxford University Press.

Peiper, A. (1963). Cerebral function in infancy and childhood. New York: Consultants Bureau.

Peritto, L. A. & Marentette, P. F. (1991). Babbling in the manual mode: Evidence for the ontogeny of language. *Science, 251*, 1397–1536.

Piaget, J. (1966). *La Psychologie de l'Enfant*. Paris: Presses Universitaires de France.

Piaget, J. (1973). *Introduction à l'Epistémologie Génétique*. Paris: Presses Universitaires de France.

Piatelli-Palmarini, M. (1980). *Le Langage et l'Apprentissage*. Paris: Le Seuil.

Premack, D. (1971). Language in chimpanzees? *Science, 172*, 808–22.

Premack, D. (1976). *Intelligence in Ape and Man*. Hillsdale, NJ.: Lawrence Erlbaum.

Premack, D. (1988). "Does the chimpanzee have a theory of mind?" revisited. In R. W. Byren & A. Whiten (Eds), *Machiavellian Intelligence*. Oxford: Oxford University Press.

Premack, D. & Schwartz (1966). Preparations for discussing behaviorism with chimpanzees. In F. L. Smith & G. A. Miller (Eds), *The Genesis of Language*. Cambridge, Mass.: MIT Press.

Querleau, D. & Renard, K. (1981). Les perceptions auditives du foetus humain. *Médecine et hygiène, 39*, 2102–10.

Quinn, P. C., Siqueland, E. R. & Bomba, P. C. (1985) Delayed recognition memory for orientation by human infants. *Journal of Experimental Child Psychology, 40*, 293–303.

Quinn, P. C. & Bomba, P. C. (1986). Evidence for a general category of oblique orientations in 4-month-old infants. *Journal of Experimental Child Psychology, 42*, 345–54.

Reason, J. (1989). *Human Error*. London: Cambridge University Press.

Sacks, O. & Wasserman, R. (1987). *The New York Review of Books*.

Savin, H. & Bever, T. (1970). The nonperceptual reality of the phoneme. *Journal of Verbal Learning and Verbal Behavior, 9*, 295–302.

Schiffman, H. R. (1990). *Sensation and Perception: An Integrated Approach*, 3rd ed., New York: Wiley.

Schneider, B., Trehub, S. & Bull, D. (1980). High frequency sensitivity in infants, *Science, 207*, 1003–4.

Segalowitz, S. J. & Bryden, M. P. (1983). Individual differences in hemispheric representation of language. In S. J. Segalowitz (Ed.), *Language Functions and Brain Organization*. New York: Academic Press.

Segui, J., Frauenfelder, U. & Mehler, J. (1981). Phoneme monitoring, syllable monitoring and lexical access. *British Journal of Psychology, 9*, 281–88.

Seidenberg, M. & Pettito, L. A. (1979). Signing behavior in apes. *Cognition*, 7, 177–216.

Sheperd, P. A., Fagan III, J. F. & Kleiner, K. A. (1985). Visual pattern detection in preterm neonates. *Infant Behavior and Development, 8*, 47–63.

Signoret, J.-J., Van Eeckhout, Ph., Poncet, M. & Castaigne, P. (1987). Aphasie Sans amusie chez un organiste aveugle. *Revue de Neurologie, 143*, 182–88.

Sinnott, J., Pisoni, D. & Aslin, R. (1983). A comparison of pure tone auditory thresholds in human infants and adults. *Infant Behavior and Development, 6*, 3–17.

Siqueland, E. R. & DeLucia, C. A. (1969). Visual reinforcement of nonnutritive sucking in human infants. *Science, 165*, 1144–46.

Skinner, B. F. (1937). *Cumulative Record*, A selection of papers, Century Psychology Series, New York: Ace, p. 127.

Slater, A., Morison, V. & Rose, D. (1983a). Locus of habituation in the human newborn. *Perception, 12*, 593–98.

Slater, A., Morison, V. & Rose, D. (1983b). Perception of shape by newborn baby. *British Journal of Developmental Psychology, 1*, 135–42.

Slater, A., & Morison, V. (1985). Shape constancy and slant perception at birth. *Perception, 14*, 337–44.

Slater, A., Mattock, A. & Brown, E. (1990). Size constancy at birth: Newborn infant's responses to retinal and real size. *Journal of Experimental Child Psychology, 49*, 314–22.

Sober, E. (1984). *The Nature of Selection*. Cambridge, Mass.: MIT Press.

Spelke, E. S. (1976). Infant's intermodal perception of events. *Cognitive Psychology, 8*, 553–60.

Spelke, E. S. (1981). The infant's acquisition of knowledge of bimodally specified objects. *Journal of Experimental Child Psychology, 31*, 279–99.

Spelke, E. S. (1982). Perceptual knowledge of objects in infancy. In J. Mehler, E. Walker, E. Walker & M. Garrett (Eds), *Perspectives on Mental Representation*. Hillsdale, N.J.: Lawrence Erlbaum.

Spelke, E. S. (1985). Perception of unity, persistence and identity. In J. Mehler and R. Fox (Eds), *Neonate Cognition: Beyond the Blooming Buzzing Confusion*. Hillsdale, N.J.: Lawrence Erlbaum.

Spelke, E. S. & Owsley, C. J. (1979). Intermodal Exploration of knowledge in infancy. *Infant Behavior and Development, 2*, 13–27.

Spence, M. J. & DeCasper, A. J. (1987). Prenatal experience with low-frequency maternal-voice sounds influences neonatal perception of maternal voice samples. *Infant Behavior and Development, 10*, 133–42.

Sperry, R. W. (1974). Lateral specialization in the surgically separated hemispheres. In F. O. Smith & F. G. Worden (Eds), *The Neurosciences: Third Study Program*. Cambridge, Mass.: MIT Press.

Starkey, P. & Cooper, R. G. (1980). Perception of numbers by human infants. *Science, 210*, 1033–35.

Starkey, P., Spelke, E. S. & Gelman, R. (1983). Detection of intermodal numerical correspondences by human infants. *Science, 222*, 179–81.

Strauss, M. S. & Curtis, L. E. (1981). Infant perception of numerosity. *Child Development, 52*, 1146–52.

Streeter, L. A. (1976). Language perception of 2-month-old infants shows effects of both innate mechanisms and experience. *Nature, 259*, 1–8.

Thomas, A. & Autgarden, S. (1966). Locomotion from pre- to post-natal life. *Clinics in Developmental Medicine, 24*. SSMEIU. London: Heinemann.

Thompson, P. (1980). Margaret Thatcher: A new illusion. *Perception, 9*, 483–84.

Tinbergen, N. (1953). *Social Behavior in Animals.* London: Methuen.

Trehub, S. E. (1976). The discrimination of foreign speech contrasts by infants and adults. *Speech Development, 47*, 466–72.

Trehub, S. E. & Chang, H. W. (1977). Speech as reinforcing stimulation for infants. *Developmental Psychology, 13*, 170–71.

Trehub, S. E., Schneider, B. & Endman, M. (1980). Developmental changes in infant's sensitivity to octave-band noises. *Journal of Experimental Child Psychology, 29*, 282–93.

Trehub, S. E., Bull, D., Schneider, B. A. & Morongiello, B. A. (1986). PESTI: A procedure for estimating individual thresholds in infant listeners. *Infant Behavior and Development, 9*, 107–18.

Treiber F. & Wilcox, S. (1984). Discrimination of number by infants. *Infant Behavior and Development, 7*, 93–100.

Van Giffen, K. & Haith, M. M. (1984). Infant visual response to gestalt geometric forms. *Infant Behavior and Development, 7*, 335–46.

Vargha-Khadem, F. & Corballis, M. (1979). Cerebral asymmetry in infants. *Brain and Language, 8*, 1–9.

Wada, J. (1949). A new method for the determination of the side of cerebral speech dominance: A preliminary report on the intracarotid injection of sodium amytal in man. *Medical Biology, 14*, 221–22.

Walk, R. D. & Gibson, E. J. (1961). A comparative and analytical study of visual depth perception. *Psychological Monographs, 75*, 15.

Warrington, E. & Shallice, T. (1980). Word-form dyslexia. *Brain, 103*, 99–112.

Warrington, E. & Shallice, T. (1984). Category-specific semantic impairments. *Brain, 107*, 829–54.

Weiskrantz, L. (1986). Blindsight: *A case study and Its implications.* Oxford: Oxford University Press.

Wellman, H. & Bartsch, K. (1988). Young children's reasoning about beliefs. *Cognition, 30*, 239–77.

Werker, J. F., Gilbert, J. H. V., Humphreys, G. W. & Tees, R. C. (1981). Developmental aspects of cross-language speech perception. *Child Development, 52,* 349–55.

Werker, J. F. & Tees, R. C. (1983). Developmental changes across childhood in the perception of non-native speech sounds. *Canadian Journal of Psychology, 37,* 278–86.

Werker, J. F. & Tees, R. C. (1984). Cross-language speech perception: Evidence for perceptual reorganization during the first year of life. *Infant Behavior and Development, 7,* 49–63

Werker, J. F. & Logan J. S.. (1985). Cross-language evidence for three factors in speech perception. *Perception and Psychophysics, 37,* 35–44.

Wertheimer, M. (1971). Psychomotor coordination of auditory and visual space at birth. *Science, 134,* 1692.

Whorf, B. L. (1956). *Language, Thought and Reality.* Cambridge, Mass.: MIT Press.

Wimmer, H. & Perner, J. (1983). Beliefs about beliefs: Representation and constraining function of wrong beliefs in young children's understanding of deception. *Cognition, 13,* 103–28.

Woodruff, G. & Premack, D. (1979). Intentional communication in the chimpanzee: The development of deception. *Cognition, 7,* 333–62.

Wynn, K. (1992). Addition and subtraction by human infants. *Nature, 358,* 749–50.

Yakovlev, P. I. & Lecours, A. R. (1967). The myelogenetic cycles of regional maturation of the brain. In A. Minkowski (Ed.), *Regional Development of the Brain in Early Life.* Oxford: Blackwell.

Yonas, A., Bechtold, G., Frankel, D., Gordon, F. R., McRoberts, G., Norcia, A. & Sternfels, S. (1977). Development of sensitivity to information for impending collision. *Perception and Psychophysics, 21,* 97–104.

Yonas, A. & Granrud, C. E. (1985). The development of sensitivity to kinetic, binocular and pictorial depth information in human infants. In D. Ingle, M. Jeannerod & D. Lee (Eds), *Brain Mechanisms and Spatial Vision.* Dordrecht: Martinus Nijhoff Press.

Zelazo, P. R., Zelazo, N. A. & Kolb, S. (1972). "Walking" in the newborn. *Science, 176,* 314–15.

Index